LIFE SPEAKS TO YOU

Magdalena Julita Byra

Copyright © 2022 Magdalena Julita Byra
All rights reserved
First Edition

NEWMAN SPRINGS PUBLISHING
320 Broad Street
Red Bank, NJ 07701

First originally published by Newman Springs Publishing 2022

ISBN 978-1-63692-354-3 (Paperback)
ISBN 978-1-63692-355-0 (Digital)

Printed in the United States of America

Contents

Foreword v

Chapter 1: What Is Life? 1
Chapter 2: Can We Trust Life? 16
Chapter 3: How Does Life Work? 33
Chapter 4: Who Are We? 69
Chapter 5: Can We Be More Surrendered to Life? 133
Chapter 6: Can Our Hearts Be Healed? 148
Chapter 7: What Makes Our Mind Peaceful and Safe? ... 161
Chapter 8: What Is Our Function Here? 177
Chapter 9: How Would You Like Your Life to Look Like? 201
Chapter 10: What Is Your Calling? 225
Chapter 11: What Is Abundance, and Can We
            Experience It without Pain? 248
Chapter 12: Healing Is Always Certain 275
Chapter 13: Life Always Speaks to You 314

Afterword 331
Acknowledgments 339
List of Books 343

Foreword

My work is to spread love and understanding of who we really are. My intention is for this message to reach everyone to bring peace and love to the whole world.

This book is for you, my reader, to find yourself in this book and reach out to the biggest potential of yourself and find your true calling.

What Is Life?

There is one Life Principle: That Life is God and God is Love.

How can God be called Life if he is somewhere else, if he is an old man with a beard who tells us that we need to be on our knees; beat ourselves on the chest; and repeat, "This is my fault?" How can God be Love if life is a struggle; if we are misunderstood; if we need to fight for respect; if we feel unworthy, unloved, and unhealthy; if we are not loved the way we expect to be loved; if we need to lose ourselves to please others; if we are not able to express ourselves; if we are afraid of life?

The image of God as a being above humanity is one that was imprinted in me by the Catholic Church and the society that I grew up in. I was born in Poland, and I spent most of my life there. When I was a small girl, I thought of church as a place where people worked. I didn't like going to church, repeating things I did not understand and spending an hour or more on something I felt was a waste of my time. But I was also afraid that if I didn't go to church, God, the old man, would punish me or my grandmother would be upset. So who was God to me? Was God a man in the clouds; my grandmother; the priest who was *closer* to God; or the people who raised me, my mother and stepfather? Whom did I need to please? And why didn't I fit in anywhere? What was important for me was never important for other people. I compared myself to others, and I felt lost and disappointed.

When I was a teenager, I stopped going to church regularly. I only went during special occasions, when the whole family would go, like Christmas or Easter. I felt guilty that my friends went to church and I didn't. I felt torn because the whole community went to church, spent time on the benches, and they were okay with it. Why wasn't I?

It was strange to me that people complained about the church and the priests but still went anyway. They were looking for a way to connect with God: kneeling before him, feeling bad about themselves, and letting priests dictate how they should live their lives.

Now I understand why people do that. They were just doing what they were taught by their parents and their communities. Those teachings became their beliefs. It shaped their ideas about what to do and how to behave. They never knew they had a choice to act differently.

We don't believe that God is a part of our lives because we were taught to see God as a deity, which was made up by religion. Most of us don't know who or what God is. Since we don't know what "true God" is, we believe that He only exists in the church; that a priest is the only link we have to Him; and that when we leave the building, we are left by ourselves, alone. We think we can go back to our old behaviors. Going to church every Sunday is a habit for people. Some go to get strength, because they are struggling in their lives and feeling guilty. Some go to ask God to punish the people who hurt them. Some go out of fear that God will punish them if they don't go. Some are so self-centered that they use the church and the clergy to help them with their own careers: "If the church supports me, I will support them when I finally have power." Some people go to church to see what other people are wearing and then gossip about them. There are plenty of reasons people choose to go to church. But who has sincerely asked the question, "Who is God?"

I was taught by my religion that there was only one God. Looking at the altar, seeing a crucified Jesus Christ surrounded by pictures and statues of saints and being taught to pray to them, it was difficult to see this One God. There is a commandment: "*There are no other gods before me.*" What does it mean? Is there a contradiction in the church teachings? People pray to the pictures, to statues of people called saints, to Jesus Christ suffering on the cross, and they see themselves suffering in their lives. Some people see a priest as a god because what the man preaches is most important to them. People are ignorant to find the Truth by themselves. They are lost in the pictures and opinions of other people. So who or what is God?

When I was a young girl, I didn't ask these questions either. God and Christ were taken away from me by the church. The church called Jesus Christ the only Son of God. What about me and others? What was wrong with me that I could not be worthy of God's love and be His only child? I just stopped believing in any god.

I wanted to take my life into my own hands. I believed that life was for me. I wanted to start my own life because I didn't feel safe at home. My stepfather was unpredictable. When I graduated from high school, I took an exam for a school in Warsaw, but I didn't pass because my English skills weren't good enough to study there. The level of English taught in Polish high schools wasn't enough to pass the exams for higher education. I didn't ask for private English lessons, and my parents didn't offer to help me. We were always short of funds. There was only one time when my parents had enough money, and it was when my stepfather worked abroad as a cook. But it was only for a short period of time, about two to three years.

So I started my adult life at nineteen years old. I left Poland for Madrid, Spain, for a "better" life. I felt happy and hopeful that my life would be better than my mom. But it didn't turn out better; instead, I started believing in a life where we needed to struggle to survive.

When I came to Spain, I was invited to work as a cleaner. My dreams were different than what I was offered. I dreamed about modeling, but there was no person next to me who believed that life was about dreaming and fulfilling them. I wasn't in the space where there were people that I could talk openly about my dreams. As a young girl not knowing Spanish, I didn't even try to pursue my dreams. I didn't know how, and I was afraid to ask my cousin about it. I didn't believe in myself at all, but my life experiences were brighter. There was always hope in me, but that was until I met my future husband.

A month later after I arrived in Spain, I met a young man, and I fell in love with him. After three months, I got pregnant, and at twenty years old, I became a mother. We both were young, and I believed that we both would create our lives in love and understanding, have dreams, and support each other in our pursuit of them. I believed that we could be a real family and that our son would grow with us in a loving atmosphere. I really wanted that kind of family after many years of quarrels with my stepfather and listening to my parents' arguments at home. Many years later, when I became aware, I realized that I put myself to the exact same kind of relationship and marriage that my mother had.

It turned out that my life wasn't different from most women in my family and society where I grew up. I stopped having dreams, and I was afraid of life.

My partner liked alcohol and his friends. At the beginning, I had a feeling that he was ashamed of me in front of his colleagues. I received some kinds of comments about my look. I didn't know why and I didn't ask. From the beginning of our relationship, there were misunderstandings. It turned out that we had different ideas about life and how relationship is supposed to look like.

One incident changed my life: the first time I was hit by my partner. On that day, he came home happy and drunk from work. He fell asleep. It was daytime. I came into the room and wanted him to wake up and be with me and his two-month-old son. I walked into the room with a joyous attitude, trying to wake him up. He didn't respond, so I sat down on his belly and, like a child, bumped him a little to wake him up. He woke up and threw up. I barely turned when I felt a hit at the back of my head. I didn't know what happened. When I turned around, I saw he was holding a mop stick. At first, I didn't know how to react. It was really unexpected. When I looked into my partner's eyes, we had a few second silent communication in which I understood what he was trying to communicate: "I will hit you again if you try to disturb me." I started being afraid of him right away. In my eyes, he put himself on a pedestal where he would tell me how I was supposed to act, think, and behave in relationship. He put those boundaries from the very beginning. I lost all hope in having a harmonious relationship and lost trust in him. Next, I felt shame and humiliation, and I started thinking that I deserved it. I convinced myself that it was my fault that my partner hit me: "If I didn't bump him, he wouldn't have hit me." I felt humiliation because there was a witness of this situation: a tenant, and she started laughing. I went to another room and started crying. At the same moment, I decided that I had to be strong. I was on my own, I couldn't tell anyone about this, including my mother, and I couldn't ask for help here because I would not be able to receive it. I had no choice but to stay in this relationship. At that time, my partner was the only provider in our household. The person who I had loved and trusted one minute ago became a stranger to me. I started shutting down and stopped feeling joyful when I saw him. I convinced myself that all men were the same and that the life I really believed in—one with mutual respect and love—was over.

Because of that incident, I started believing throughout my early adult life that I deserved to be treated badly in my relationship and I had to deal with this by myself. Because of that, I started disconnecting myself from my feelings and source of life. I felt alone even when I was in a relationship. My whole life and hopes came to nothing. I was hit by a man whom I truly trusted. I chose him as the father of our son. I felt like a failure. I blamed myself that I trusted the wrong person. I started pretending that everything was all right in front of others. I started operating in survival mode. I became a submissive person to avoid being hit again but to no avail. And I started having my own negative dialogues about myself and life.

I went back to Poland with Martin, our son, three months later. In July, my partner came for the holidays to Poland, and we got married. Then I joined him in Spain two months later. I left Martin with my mother, and my ex-husband's parents helped her take care of our son.

In November 1994, about nine months after the incident, I started losing consciousness. When we came back to Poland the following year, I fainted at my new workplace and was taken to the hospital. A physician diagnosed it as epilepsy. I was twenty-two years old then. My life started to revolve around the disease. I had taken pills since that time. I was more cautious. I felt worse, and I worried about myself and cautious about my body. I started to feel older and unattractive. I didn't see any purpose in my life. I started to have a very cloudy life hoping that one day it would change by itself.

In our marriage, we were fighting all the time. Even though I thought that he was the only person in my life, I didn't understand why he wanted me to change so badly and why everything had to be his way. He wanted me to be someone that I wasn't. I had feeling that he wanted me to change into his mother who had no voice by herself, only believed what her husband said, and agreed with him. Her place was in the kitchen, and she had to listen to her husband's decisions. She was very convinced in this belief. Because of that, I was losing myself more and more. I didn't know to whom I should believe and what was right as being a mother and wife. Friends, alcohol, and his parents were more important to him than his own family. Everything was forced on me and our son by him from the very beginning.

When Martin was three years old, he was beaten by his father because he peed in his pants in the grocery store. One time, when I was in the hospital, he fell into an icy swamp. Martin was eleven years old. His father, instead of being happy that his child that was under his care was alive and was able to come out by himself, beat him. Martin lived in terror of his father all the time. Instead of taking responsibility for his own child by being more attentive, loving, and caring, he punished him. His way of caring was being violent when something wasn't done his way. I know now that my ex-husband wasn't treated in loving way by his father when he was a kid. He only duplicated his father's behavior toward him and his wife.

When Martin was a small boy, I struggled all the time to leave him under his father's care. It was madness. Ever since Martin was a small boy, he was treated by his father as an adult, and all the time, he was shown that there was something wrong with him in his father's eyes. I thought that things would change for the better, but it turned out worse. There was more fear, more violence. Alcohol played a big role. I was also blackmailed into having sex. If I denied it, there was a quarrel. Our son grew in this atmosphere. When I wanted to go back to school, I had to force my ex-husband to let me go to college and get a vocation. I was fighting all the time for my own rights.

I started protecting myself from my ex-husband and also started cheating on him with everything. We both did it and pretended something else. I fought for freedom of being myself. What I learned later was that when we fight against something, the more we attract these kinds of situations. This is the law of attraction. Also, the more you fight against that person, the more you become like that person. This is the reciprocity effect. We cannot be different from the person or have different views on life if we use similar words or act like them who offend us in our mutual interactions. I started losing myself and became more like he was. I took his beliefs about life: that life was hard, we needed to work hard to have enough money, and everything that could happen was only bad.

I didn't feel strong enough to end our toxic relationship. I was so afraid and had so low self-esteem that I didn't know how to say no to this marriage. I was afraid of the unknown. How would I support myself and my son? I grew in a society where the man was the provider of the family and he was supposed to make enough money to support his own family and he was always right. It wasn't true in my experience, but I stuck to this belief.

My husband earned more money than I did, but it wasn't enough. We struggled from month to month, but I was afraid of leaving him. Being in that kind of relationship, I believed that life meant fighting, and even cheating, to get what you wanted. When I had enough of fighting, I stopped asking and I didn't get what I wanted. I started believing that life was not for me. It was a very tough time. Through my experiences with the people that surrounded me in the past, I believed that life was that way: tough and cannot be changed. There was no other way. Wherever I looked, I felt stuck and I saw walls. No matter how much I tried to improve my life, I wasn't able to do it. There is a proverb: "With who you surround yourself, you will become the same." In other words, our surroundings determine our way of being and believing. Our experiences with others determine how we look at ourselves and at life. My self-worth was low, and I believed in a life that others saw but not in life itself.

When I was a teenager, I was open to life, I saw only good in my future, and I wanted to be an adult. I thought that my life would be better than my mother's because I wasn't her, was I? What turned out was that my life wasn't better than hers. I met my future husband, we had a family, we went to work, but there was a lack of money, arguments, physical violence, and no mutual understanding or intimacy. My whole scenario was not so bright as I had thought. From being a healthy person, I became ill. Instead of having a partner and friend in my marriage, I had a stranger whom I couldn't speak openly to and be myself. I felt like a victim of life. I put on masks depending on the circumstances. It depended on whom I met during the day or whom I was with.

When I was with my mother, I was a daughter listening to my mother's beliefs about life and arguing when I didn't agree with her. When I was with my son, I acted like a parent who kept control over her child. When I was with my husband, I acted like a victim wife fighting for love and understanding. When I was with my friends, with whom I felt better, I acted more myself but not enough to freely speak and be different. I accepted what society agreed with, and I melted in it. When I met strangers, I put on a mask for a stranger. I was very nice and kind. When I was talking to the boss, I acted as an employee. I listened to my boss and did the assignment that he gave me. I did the best to satisfy all those people. All the time my act was that I should meet the expectations of others. I was in survival mode all the time, never myself. When I was with myself, I wanted to escape. I didn't like myself. Why should I? I didn't mean anything. Life was happening next to me, not for me. I never asked myself what I really wanted to do. At that time, I didn't know that I have a choice, and I am the cause of the change in my life beyond what others do, think, or believe. None of these masks I wore were true, and I was fed up with them. I wanted to be myself and be loved the way I was. Worst of all, I denied myself. I could see myself clearly now—how I didn't like myself and how I didn't care about my life. I let my ex-husband abuse me physically and verbally, and I didn't do anything about that. What was with my mind that it believed that I had to listen to the person whose consciousness was lower than mine? How many of you believed that you were stupid because your husband or someone close to you said this to you? What I had learned later was that by denying myself, I denied God.

Ironically, I wasn't going to church because I knew that this was an institution and people were working there, but my whole life was mirroring exactly how I understood God to be: cold and separated. The image that was imprinted when I was a child stayed with me for over forty years. I felt separation from others. I didn't feel loved. My friendships were fine, but our conversations were about how life was bad. We talked about unfairness. We talked about others but very seldom about ourselves, because what would we tell about ourselves when we had nothing to say? Our lives were ordinary, nothing special, just the usual ups and downs. Nevertheless, we thought that couldn't change anything. Life was happening to us. Our bodies suffered, and we didn't know why. We were so righteousness about everything in our lives that none of us thought to let go of what didn't serve us and that everything would turn out fine by itself. When some kind of *tragedy* happened to others, we felt sympathy and pity for them. We didn't know why something *bad* occurred in the lives of others or in our own lives. We didn't know that it was happening for a higher purpose. So mostly we complained, were worried, and made fun of others—very often our partners—to release anger and express resentment and resignation over our not working relationships. We thought that we had nothing common with how others behave toward us. We didn't take any responsibility for our own lives, feelings, behaviors, and helplessness. We all took responsibility for others and then blamed them for not being the way we wanted them to be or for not doing what we wanted them to do. So it was easier to talk about them and then feel better about ourselves. There was always somebody to blame for our unhappiness: our families (including children), our bosses, acquaintances, politicians, etc. I really believed in that kind of life, and I didn't know how much I was disappointed with it. We all were, but we didn't say it out loud.

After five years of suffering from the violent behaviors of my husband, we broke up. We both had enough of trying, and I believed we both were tired of that. Before we broke up, he took out from my purse the document from the medical examination that said he abused my body physically. I noticed it many months later, and I was angry with myself that I didn't see this before. But later, it turned out to be a blessing in disguise. The divorce went smoothly.

I moved with our son to my mother's. Then I got an opportunity to go to United Kingdom for six months. I received a job opportunity there. I left Martin with my mother, not telling him that I was leaving for London for a while. Later on, I found out that this small incident left a huge imprint on our mutual relationship for many years.

Being in London, I found out that my husband had filed for divorce. I pitied myself and cried for two to three days. After that, I felt relieved and really happy. I knew that I wouldn't be able to file for divorce for myself at that time. I was afraid. I wasn't able to stand up for myself and take responsibility to finish our relationship involving other institutions, and I had huge fear of not having enough money to deal with it. So in the end, my ex-husband did me a favor by filing for the divorce. When I came back from London, I went to the court and said yes when the judge asked if I agreed to the divorce. Then it was over. It was so easy. I didn't even see my ex-husband at the court. We had different date hearings. My lawyer said that it was the first time he saw a happy person who was divorced. I really was. It was over. Our marriage stopped existing. I was free.

At that time I didn't appreciate what life gave me. That's why my next move wasn't reasonable. I came back to work in my previous company, and after a while, I received a huge apartment from a town council. I was so happy that we had our own place to live with Martin, but later on, it turned out that the costs of keeping up my apartment were nearly equal to my salary or sometimes even higher. I became upset again. That time my ex-husband came back from abroad where he had worked for two years. We rekindled our relationship "for the good of our child." It was Martin's first communion. He was eight years old at that time. We tried very much to be better for ourselves, and though my ex-husband treated me better somewhat, his violence turned toward our son again. I obeyed my partner, even when I felt differently. I accepted what society said that "a man is right." It was the most difficult thing for me to do—to forgive myself as a mother who allowed violence toward her own child to keep the household from having quarrels.

My apartment was too expensive to keep, and my partner (ex-husband) had an idea to swap the apartments. He went to the real estate agency, and we swapped this huge apartment for the smaller one. I got the difference for the measurement, and for the very first time, I bought my own small apartment. I rented out this place, and we all moved to my ex-husband's a little bigger apartment. He bought it after he had come back from abroad. We started our life as a family again, but the ideal setup was over. We went back to our old behaviors.

After a few years, my ex-husband got a job in Ireland. I joined him a few months later, and our son started attending college there. Our life in Ireland had its ups and downs. We had quarrels all the time, and we apologized over and over. My health was getting worse. Instead of facing the problems in my relationship, I was escaping from them. I was watching *SpongeBob* and *Dog Whisperer* and learning English from books, which I loved to buy. I was attracted to video recordings about Machu Picchu and other ancient sacred places. I dreamt of visiting them one day when my partner would maybe want to go. I knew that it would not happen with him because my ex-husband's dreams were very mundane and selfish: having a car for himself, building a house, going fishing, spending time on indulging his taste buds; and that was all. He did what made him happy without asking what really made me happy. I wanted travel and really be free to choose what I wanted to do or not instead of being pushed to things that weren't for me. Every time I was able to express myself and tell him what I really wanted, my words would be twisted by him. He would say that I was wrong and that we didn't have money. I never appreciated my contribution of work and money to our relationship, and I believed him when he said that I didn't deserve to live my dreams. I was very dependent on him, on what he wanted me to believe about myself, and on his opinion of what life should be. So I gave up on myself, and I was involved in his dreams, which made me more and more unhappy and unfulfilled. I was miserable. I didn't see way out from this relationship at that time, and I knew that my partner would not change.

One day, after another quarrel with my ex-husband, I sat on the bed crying and I asked the question to myself: *Is there a different life?* I knew deep in my heart that there were relationships where there was love, respect, support, joy, and more fulfillment. I had really enough. My body was ill, and I felt unhappy, but I still believed in a better life. I really wanted to live.

Our son, Martin, also had ups and downs in a new environment. He started attending a college only for boys, and he didn't like it. He was oftentimes complaining about a stomachache. He stayed home very often. Thanks to that, he learned English very well by himself. He was twelve years old at that time. He said that it took him three months to speak the language fluently, and he looked up words in the dictionary only once. His spelling was good before he came to Ireland. In Poland, he played online games, which let him practice English with peers around the world. He shared with me that his spelling and computer skills were much better than his Irish classmates'. He was very smart and did the best he could to adjust himself to the environment. After two years of education in this college, we moved him to another one—a mixed one where boys and girls could learn all together. The reason for this move was that Martin was bulled there. His classmates were very nasty to him. Even Martin's father showed his compassion for him. It was the first time he really showed, in a loving way, that he loved and cared about Martin. The last time I saw him care about our son this way was in a month or so after his birth. I took the picture of them both sleeping together. Martin was sleeping on his father's chest. It was unconditional love between them both. In a new school, Martin found himself very fast. He loved going there, and he made a lot of friends.

At that time our son had finished his first three years of college in Dublin, and we needed to decide if he was staying for another three years or would finish his school in Poland. We decided that he would continue his education in Poland and I would go back with him. I had just finished my work in a nursing home.

It was the best decision we had ever made. When I came back to Poland, I felt more confident because I had my own savings. I had been receiving unemployment benefit from Ireland for a few months, and I got the whole family allowance savings. In Ireland, every family, rich or poor, who has a child receives this allowance until the child turned eighteen years old. It gave me a little peace of mind, and I wanted to stand on my feet without my partner (ex-husband).

One day, I said to my ex-husband "Enough" when he tried to get closer to me. I wasn't able to continue this relationship any longer. At that time, I wasn't even angry with him. After all those years together, over eight years of our relationship as a divorced couple, I became aware that I could not change him and he wouldn't change by himself. I couldn't stand him touching me, and I felt pity for him. I felt resigned. When I recognized these feelings for the man in front of me, I wasn't able to do anything else only to break up and tried to move forward by myself. It was over for me. I was afraid but I had nothing to lose. My health was ruined. My self-esteem was very low, and I felt if I stayed one year longer in this relationship, I would literally die. I didn't know that my intuition was waking up then. We cannot help or save another person by feeling pity for him or her and condone their behaviors. It took me a lot of years to understand that. We only lose more of ourselves, and we don't give opportunity for this person to grow and move forward. We imprison ourselves and others in a relationship that is toxic for all involved, including our children, when we have them.

Later, I learned that my decision was supported by a book that I didn't know I had. I bought it in Ireland. It was *The Secret* by Rhonda Byrne. Letting go of my ex-husband was a blessing for him and for me even if we both didn't understand it that time. I gave him freedom to build his new life again, and I was learning how to be independent and trustful that all my needs and my son's would be met, that I would be capable to meet the demands as a sole parent and keep up our small household at the same time.

One year later my ex-husband had a new wife and a new child. But if we are on the consciousness of "eye for an eye, tooth for a tooth," there is no understanding. We feel hurt and angry, and we want to get back. When he understood that our relationship was over, he started playing very low.

First, he started to set our son against me. For a while he accomplished what he wanted. He sued me to decrease the alimony payments for our son. He forced Martin to sign false statements that he had paid alimony on him when he didn't do that. When Martin was of age, he sued him. It lasted over eight years.

What can I say? When we know only separation, we do everything to live that way and our lives and the people around us become more miserable. We become bitter and resentful. Thoughts of anger and hate impact our bodies and cause disharmony and illnesses, and they were getting older.

By that time, I started my own journey to know *who I am* and what God is and to trust that everything will unfold in the right way. I didn't know that I was being guided to find the truth of life. I was thirty-seven years old then. It was 2010.

That year I got a tattoo on my left shoulder after searching for four days and nights for the right one. Every tattoo has a meaning. It is important when we do such a thing, because we would have it on our body for the rest of our life. My tattoo was of mountain lion—a puma, very often called cougar. My decision to have a tattoo was an impulse. I never thought that I would have it. My son was fan of it. He watched programs about tattoos, and we played with henna. He drew a beautiful flower and two birds around it on my shoulder with henna. I was looking forward to when this tattoo would be washed away. I told myself, "This is not for me. I don't like it." But one day, after seeing my brother's and his ex-wife's tattoo images, a thought suddenly appeared in my awareness: *I have to have a tattoo.* I thought that the reason I wanted this tattoo was to cover my two-centimeter scar and had the meaning suitable to my awareness at that time. Over seven years later, I found out that mountain lion means that your intuition is knocking on your door. When I started my own journey in 2010, I didn't know what intuition was, but I started following it unknowingly. Thanks to following my heart, universal spiritual principles were unfolded to me, which I will share with you in this book.

God is omnipresent, omniscient, omnipotent, and omniactive. All Existence is the manifest form and activity of Spirit. This Presence is equally present in all space, time, places and in all persons, as well as beyond time, space, and manifest creation. Ours is a holographic Universe in which every part—that which is seen and that which is unseen—is an emanation of the unmanifest Whole.

—*Agape Spiritual Principles and Practices*

CHAPTER 2

Can We Trust Life?

It is a law of my life that wherever I go the way shall be prepared before me, made immediate, perfect, plain, straight and easy.

—Ernest Holmes

Now I can say *yes*.

During the last eight years, I thought that I was alone because I didn't have like-minded people around me. But now I understand that I was always guided, protected, and supplied; never betrayed, never judged; only loved and supported by Life.

When I read *The Secret* and watched the movie, honestly, I didn't understand a lot. But I took the most important thing for myself: see good everywhere, in everything, and in everyone! If I couldn't see it at the first time, I would look for it deeper and I would always find it. Thanks to this book, I made the best decision in my life: I *stopped listening to others*, what they thought about life and how I was supposed to do or act. I wanted to explore life by myself and prove to myself and others that life is not the way we were taught. My whole life, I was taught that our brains are the most important organs and that we depend on them for our intelligence, which determines how smart we are in the eyes of others. I was taught that we needed to make decisions based on it and try to predict which decision would be right for us by making a list of pros and cons before making a choice. People call that "a smart choice." But when we make "a mistake" based on that kind of knowledge, we start regretting. We'd call ourselves different names like stupid, failure, and so on and so forth and do nothing about it. Instead of letting go of judgment and asking for help to solve the problem, we keep ourselves stuck on this problem by ourselves, and our lives start revolving around one mistake we made in the past. Even getting pregnant without planning to isn't a huge thing unless our closest family members show us differently. When we were young, we wanted be loved and not judged, but mostly, what we received were feedbacks that were different from those we asked for. Adults wanted us to be responsible for everything and everyone, and even we were not capable of doing that. Nobody taught us; they only demanded us to be like adults, to act like them and think like them. When we tried our best, they mostly judged us and pointed out that this or that was wrong. "You're supposed to do it that way and not this way." In most cases, we had people around us who made the same mistakes, and instead of seeing the possibility of loving and supporting us, they treated us the same way they were treated in a similar situation. When I made choices without reasoning and judgment of what I was doing, I found out that the headquarters are in our hearts and that intuition is the most important tool to follow. At the same moment, my own journey started—the journey to my greatness, to who I can become as a human being for myself, and to find the truth of our existence and share it with others. Intuitive guidance has nothing in common with cons and pros; it only leads us to fulfillment and guides us safely in every situation.

So I had a book that promised a better life, and I had people around me that I was listening to all my life, but their lives weren't happy and really fulfilled. They made a lot of mistakes, had a lot of regrets, gave up on themselves, and they taught me how I was supposed to live. They wanted to protect me, but I wanted to give myself a chance to understand that Life was always *for* me, not *against* me. I stopped taking my family's pieces of advice and other people who said that they "know life," and I started watching my thoughts, making sure they were more positive.

It was a struggle, going from one mood to another, but I was stubborn. I tried my best. During the following three years, two books were released by Rhonda Byrne: *The Power* and *The Magic*. The last one was a salvation for me. I became grateful, more faithful, and more open for good. I started to trust myself more. I started knowing what I wanted and started to focus on it.

At that time, the word "God" didn't feel very trustful for me and sounded very strange, so I preferred to use the name "Universe." Later, as soon as my awareness grew, I started calling it Divine Power, Universal Mind, or Divine Intelligence.

I read books such as the trilogy *The Science of Getting Rich*, *The Science of Being Well*, and *The Science of Being Great* by Wallace Wattles. I also read *The Master Key System* by Charles Haanel and *Think and Grow Rich* by Napoleon Hill. I was hungry for these kinds of books, and my consciousness was growing. All these books had many things in common: it showed how to use our minds, imagination, concentration, goal-setting, and gratitude and how to apply the law of attraction to it.

All these books came to me in the period of 4–5 years, and all of them I read in English. I was learning to visualize and spent a lot of time watching movies that brought me joy. I also read other books that I could laugh myself to tears, mainly Polish authors.

Mostly, my goal at that time was to bring prosperity to my and my son's life. Honestly, I wasn't successful in it, and the reason was that I didn't know how it could be possible. Unconsciously, I felt unworthy of having prosperity in my life. I wanted money. I was appreciated for all I had, but my financial situation weren't changed a lot. I earned more money, but it wasn't enough to meet all the needs at that time. I felt that money is for others but not for myself. That's why I received only what I believed in the matter of finances, how worthy I was of it: ups and downs.

I stopped socializing with my old friends and avoided visiting my mother. The reason was that I stopped complaining but the others were doing it all the time. I wasn't so sure at that time what I was doing. That's why when we met occasionally, I would put my words in a positive way, but I didn't know how to react to the complaints of others. I didn't know how to explain to them how the Universe worked because I had just started crawling into this topic by myself and I didn't understand a lot. But again, I was stubborn to do what I was doing: using gratitude and reading more books on the topic. I felt like I was from a different breed, a different planet.

At that time, I got from the Universe a person that I could speak with openly what I had learned. I was really grateful for our time spent on the phone because he was the one that I was able to share my dreams and I was also able to help him see things differently. But there was something not right, because after our phone conversations, I would feel empty, like I was robbed of something that was very important to me, and I didn't know what. I gave myself wholly in these conversations, all my passion, and I did not receive them back. I was losing myself again. Then one phone call became the final straw for me, and I needed to cut myself from our conversations. I needed to recover from this distant relationship. After a few months, we started communicating again, but it was on a different level. I had a new job, and my conception of myself was different. I could be open again, but I didn't lose myself. Thanks to that, we became really good friends.

At that time I didn't understand why people were not excited about what I was learning, practicing, and sharing. They had a secret of life to solve their problems, and they rejected. They didn't want to accept that life can be really easy and joyful: Ask, believe, receive, and joy is a main tool in this process. I didn't get it. I was in the process of letting go of my attachment to other people's way of being, specifically the people who are resigned, waste their lives and health by accepting life the way it is, and believe in aging. Fearing and misunderstanding life causes them to reject their own well-being and role in this world. We are from the same source, but our consciousness are different. And because of that, we operate on a different plane.

> *Wherever I am a small or big wave of being,*
> *the same Ocean of Life is behind me.*
>
> —*Paramahansa Yogananda*

We are from the same Source, but not the same. When I shared with my family, I was offended, judged, and I was taken as an irresponsible person and mother because I was doing what I felt I needed to do, not what they thought I should do. I believed that I could get my dream job, so I wasn't looking for just any job. I packed my son, and we lived separately for three months because we weren't able to talk to each other. Martin was receiving alimony, granted by the court from his father, and because of that, I knew that he would be able to keep himself up.

I introduced Martin to *The Secret*. He used tools given in the movie from time to time with positive outcome, but he didn't believe that the law of attraction apply to all areas of our lives. There was one of many reasons that we had misunderstanding in our communication. His judgmental way of being about my behavior and what I should do or not to do only made the case worse. Also he was under his father's influence and others, and we argued all the time. I had enough. I remember how I was crying when I packed his stuff. He was at his father's on holiday at that time. I knew that I had lost my son and what I would say to him, he would reject. He rented a room, and I left him alone. I stopped controlling him because he always was between his father and I. I went to his school to find out about his grades, but I let him be by himself, and I trusted that I would have my son back home one day and our communication would get better. However, my ex-husband wouldn't stop controlling our son, even if he had a new family and lived 780 km away. He called Martin every day with demands and pretensions.

After two and half months since Martin had lived on his own, I received a phone call from the hospital with the information that he had overdosed on some tablets. I found out years later from him the real reason why he took the pills. He said that his father told him by phone that he couldn't afford food and clothes for his newborn daughter because he was paying alimony to Martin.

That year Martin's father came back from Ireland, where he had a well-paying job through many years. Martin himself went to the hospital to have a gastric lavage. It was a sign for me that I could take steps to make my son come back home, and I knew that he would agree to do this. He was reluctant about it, but he moved home back after two weeks. I asked him to change his telephone number to stop receiving phone calls from his father. When he saw the word "father" on his cell phone display, he froze and was afraid not to answer the phone. I had the same issue when I was in a relationship with his father before. What a huge power fear and guilt had over all of us that we are unable to make own choices and let go of people who make us believe that life is about control and fear. Martin was eighteen years old at that time.

One month later, he met a girlfriend, and very soon after, he asked me to change his phone number. It turned out that his phone network service was expired, and he didn't give his new telephone number to his father. Also, he kept this number away from his father's mother. He didn't trust that she would keep her promise of not showing Martin's phone number to her son. He kept a distance from his grandmother for over one year. During the few months he stopped receiving phone calls from his father, he started learning better, and he graduated from a technical school with very high grades, which surprised even him. Our lives started to become more harmonized. I got a new job. My son started studying at the University of Technology in Stalowa Wola, where we used to live. After two years of studying, he quit and I supported him in this. He chose business studies in English at the University of Technology in Wroclaw, from where after three years he received a bachelor's degree.

At that time, I thought that my new job was a dream job. I could use English, develop myself, and later travel to the United Kingdom for sport trophy's fairs and business trips. Before this job, I had a commission work for the cinema. It was a blessing for me then. I could watch movies that I liked for free any time I wanted, and my son could earn extra money after school. I was grateful for this experience and the friendships that I got then.

My "dream job" turned out very stressful. Mostly, I had to learn all by myself. The person I was assigned with was very reluctant to teach me. I needed to ask him all the time and struggled to get a response. Then I decided that I would go to those who were open to support me in learning my job duties. These people were from the management level. My coworkers loved to gossip, complain, and were bored with their job. They stuck together in their way of being. What was precious about them was that they were very good employees who couldn't see the way out to follow their own dreams. I felt like an outsider. I didn't complain or gossip, so we had nothing common to talk about. I always spoke about others kindly and encouraged them, and I really was appreciated for my work. It was very challenging for me to work with these people. At that time, I took everything personally, and I didn't understand why some people were disrespectful toward me and why they treated themselves so low.

Sometimes when I had enough, I would cry at home. I had a lot of resentment toward some of them. Now I understand that they were my great teachers. They showed that I was disconnected from myself so their behavior had an impact on how I was feeling about myself in current situation. Later on, I read the book *Four Agreements* by Don Miguel Ruiz in which was given four the most important agreements with yourself: *be impeccable with your word, don't take anything personally, don't make assumptions, always do your best.* I didn't have good relationships with my coworkers, even we tried our best, but my work and attitude were noticed by the management.

Because of being grateful, the magic was happening all the time. The English and Irish markets for which I was responsible grew so much that during two and half years, from three to four clients, we were preparing to open a branch of our company in the United Kingdom. It was really magical. When I got my first sales plan in July 2014 on an amount of €3,000, I didn't know how it would be possible to reach that amount, but the sales plan was reached. It came by itself. I was grateful in advance for this and believed it.

When I was not sure if the sales plan could be done monthly, I would repeat over and over until I believed in it: "Thank you, thank you, thank you for a sales plan this month." I started feeling better and trusting the Universe that it was done.

I found the power of affirmation, "*I am whole, perfect, strong, powerful, loving harmonious and happy,*" from Charles Haanel's book. This affirmation was the best for me when I was stressful and I wanted to fall asleep and needed to wake up in the morning the next day.

Every morning I wrote ten things that I was grateful for. Also, I used the "magic rock" at night to be grateful for the day that I had before I fell asleep. I did what I had learned from *The Magic* book by Rhonda Byrne.

I appreciated everything: for the sun and clouds, for the breath I take, and for my healthy body. I appreciated that I could walk, I could write, and I was able to take care of myself and for the smallest things that I received or I could afford to give. I was really grateful. I taught myself to love life, that life is good and abundant in other ways than only money. The salary wasn't so high—it didn't match the amount of work I was responsible for, but besides increasing sales, I received many more amazing gifts from Life because of gratitude.

For example, when I was on business trips in the United Kingdom, I always had big beautiful rooms. My workmates always had the worse ones for the same price. Our employer paid equal for all of us. I had an English client who always invited us to very delicious and rich dinners. He appreciated our presence. I was respected by English local suppliers, and life was really good.

When the United Kingdom market became bigger, it was divided into two parts: the south and north. The reason it was done this way was that the south was developed well by me but the north had a smaller base of clients. I was assigned to develop the north, and another girl received the south to continue developing it. Her name was the same like mine, Magdalena, and she was great at what she did.

In 2016 our superior decided that there would be two business trips to the United Kingdom: one to the north, where he would go with me, and another two months later to the south part, where he would go with my workmate.

At the beginning, I was a little disappointed that I would only go to the north part. I really dreamed to see London again and have a ride on the London Eye. I kept this picture on my refrigerator which also served me as a vision board. Also I knew that I deserve to be in the south part to meet our clients. I had worked hard over two years to develop this market.

On our first business trip in March, my superior that time and I started in Scotland. Our first client was there. She always said, when we spoke on the phone, that it was raining most of the time in Scotland. When we arrived, it was an astronomical spring. It was warm, the sun was shining, and the sights were beautiful. It was the opposite of what I was told. It was a joyful experience. I was grateful that the weather was always on our side. The last client was in Nottingham. So we were able to see a lot of the northern part of the United Kingdom.

On this business trip, I bought the book *Wishes Fulfilled* by Dr. Wayne Dyer. It was the best investment that I did at that time. I always received books that I needed at the right time and I still receive them. I started reading this book during my flight back to Poland. When I finished at home, I sat in my armchair, and I received an image that I was in London walking on the bridge. The image came by itself and was so real. Later on, I was told that it is my gift to *see*. I started being guided by receiving images of my future or others' futures when it was needed.

A month later, I was asked to my superior's office, and he said that my workmate who was supposed to go to the south part of England got pregnant and I would need to replace her on this trip. I was so happy and thankful. My coworker and I received what we wanted the most and were ready for it. I received my job and traveled to south part of England, and she received a new family, which she really desired. Thank you, God.

When my boss and I came to London and finished visiting our clients there, I bought a ticket for a ride on the London Eye. When I stood in the line to get there, I felt like time stopped. There were plenty of people, but I was in my own world. I was smiling to myself with a wide smile, and I felt perpetual joy that one of my dreams came true. Thank you, again, God.

In 2016, I was in the United Kingdom four times. I was so happy. At that time I felt powerful, and I thought I was in control of my life. Also, I felt lonely in my journey. The reason was that I didn't have people around me who thought the way I did. I was so positive and happy. Many times it would cost me a lot of energy to bring myself to this state. As I mentioned before, there were ups and downs. But I did it. Also, I was committed to helping others in seeing good things in the world and their lives. I uplifted people all the time. Sometimes I was surrounded by people who were like vampires and they sucked my energy. They were hungry for positivity because it made them feel better. They weren't able to see the good things in their lives by themselves.

Every time I went to the United Kingdom, I had with me the best book for me ever: *The Alchemist* by Paulo Coelho. One day I suddenly needed to buy it and read it again. The first time I read this book was years and years ago, and I didn't understand it. It was just a good book. But when I started dreaming again, knowing more how life works, I started understanding the book.

Building the brand for the company in the English and Irish markets, I saw myself in Santiago's experiences. When he made the crystal seller's store prosper in a very short time, I saw how magically fast the English and Irish markets grew. When I read the part about his meeting with Fatima at the well and them knowing that they were meant for each other just by looking at each other's eyes, I saw my dream of meeting that kind of person, my partner, a person that was given truly by God, not chosen by my small ego, which was always cheating itself by convincing me that this or that man would be the best for me.

The sentence said during the wedding ceremony, "What God has put together let no man put asunder," is so much misunderstood. We all believed that the wedding in the church was God's will and the person next to us at the altar was meant to us by God. But maybe relationships are meant for partners to learn something, not to take this person as husband or wife for our all life. The truth is, in most relationships, people don't fit with each other. They have different expectations, they like very different things, and they have different ideas about love and being in a relationship or marriage. A lot of marriages are kept because of obligations mostly given by society. People don't love each other only work hard to adjust themselves in the relationship and their cultural environment. Because of that, they spend less and less time with each other. Some marriages connect only through their children, who are not happy seeing their parents unhappy with each other. They think that it is their fault.

There are so many mistakes that people make by getting married from the very beginning. They manipulate and push, and after that, they lie to themselves by convincing themselves that after the wedding, the husband or wife would change to the kind of partner they want and that the relationship would look how they think it's supposed to look like. Others are victims of society and cannot say *no* to marriage even if they don't feel the calling to it right now. They get married because they believe that's how it should be, convincing themselves that their current partner is the best for them and the one. There is a lot of fear in it and cultural influences on what life is supposed to look like, which does not give yourself time to grow and learn. In my culture, most women have this kind of attitude. There is no other man. I believed in it, and a lot of people who are divorced now or not had the same belief system. The biggest mistake is that people keeping their marriages because it is said that God connects them through the wedding in the church. Some people who have a very Catholic background stay in toxic relationships forever. Very often a woman and a man meet each other and think that the love will last forever because they are "madly in love," but this emotion does not last very long as routines come in their marriage. They become bored. Some of them cheat to feel better about themselves, and they are afraid to admit that their marriage is not working.

Some women got married because they got pregnant. In the past, a lot of women had to endure stigma from society when they got pregnant with no husband. It is still in the society's consciousness. Our relationships are mostly made with logical force by convincing ourselves that this person is the right one even when our intuition says differently. In these kinds of relationships, we get hard lessons and a lot of emotional pain. We lose ourselves to keep control of our partners. We don't feel confident; we are insecure. That's why struggle starts in the relationship and in the marriage.

From our first date, we already knew that the person was, or wasn't, the right person for us. We put so many expectations on each other that love changes to resentment and hate. However, if it is with the right person from God, it feels like home. We can be open from the very beginning. We are relaxed when being with that person. There is no doubt that we are loved for who we are and the way we are. We are listened to, and it matters to the partner what we speak. Our values are the same, and no one has to be pushed or manipulated. We give and receive. We are tolerant of our differences, and we respect them. No one wants us to change, and we don't want to change the partner. We both are perfect. We feel like we've known each other for ages. Our affection grows and grows for each other, and the relationship brings out the best in us on many levels. How many times have we said to ourselves that he or she is the one, but it turns out after a few years or even months, there is more struggling than joy? And we do the same mistakes again and again, instead of trusting Life that the right person will appear in the perfect time when we are really ready. The madness of looking for the person to fulfill us would be finished. There would be less emotional pain; fewer divorces; and more love, joy, and trust in relationships and marriages.

Life loves us and wants us to be happy, wants us to have really meaningful relationships where we can be ourselves and not pretending to be someone else to meet the expectations of the other person. Life is easy. Life is meant to be joyous and harmonious, filled with love. We need to learn how to love and trust ourselves first, and then the right person will enter our life with ease and joy. The relationship can only evolve to a higher and better level of love, joy, compassion, and understanding. Everyone has their own "the One." We need to be patient and stop looking at what other people do and what they understand what happiness is. Only then would the right person given by God appear.

My "dream job" absorbed my life. I lived it. It was my passion. I loved seeing how the markets were growing. It was magic looking at this. The English market had eight big local suppliers from our branch, and we were growing constantly even when we operated from Poland.

In 2016 I was assigned to prepare a business plan for our branch company in the United Kingdom. I was asked to find a warehouse, an accountant, and a solicitor and I also had to do my daily duties such as the monthly sales plans. I worked for three people, but I didn't complain. I loved to see how I was expanding. Everything was found and done. I was waiting with joy to introduce the project to the board at the end of August 2016.

During that year, I had my first spiritual experience. In July, I was on a holiday in the family house in the town where I was born. I was sitting in the garden of my grandparents. I was wearing white jeans. Suddenly, I noticed a monarch butterfly sit down on my lap and start cleaning its left antenna. I was afraid to move. I wanted it to be on my lap the longest possible. After a while, it flew away. It was an amazing experience. I knew that I was prepared for something new, because a butterfly is a sign that we are going to enter the path of our soul and transformation.

I shared this to the members of my family who were with me at that time, but they minded their own business. They weren't so amazed as I was. At that time I knew that they could not see and could not hear. So I was on my own with my journey.

I also had a dream the same night. I saw a pack of white wolves. They were beautiful, and they were running. Some of them were in the mode of attacking. I wasn't afraid, but I took my mother and son to the place where we were all safe. The white wolf means protector of a household. I was chosen to be a protector of my family and lineage. I was the first who was waking up. And I kept it all to myself because those who surrounded me did not understand. I was awakening step by step, but even I didn't understand it at that time.

The day for my presentation in my company came. I was ready and prepared. That day more employees had their own presentation in front of the board. When my time came, I was relaxed and everything went flawless. I got the answer the same day. The first thing that I found out was that I was evaluated during my introduction. I got good rates, but the feeling wasn't nice because I didn't do it to be evaluated. What I was doing was giving my heart to this job. The second surprise for me was that the management said *no* to the project. I was astonished. It caught me by surprise. I felt like all my zeal for this job was gone—my whole work, what I did, my time, and my enthusiasm. The entire work that I had done during the two years was not appreciated as I expected. Those were my first thoughts. I knew that I had the possibilities to learn a lot during these years, and I took the advantage of it, and I did my best. But I also had big professional expectations with the United Kingdom project. If it passed, I would be promoted and get a raise. I would be in the United Kingdom more often and have a more permanent contact with the English language. I would visit clients to increase the sales, meet new clients, and would grow personally and financially.

As the mother having a son who was studying at a university in a different city, I needed to take a loan in the bank because my income wasn't enough to maintain two households. I thought that when I got promoted, I could pay up my credit easily. But it turned out that that was beyond my reach.

I started thinking about how I could get out of the job without losing my reputation as a good employee. I didn't have any other job prospect. I started losing interest in the job, and I knew that it would affect the sales plans. I knew that even if I was disappointed with this situation, it was for a reason: life wanted to take me to a better place. I trusted. I started trusting life ever since I started practicing gratitude. But I didn't see where, how, and when. At that time *how* was in my focus. That's why I wasn't feeling good about the situation, but I did my best to uplift myself and be grateful.

Once when I spoke to my superior, he said that we would open our branch company with the United Kingdom address, phones, etc., without warehouse and we would operate from Poland. I prepared another business plan, and I got the answer before Christmas. *No* again. It was the final straw for me. I was only grateful that it was the last day of work that year and I had about ten or more days off. I knew that I would not stay in this company for long, because from what I had learned, developed, and given my heart to, I could not sit by the phone as a call center agent and attract clients to make bigger sales. I wanted growth, and my deepest dream was to teach what I had learned from the books about the law of attraction and gratitude.

That year, in November, I had another spiritual awakening. I went to Warsaw to Pulsar publishing house for a Tzolkin workshop led by Hanna Kotwicka. Tzolkin is the sacred round of the Mayan calendar, a galactic matrix composed of twenty archetypes and thirteen numbers in combination. The Pulsar website is www.maya.net.pl., which can be also opened in English pages.

The workshop was for two weekends. On the second weekend, I started to be more awake. It was the first time that I started noticing the signs and guidance. When I was getting dressed, I saw a jaguar label that was stuck in my cousin's room in Warsaw. It had been there for a very long time, but it was the first time that I noticed it. The next day, the jaguar caught my attention during our workshop break. I noticed this animal on the wall calendar behind Hanna Kotwicka's desk. On the third day, I understood that a jaguar really showed up in my life to guide me. We were all finishing our workshop and we were asked to pick up a pebble from a sack. It had a number assigned to an animal. I remember myself thinking before my turn, *If the jaguar, which I started noticing during this weekend, means something, I would pick up the pebble with it.* Guess what? I took out the pebble with no. 12, which was assigned to a *jaguar*. Then I knew that the jaguar put its imprint on my journey and would guide me.

Most importantly, I stopped doubting the signs that Life had given me. I read the meaning of a jaguar. I read that this animal shows up very rarely to people, and I got an affirmation that *I am at the right place, at the right time, and I do what is right. I am ready to wake up to my true greatness.* I was amazed and happy, and I repeated this affirmation very often. Also, it was written that a master was waiting for me. It turned out that even if I repeated it, my mind wasn't so ready for what life have offered me few months later, but this wasn't important. Life took its course. I affirmed, and my soul started taking back control of my smaller part called *ego*. We all know the sentence: "You askth and you haveth received it." We need to own it. A great master, Jesus, said these words over two thousand years ago.

Thanks to this workshop, I learned about I Ching, which is connected with Tzolkin. Mayan Calendar speaks about the fourth and other dimensions in the moment *now*, where spiritual cleaning and becoming is. I Ching, on the other hand, speaks about life in the physical world. Our three-dimensional reality is where there is cause and effect. We received information about our life in this incarnation and the root cause. The root cause tells us what our assignment is in this incarnation. My root cause was to let go of all burdens. I didn't understand it that time when I read it, but I did understand it subconsciously. Now seeing my journey and how I have cleaned things, I am still in the process of releasing everything that doesn't serve or limit me to the point where I cannot show my true nature and greatness. Also, I'm clearing up everything that I had done that wasn't in harmony with my soul and only with my ego consciousness, where there was fear and uncertainty. It's like I am guided to finish things I had started and wasn't able to continue when I was younger to fulfill the purpose of my soul's incarnation. The new desires have arisen, and the ones that were buried have awakened.

We need to stop being afraid of death. When ego identification dies, we allow guidance from our higher self, where death does not exist. In death, we can understand that the old "I" dies and a new person arises like phoenix from the ashes or butterfly from the cocoon. By letting us die to our old identifications, we can understand more things, situations, people, and what we experienced. When we let go of what doesn't serve us, there is a place for a new life, for something better.

Every morning we wake up as a new person, but mostly, our experiences are the same, because we code our subconscious mind with old, unpleasant thoughts about things from the day before, and when we wake up in the morning, we repeat it instead of changing our thought patterns. Only then our life can be changed and transformed. We don't have to be afraid of transformation because with it comes our expansion. When we finish our incarnation, we release our physical bodies—a process we call death, and then we meet our loved ones, who are waiting for us in another realm. Our expansion is added to the universal bank for coming generations. We all leave a legacy for a new world. That's why TZOLKIN guides events in the global consciousness and the individual ones. When each of us takes responsibility for ourselves, growing into a consciousness of love by simply starting to dream, the global awakening is certain.

MAGDALENA JULITA BYRA

In the Tzolkin workshop, I met a friend who was learning psychological tarot. There are five or seven levels of tarot. The first one is when we want a psychic to read from the tarot cards. But this is only a foundation, and it is not constant, because our thoughts are changing and this basic reading doesn't have to be fulfilled. The reason is that we are creators of our experiences and what we believe we receive. I am a good example. The psychological tarot is read from the date of birth, and it says where we came from, what traits we possess, the past karma we have, etc. Also, she did an astrological chart for me, and it turned out that in this incarnation, my soul finishes the journey to love, which started in my previous incarnations.

> God is Absolute—the same yesterday, today and forever, constant, changeless, eternal *because time, space, and form are variable and God is not. God is absolute because God is One. God's nature is unchangeable.*
>
> —*Agape Spiritual Principles and Practices*

CHAPTER 3

How Does Life Work?

Life always gives us and gives us abundantly.

When I came back to work after New Year, we started preparing ourselves for the fair in the United Kingdom. That week, I was at the doctor's office. The doctor and I decided that I would stop taking the last small dose of the medication because I hadn't had a seizure in nine years. The last time I had it was in Ireland when my health dropped because of the huge stress I had in the relationship and from working for a while at the cash register in a department store where displays were flashing all the time and I didn't have enough rest. By the way, in Ireland, I took the biggest dosages of that medicine since I started using medications at the age of twenty-two, and they didn't prevent me from passing out. They only caused dizziness many times. As I mentioned above, I was functioning normally for nine years. And despite having stress lately from work, I was on the smallest dosage, and my body functioned great. The doctor said that the small dose that I took was impossible to prevent the seizure. I was happy, and I thought that I was healthy.

Two days later when I stopped taking a tablet, I received the e-mail from the client. He complained about something. I remember thinking, *I have enough*, and I woke up in the emergency ward at the hospital. I was connected to my doctor by phone, and he suggested I take the biggest dose of the medicine twice a day. When I left the hospital room the same day, I started taking the medicine, but I decided to increase by half the dosage that I used to take and only took it once a day. Honestly, I became my own doctor since I discovered that our mind and thoughts create health or illness in the bodies. I needed the doctor to prescribe me the medication and lead me to health until I am able to regain my health completely throughout my spiritual work and understand the cause of the disease. And it worked for me. It turned out later that our phone conversation from the hospital room was the last one. I found out a few days later that Dr. Stanislaw Sajdek had died in a car accident a day after our phone call. My first reaction was disbelief. After a few moments, when my mind adjusted to the thought that I would not see my doctor anymore, one who I trusted, I started being thankful that he was there for me and others when we needed him the most. His life was meaningful because of being of service to others.

Also from the emergency room, I texted my boss that I was fine and I could go to the fair, but he responded that he couldn't let me go. It was a sign for me that my pleas had been heard. I knew that the universe gave me a way to get out of a job that I had lost interest in but still with a reputation of being a good employee. Life is good when we believe in it, and we will always fall on our feet when we begin to trust Life.

This was another sign for me that I needed to take care of myself more now. I didn't know where I would get my income or what I would be next. I knew only that I needed to take an advantage of what Life gave me, and I did. I was on sick leave for over two months, and I resigned from my "dream job" in March 2017. I was to receive income for two more months, so I was supported for a while.

Every day I was grateful, and I trusted that everything would be all right, that I would be provided and I would find a place where I could start my new life.

My first step was to Atelier Soul and Body in Stalowa Wola, in the town where I used to live. A beautiful girl, her name Aldona, helped me connect my head to the rest of my body. I was so in my head that I didn't feel my head as a part of my body. From my neck to the feet was the body, and above was my head. I noticed this during the session. I needed to take care of everything at work, so my head never was quiet. I had thousands of thoughts about what next I needed to do to be able to do the work of three people by myself and on time. My mind controlled everything, disregarding a deeper connection with my body's needs, and I wasn't aware of it.

During the healing, after my whole body had been energetically connected with my head, I saw a picture of me when I was a two- or three-year-old girl, and back then, my grandmother held me lovingly and said, "Poor Magdalenka. She doesn't have her father." At that moment, I felt anger at her even though she was in the unseen realm. She made the transition three years before. Because of her beliefs, I started feeling incomplete, and that was something wrong with me. As children, we see ourselves perfect the way we are. We don't believe that something is lacking in us; but in the company of elder people, who see us differently because of our circumstances, they speak to us in words that we don't understand. But our subconscious listens to it and takes it as true and creates our lives with these false beliefs about us. We feel incomplete, and we will only become complete if we have two parents, if we have plenty of money, if we are slim, or if we have the things that an ideal family or environment has.

Because of this picture, I started to understand why I didn't feel complete. My way of being and the inner dialogue I had as a teenager and as an adult person only mirrored subconsciously implemented beliefs. My whole life, I was looking for something and proving that I deserved to be loved, that I deserved to be appreciated, that I deserved to be respected no matter what age, and deserved to have money to buy things that I like. I felt abandoned and unworthy. As a teenager, I missed my father, and I blamed him that he left me and my mother and I had to be brought up by my stepfather, whom I had never accepted. I remembered like I was sitting on my bed crying after another quarrel with him and realizing that no one would come to save me. I was on my own. Since I was a small innocent child, I had to compete for my mother's favor with him. Ironically, he was the one who mostly won. I was neglected many times. They both made me believe that I was wrong. In their understanding, I was the needy one, and as a child, I believed them. But the truth was different. I needed to meet their needs to survive with them. After healing my inner child, I recognized that as a child I was attuned to myself very much, and I saw more than they did. Sometimes, they wanted me to become their parent, and I played a role as an emotional one. They both were like children who requested from me a small child to meet their needs of abandonment and lack of love in their own homes and relationships. They sucked my energy, and I needed to pay attention to them both, but my stepfather was the most needy one. As a result, I gave up my true nature and believed them that I was a cause of their unhappiness, and as much as I wanted for them to have relief, I couldn't bear this. I was only an innocent child and later teenager who had to be involved in their illusive game of playing a role of the adult parents.

My stepfather tried his best to prove me many times that I was a bad child and inadequate person. He wanted me to change all the time. He was unpredictable. You didn't know what would bring him out of balance, and I was the one who was blamed for his lack of control toward me. Everything that I did was very often wrong according to him, even I did things better and faster than he would do or think. Instead of appreciation, I received feedback that I am not good enough and I was too young to dictate how things in life supposed to be done. It was his own fear of losing control over others. He never felt enough to be wanted and appreciated because he was. His feelings of unworthiness were projected on me and later on my younger brothers Bartosz and Pawel. As a result, I was afraid of him all the time.

I always wanted to meet my father and I did. I was twenty-three or twenty-four years old, and I was working in the biggest steel company in the southern east part of Poland called Huta Stalowa Wola. I was asked to be a part of the crew for the building machines fair in Poznan as a hostess. There I had the opportunity to meet my father, Wieslaw, his second wife, Teresa, and two younger half-brothers, Michal and Piotr. After the fair, I was invited by my father and Teresa to visit them for the holidays. I went with my son for two or three weeks and spent a longer time with my father's family. The idea I had of my father was different than he was at that time, but it was good to be there. Also I met his younger sister, Hania. We all kept in contact for a while, and then we stopped. At that time I assumed that I had more need to contact him than he did that I decided to stop calling him.

It was good for me that I met him because I stopped missing him. But I still kept my resentment toward him for years although I wasn't consciously aware of it.

After connecting my head with my body, I was at a family constellation workshop in Wroclaw. I got a contact from the girl, my first healer. All the time I was guided, step by step, from person to person, from workshop to workshop.

I didn't understand why I was doing all this stuff, but I did, and it was a very strong feeling. I knew that I was safe and everything was for my highest good. I just followed my heart's desire. I was looking for healing and, most importantly, who *I* really *am*.

My intention when I joined a family constellation workshop was to meet my soul mate and to have a truly supportive, loving relationship. I was told there that before my mother, my father had a girlfriend who left him and I played her role all the time. He felt hurt because of that, and my mother was the person who was supposed to quench his pain. I was told that because of that, my relationship with my mother was in disharmony. I acted more like a colleague of hers than a daughter. Also, I was told that because of that, I was never chosen as a first woman. Only men who were in relationships were interested in me, but I wasn't interested in playing the role of second woman. I was tired of that.

Also it was pointed out that my family from my mother's side behaved rigidly and conservatively. When I watched the scene, I noticed that it was true. Also, we were told that whoever has mother in their hearts, that person will always have work. It will come to them very easily. The person who has father in their heart has enough force to push themselves to get up and go to work.

So it was a very informative and clearing workshop. A lot of people released emotional pain. They found out what pulled them down through their ancestor's karma, and they cleared that.

When I came back home, I found on YouTube Louise Hay's affirmations and started to use them. I found out also about Abraham-Hicks teachings, which I started to be familiar with later. We need to be ready for new information and have open minds.

One day after meditation (I was learning by myself from YouTube), I was in my apartment and got the thought, *Louise Hay*, but I didn't know what I needed to do in this direction. I was in a small town in Poland without income, and I didn't know where she lived. I only heard that she had a school or something like that, and I wasn't able to find anything on Google. I found information about her on Wikipedia and noticed that I had the same birthday she had—October 8. I knew that it was the right direction. She did what I wanted to do as my occupation, but it looked impossible for me. The question "*How?*" appeared in my mind again, and I let go of this thought.

After the family constellation workshop, I went to Warsaw for the soul body fusion and transformational breathwork workshop for the weekend. It was a wonderful experience, and there was a beautiful feeling of caring. Transformational breathwork is also called rebirthing. Soul body fusion is very useful when we want to live long and happy. Our soul many times doesn't want to be in the body because of a disagreement with what the ego wants or does. When the ego takes over the body, the soul cannot navigate the person, and then the soul has the right to finish the incarnation without reason. Many times, there are young healthy people that suddenly don't wake up or have an accident that finishes their lives, or the soul cannot navigate the middle-aged person. That is when it chooses to let go of this incarnation and turns it over to the ego to stop hurting others or its own body. The simple soul has lost control over the ego, which is attached to the body and has no possibility of continuing its path that it chose for its current life as a person. When the soul is not 100 percent in the body, there are many diseases, a lack of compassion, unforgiveness, a lack of understanding of what life is for, negative thinking, getting older, and many other disharmonies. The soul cannot receive intuitive guidance not being in the whole body to follow its path because the ego took over everything. For example, my friend checks how much soul is in her clients' bodies with a pendulum. Sometimes it is only 20 percent. After soul body fusion, the client comes back to a harmonious life and starts feeling joy, love, their body starts healing itself, and getting younger. And the person starts taking care of themselves. That's why it is important to invite our soul to our bodies by soul body fusion practice and guide ourselves to unfoldment and happiness in our lives.

We all really cared about one another even if we hadn't met before. People who are on a spiritual path are changing, and they care more as *we*, not *me*. People started feeling more love for themselves and others and started being more open, becoming more true to themselves. This is a long healing process. From those kind of workshops, true friendships can be born.

Being on this workshop, I received contact to Jerzy Gorak, who does the transformational breath sessions as a professional breath seater in Wroclaw. I was told that to make changes in our lives, the best is to have ten or more private sessions. Even if I didn't have work at that time and had only money for a journey and one session, I went without hesitation. I contacted Jerzy Gorak in Wroclaw, and I made an appointment with him.

I intended to heal my body and my life and grow. This was the most important thing for me and still is. I kept faith that all my needs would be met and that life was given to me all the time: guidance and money, people and books. It was only my decision if I say *yes*, and I did. Gratitude opened new doors for me, and my consciousness was growing.

I bought a book, *Live on Your Own Terms* by Osho, at the time when I had my first transformational breathwork session. It was magical how I received what I needed at the exact moment to move forward and grow independently.

From the very first session, my body started to be more vital. When I spoke about my experiences, my body shivered and I felt cold. I was cold. During the rebirthing session, I saw myself as a small girl in the crib or bed and saw my mother. She was saying lovingly my name and reached out to me. At the same time, laying on the bed as an adult, I felt energy moving through my brain on the right side. It was a strong experience. The healing was started.

Transformational breathing meant to help us release emotions. The goal is to process blocked emotions and energy, leaving us free to form trusting, healthy attachments. Rebirthing is called healing breath because it comes from the Spirit. We start breathing from the diaphragm without pause between inhaling and exhaling. There is the whole circle. Babies breathe that way. We need to learn again to breathe like them. When we breathe in this degree, we are connected to the world. If we breathe shallow, our trust in life, communication with others, and health is not good. We all know that babies and children are very connected to life, happy, and trustful. They cry when they feel hunger, anger, or pain, speak the truth of what they see, and don't worry about what others think about them. They know how to communicate. They don't expect people to read their minds. They openly show their feelings. We know when they are happy or upset. When they can speak, they tell us why they feel this or that way. We lost that kind of sincerity when we grew up. Children aren't afraid of saying what they want, and the adults give in to them with pleasure.

Sometimes the parents or grandparents don't know when to stop. We learned that if we buy more for a child or a person, we show them how much we love them. We learned to show our affection by buying things. When our behavior is very harsh to the person or our child, we buy her or him something and we stop feeling guilty. We apologize to them this way, but our behavior has not changed. We still act violently or don't have enough time for our relationship or our own child. We feel guilty because of that, and we buy another thing, but nothing has changed. We lie to each other, we manipulate for our convenience, and we are overbearing. This kind of behavior was taught by our parents, and we teach them to our children.

We buy love that way from others. It is easier than changing our behaviors or habits. We believe that we can fill in our inner emptiness by buying unnecessary things for ourselves or for others. We need to learn again what true love is, such as caring, a warm word, helping without expecting to receive something in return, encouragement, hugs, kisses, listening, and open communication with each other without fear that we can hurt the other person by saying our true feelings. We can offer others help by relieving them of their duties because they took on too much on themselves to prove their love and they don't know how to stop. Mostly women have that kind of attitude: to bear all for others. We also need to learn how to be open to receive love. There is the whole cycle: giving and receiving. The breath show how life wants us to live: inhale (receiving), exhale (giving). There is no other way. There needs to be a balance between giving and receiving.

After the first session of transformational breathing in Wroclaw, when I came back home, I woke up the next morning and I got a thought: *sell the apartment.*

I didn't trust first that thought. It was strange. *Why do I need to sell the apartment?* But when I was walking, I went into the real estate agency by chance in my town and the process had started. It turned out that the person whom I hired wasn't good at what he was doing. He was giving untrue information about the address of my apartment and other small details and wanted me to convince that what he was doing was right to sell the place. Thanks to that, when I met my friend from high school who was a realtor, I could release the first broker from the contract without any additional charges on my side and start a partnership with her. She took care of everything, and the apartment was sold in less than one month. The whole process lasted one month and a half.

When I had doubts if my apartment could be sold, I took from my shelf another book by Rhonda Byrne: *How the Secret Changed My Life*, which was released at that time. I read how the girl shared her story about selling her place. I did what she did. I sat in my armchair, and I felt that my apartment was sold. I wasn't so good at visualization, but I was very good in saying "Thank you" and believing that it is done. The buyers showed up soon.

Meanwhile, I packed my stuff, and I transported them to my mother's basement. My best friend Donata helped me. I played the game of make-believe.

Because I grew spiritually in this apartment and I loved this place very much, I released intention that I wanted to sell this place to a family. This apartment deserved it. And it happened. The apartment was bought by a young family with a four-year-old daughter, and the other girl was on the way. The mother was eight months pregnant. The four-year-old girl showed me how *The Secret* works. When she was with her mother to see the apartment, the girl was talking to her. "I would have my toys here. There I would sleep…" They both planned what they would do in the place. I knew and had hope that they were the buyers, and I needed the money so much. I was right. This was the family who bought my place. The apartment was sold with the first price, which was given to me. A thought flowed from my heart, but I didn't trust that thought again and raised the price later, as others always do. But when a young family put the price that was given to me at the beginning, I started understanding that I was about to listen to that inner voice and stop doing things what others do. I couldn't argue with the Universe. I was only amazed at how it really worked every time.

Thanks to this deal, I had money for my next breathwork sessions and my whole journey during that year. Also I could afford to transfer money to my son's bank account to support him in his last year at the university in advance. I was free to take care about myself and moving forward with my life. The steps where I was headed were shown to me one month later.

In April 2017 my stepfather made a transition, and I was the last person who saw him alive at the emergency ward. I was waiting in the hall when the physicians tried to revive his body, and I noticed a hummingbird on the curtain in one of the free patient rooms. The meaning of this bird is that the chosen path is the path of the heart where love and compassion lies.

At that time I was after my soul body fusion workshop. I was sitting on the chair, and I wanted to do soul body fusion on my stepfather's body by imagining that the body would be revived and the soul would reconnect with the body. I did the right thing, and this time, the soul chose to release the body that wasn't working anymore. Thanks to that, very often, when we enter our spiritual path, our ego dresses up in a new form and pretends to be omnipotent. I wanted to be more aware and learn to notice it to distinguish the truth from ego impersonation. It can be done only when the mind and heart are connected and are guided by the soul.

When the doctor went out, I thought that my stepfather was alive, but it turned out that he had made the transition. I went to the bed where his body was lying, and I said goodbye in my mind. I knew that his soul was there. My knowing was confirmed few months later by an audio book, which I listened to, written and read by Anita Moorjani, *I Was Dying to Be Me*. Thank you for her coming back to share her story with us, what the truth is. Our loved ones surround us all the time. We cannot see them through our five senses, and we cannot connect with them by feeling grief because of their transition. We can feel their presence when our hearts are open and happy. They come to visit us all the time.

I made phone calls to my mother, half-brother, Bartosz, and my stepfather's brother. I wasn't able to speak differently than what I knew, and for sure, they didn't understand my words. My stepfather's brother was more focused on the lack of the person and blame than the good news that the body was not suffering anymore and the soul was in a different realm tangibly surrounded by unconditional love.

The room where my stepfather lived was renovated, and I could move to this room for a few days after selling my apartment. This room used to be mine when I was a teenager.

At the end of June, I moved to Wroclaw. I had the opportunity to live in my son's rented room, and he paid for this from the alimony. I appreciated what he did because I could save the money for my next step. At that time Martin was on a work-and-travel program in the US. It was his second time in two years. I paid for it, and probably he wanted to thank me that way.

When I continued the breathwork sessions, it turned out that Jerzy Gorak knew a girl who was on a Heal Your Life training authorized by Louise Hay in the US ten years before. He connected us, and I received a link to the website called Heart Inspired Presentations LLC, to a couple, Heal Your Life coaches and entrepreneurs.

I took about five to six rebirthing sittings all together. I didn't feel like taking more of them. During one of the sessions, I saw a small blue building, and next to that was an arch with ivy leaves. I thought that it would be New York City because that arch and leaves were similar to a place in Central Park in New York City, which I saw in movies whose plot took place there.

On July 1, 2017, I went to a shamanic school in Lodz for one class to see what was that about.

The same day, we were meditating. At the beginning, the workshop leader said to us that we would see the whale, which represents the subconscious mind. Also, we were told we would see our superconscious mind, which would guide us. I started seeing myself sitting on the whale and felt a lot of love for this creature. There was a vast body of water, and we were crossing through. I looked up and noticed an eagle, which started flying above with us. He was my superconscious mind and guided my sight. I noticed a green island from afar. It had the shape of an apple. I knew right away that it was the enclave where New York City had been built. First, I saw apple orchards. After that, I saw a tower with bells. I recognized right away that it was a tower or gate from the churches that were built in Mexico. These two pictures appeared one after another. The eagle guided me to the United States. The whale, as my subconscious mind, was aligned with my soul.

During our break, we left the building to have some lunch. I started noticing plenty of signs about New York City and the United States, which I hadn't noticed before. Now looking back at my small mind, my ego didn't accept it at all because I had never dreamed about going to the United States. I felt good living in Europe, feeling familiar with this continent and its people. I got along very well there.

After I received the link to the Heart Inspired Presentations, LLC website, I saw that there were two dates and countries for me to attend the Heal Your Life training, which was facilitated by the same couple from the USA—Patricia Crane, PhD, and Rick Nichols. Honestly, at the beginning, I thought that I was going to some kind of workshop, but later on, it turned out that Life guided me to the training, after which I would be able to lead Heal Your Life workshops. Later on I found out that Patricia worked with Louise Hay and led the workshops with her. But after the Hay House publishing house, established by Louise, had become known, she gave authorization to Patricia, and she became the only Heal Your Life trainer in the USA. When Patricia met Rick, they both spread this philosophy throughout the world and certificated many Heal Your Life workshop leaders and coaches to continue Louise Hay's legacy.

The dates were July 2017, the United Kingdom, and September 2017, San Diego, USA.

Even I received guidance to the USA, my first attention was to the United Kingdom. It was logical, closer to Poland, and cheaper to get there. My brother lived there, and as I mentioned above, I was familiar with those people and culture.

I e-mailed the person who was organizing Heal Your Life training in England. I didn't get a response from her for three to four days. On the fourth day, I decided to e-mail San Diego. The response was the same day, adding the time difference, which was nine hours. I paid a nonrefundable deposit.

Next day, after paying the money, I got a response from the United Kingdom. It was too late to go back. I could only move forward, and I applied for a United States tourist visa as an unemployed person. In filling out the application form, I got help from my friend Dorota, who lived in Wroclaw. I met her at a Mayan (Tzolkin) Calendar workshop in November 2016 in Warsaw. We were great mirrors for each other at that time. We even picked the same cards about looking in our creations; truly then our lives would change. I submitted my tourist visa application online to the American embassy in Krakow on July 13, 2017. I remember how I was stressful when I filled out the document online. I wanted everything to be perfect and trustworthy. Long, long ago I decided that I would always state the truth, and filling out the form for the US embassy, I stated that I was unemployed. I trusted and played with Life. I said to myself: *If this is my direction, I would receive the tourist visa by telling the truth.* Only faith kept me in doing right.

When I communicated with my family or friends that I applied for American tourist visa, there was only one statement from me: "Thank you for receiving the United States tourist visa." On August 1, 2017, I got it. I was probably the first one who received an American tourist visa from this consul that day, and I wasn't the first in line. The consul was chatting with her assistant why I left job. She didn't ask me. Understanding English and hearing their conversation, I told her the reason that ambulance took me from my working place to the hospital, and job was stressful. It was true. Because of that she gave me a visa.

Some of my friends couldn't believe that the visa was granted to me. The best part of it was that I received it as an unemployed person. When we put the intention that we want to grow and change our lives to be aligned with our calling, follow the signs, and believe in it, then we can only expect the best outcome. We don't have to be ready, but we must allow Life to take rudders from our hands. It will lead us safely to the places where we really belong. We need to trust that Life is for us. Life is God. God's desires are in our hearts, and it always evolves us more and more. Sometimes we don't like it, but this is for our highest good. Life peels all the layers that we put on ourselves. It wants us to reach the core of our true being, our innocence and greatness.

In August 2017 I attended the Mer-Ka-Ba workshop based on Drunvalo Melchizedek's teachings about sacred geometry. His workshops were called the Flower of Life. Our training was facilitated by the same person who had a shamanic school in Lodz. She was certificated and got authorization by Drunvalo Melchizedek in Mexico. Our Mer-Ka-Ba workshop was held in a small town near nature. There were tense four days to learn how we could hop from our brain to the sacred space of the heart, and from there, to the tiny space of the heart where the whole creation of Spirit exists. Being in the sacred space of the heart, we were taught to make energetic rays for halo and activate our sleep light body called Mer-Ka-Ba. The halo and Mer-Ka-Ba were activated simultaneously. Regarding Melchizedek, our souls move in these light bodies after releasing the physical body. Mer-Ka-Ba, after activation, has the shape of the UFO. Curious, the leader told us that at the beginning, when Drunvalo Melchizedek had workshops in Mexico and participants activated their own light bodies, the military helicopters flew over the place. The radars recorded unidentified objects. Because of that, he taught the participants to put intention to Mer-Ka-Ba to be unseen, and the helicopters stopped flying over since then. In the spiritual, word is done or not. It depends only on our intention and trust. In the material world, we hesitate with our minds. We need to be firm in our intentions to grow and believe that it is done. In our training, when we activated our light bodies, we were asked to say intentions also. During activation, I saw through my third eye and felt like my light body expanded. There were twenty or more people in the workshop. In the group, we always received faster effects of our endeavors than by doing it ourselves, and when the leading person was highly awakened, there was no doubt that we would succeed in everything.

In the workshop, we learned two ways to get into the heart space: male way, like Jesus did, and female one. We would see Jesus with the halo in some pictures. We were told that his healing powers were more activated then. We also learned how to create from our heart space. When we create from the mind, we will always experience duality. Our desire will be manifested, but we also experience something that we don't want. It is more a one-sided way of what our ego wants. The reason is that our mind is limited and sees duality. In the dual world, it is white and black, likes and dislikes. With our minds, we cannot embrace and predict the future. They are more logical and need accurate data. We will find out the results of our minds' creations later, and we need to deal with them. We need to remember that when we create (visualize) pictures in our minds, we create mostly from the level of our ego, what we know about life and in what we believe how our life is supposed to look like. We compare ourselves to others, and we want to have what others have because we believe that it make us happy. It is awareness of all about me. We don't know that there is another way more meaningful. In the sacred space of the heart is unity. There is no polarity. We will not experience anything negative and it will be aligned with the person. Heart always gives the dream for the highest good to all involved. When we see pictures, they are moved from the small torus, which is around our heart, to the big one that surrounds our entire physical body, and then manifestation is very fast. The pictures are given by our soul. That's why it is very important to heal our hearts by forgiving our past experiences and by being attuned to our soul's purpose, and then the true desires will be revealed.

In the workshop, we were taught how to get into the tiny space of our hearts, where we are connected with all cosmos in the spiritual realm. There you can meet anybody whom you want to talk to or meet. Virtual meetings in the real world connected by telepathy. Our bodies are equipped in everything we need. We can communicate telepathically, see the future, and materialize our bodies in other places, but our gifts are dormant. Therefore, scientists who are connected to the energetic field of one universal mind bring to the world new inventions to let us be connected, and life becomes easier and faster.

The side effects are more pollution, less time, more artificial intelligence, and gadgets that we become more and more dependent on. We were taught very limiting beliefs about ourselves by our families from generation to generation, and instead of being in communication with the spiritual realm, we became more dependent on the outside world. We love to communicate with one another; that's why the phone is invented and we use cell phones. We love to move from place to place very quickly; that's why we have faster and faster cars and airplanes. New technology makes our lives easier, but it also causes side effects where our bodies become weaker and our minds become more scattered. Our dormant abilities can evolve only by practicing them in silence, but our consciousness as humanity is focused on the outside world, and it forces science to invent invention after invention to improve our lives. Everything that we saw in science fiction movies has become more and more real in this world. As we saw in the movies, there are a lot of side effects as new technology can help us in one way and can be dangerous in another way. There is always duality on the earthy plane. It depends on us how we want to leave Earth for another generation. Can we heal ourselves, our hearts, and remember who we really are? Then the future with technology, which is created right now, would serve all humanity instead of controlling us. We need to be role models to our children and keep them remembering where they originally come from and how they can communicate with our Real Source of Life. When we stop hurting ourselves and our children by adjusting them to society's beliefs, they will create a great future for themselves and other generations.

The Mer-Ka-Ba workshop was powerful. We had the assignment to activate our halo beams and our light body for twenty-one days. Thanks to that it stays with us permanently. In this workshop, I met other wonderful people, and I had a beautiful encounter there. The first day, when we started, we had the exercise to look at one another's eyes and say what we saw. We always see a reflection of our beauty in other people's eyes. When I looked at the person's eyes, I felt like I knew that soul behind those eyes. I felt so much love, and I knew that I was loved very much. It was an encounter on the soul level, not in the human bodies. We had never met before in this life, and we both felt the same joy from the encounter, not having any explanation as to why. During this exercise, we both had more opportunities to look at each other's eyes. It was a joyous experience and, at the same time, embarrassing for both of us. In most cultures, we were taught not to look directly into our interlocutor's eyes. Because of that, we are ashamed to look very long in one another's eyes. Mostly, we are hypnotized by the teeth of the person when he or she speaks. We always look down during our conversation instead of straight into the eyes. I was blessed by this experience. I had started understanding that there is something more, something greater and changeless. I still keep in contact with this person who had eyes of my past-life love. He is a beautiful soul, and now he is in service to others. He has become a healer.

Two years before I had a similar but a little different experience. It was like a vision of the future when my eyes made contact for a second with another person. It was a glimpse. In his eyes, I saw a small toddler girl with black curly hair. She resembled me when I was nine months old. I didn't understand that, and I didn't even accept it as true. I was very much in my head at that time. I left the place without talking to the person. I had an idea about how my life supposed to look like and where I was heading. Over one year later, I found out that I was wrong after like Life had taken its course. I really appreciate for this encounter. It gave me a glimpse of who I would become in the future for myself and others.

My last workshop in Poland was about karma. This was in September 2017. I went to Lodz again. Day before the workshop, I had a phantom surgery to remove epilepsy from my body. It was removed on the energetic level. I saw and felt it. I was asked not to do energetic exercises after this surgery for two to three weeks, but I forgot. Next day I didn't take a tablet, and I did the Tibetan rituals, which were very high energetic-level exercises. They reversed the aging process. My body passed out later.

During my phantom surgery, I saw how I was conceived. Also, I was putting back my energetic handcuffs above my ankles even though they were taken off by the healer. I was so connected to my mother and her beliefs that I didn't want to let go of her. I was scared and felt guilt that I wanted a better life for myself. Even though my conscious intention was to be free and live my own life, my subconscious mind was still attached to the old. I really wanted to believe how my mother viewed life. It would be easier. I grew up with those beliefs, but it turned out that they weren't true. I was on my own journey to really find the Truth of life and myself and share it with others.

On the karma workshop, I have learned that the child's life is based on the nine months before conception, what the parents did at that time; then pregnancy, labor, and the first year of the child's life—these periods define the path of a person's life.

As we see on an ultrasound, a fetus is transparent, like water. All the emotions of a pregnant woman are taken by the fetus as its own. Children start seeing physical separation from their mothers about the second year of their lives. Then they start saying *no*.

So as a fetus, my body took all my mother's emotions. She was left by her boyfriend when he found out that she was pregnant, even though they had been a couple for two years. You can imagine that she felt lonely, betrayed, desperate, and unloved. For sure, she was afraid of the unknown, what came next, and her internal conversations were not always positive. My grandmother was very despotic and ashamed that her daughter was pregnant. My family lived in a very small town where the church and what other people would say were very important. My grandmother was a very Catholic person, and whatever the priest said was holy. She practiced the whole Catholic doctrine and believed in them. It gave her the strength to overcome all obstacles in her life. Priests and church had a big role in her life. She invited them home and chatted with them. At the end of my grandmother's life, on her "bed of death," she told my mother that she regretted keeping with the church and their beliefs so fanatically all her life. My grandmother passed away because of cancer. All those beliefs of condemnation, sin, must listen to the husband, not having right to speak, etc., were causing her to feel resentment and unforgiveness. Also, not caring about the right nutrition for her body brought the experience of this kind of disease. All women were taught for ages by the church that our bodies were sinful and that we had nothing to say. My grandmother lived for eighty-eight years. She always was very hospitable, and she loved to learn about places and new things in the world. She loved to have guests who lived in big cities, and they shared with her their knowledge and experiences.

She had an opportunity to host a lot of professors and high-ranking people, thanks to my two uncles' (her sons') professions. Also, she was a very good seamstress. A lot of well-situated women asked her to make costumes and dresses for them. She had a small Paris in her kitchen. But the Catholic church played a huge role in her life, and she saw sin in everything that concerned her and her family. Everything was filthy. She rejected her body so much that she passed out many times when she was older. My grandmother was a wonderful woman, and the beliefs that she grew up with and kept didn't serve anyone.

She didn't have an easy life with my grandfather. Many times she had to hide herself and earned money so my grandfather didn't take from her by force. He had a lot of friends with whom he spent time drinking. He didn't hurt my mother or other children, but he was a cause of my grandmother's behavior toward them. She had to deal with everything by herself. She didn't have support, only demands and requests. My grandmother accepted life the way it was and was trying to do her best to take care of her six children.

Because of her struggling and beliefs, she wasn't nice to my mother during her pregnancy with me, and she showed it many times. My mother was vulnerable and dependent on her parents, but the main role played by my grandmother was condemnation, shame, and guilt—the Catholic church's beliefs. Guilt wants punishment, and punishment causes pain in the body. Condemnation leads to criticism, which, as a permanent habit, causes an arthritis. Through generations, the Catholic Church taught that women were sinful and worse than men. Also, divorce was a sin. A lot of marriages were kept only because of that belief. When I was born, my mother was taken to the hospital. The labor was in the small health center in Jozefow, a region of Roztocze. All children were born in this place until my mother's labor. After that, it was forbidden. The reason was that my mother barely escaped with her life after I was born.

It was said that the doctor who assisted her delivery was incompetent. He forced it instead of asking for help. From our human perspective, it was all true that he made mistakes and caused all the pain, but looking from the spiritual plane, there were no coincidences. Everything was planned there before it happened, and help was prepared. My mother was taken to the hospital in another town to get good medical care. My grandparents and my mother's siblings took care of me until she came back home from the hospital. As a newborn, I experienced first time the abandonment. When my mother came back, she registered me as Byra, her family name, because my father was hiding. She took him to court to acknowledge his paternity. When I was nine months old, the court recognized his fatherhood and I received his family name, Ferens. So in my case, the pregnancy was tough for both of us. Labor was tough; and after nine months, I was given the family name of my father, who wasn't happy that I appeared in this world.

By taking my father to the court to get alimony and let him be responsible for my appearance and to let him participate in the expenses, she did the right thing from the human-awareness standpoint. But when we know that a child's life path is defined by its parents' actions and surroundings and that the first year of a child's life is the most important, that action wouldn't be so right.

I felt abandoned, not wanted. I couldn't find my identity, and subconsciously, I believed that I owe something to others. My stepfather repeated me when I didn't want to listen that I owe my life to my mother. So if we have in our subconscious mind that kind of belief, that we owe life to others or we were unwanted by our parents, and because of that we are incomplete, there is no wonder that I felt abandoned, unloved, unwanted, and unworthy. I needed to deserve for everything, for love, for acceptance, for money. Also, I received from my mom the belief that I cannot have all that I love. When I was born, I was the most important person to her, but she also loved my father, who wasn't ready to take on responsibilities for both of us. And we both felt somehow abandoned because of that. Children don't need words to be said to know. They feel everything and take things in subconsciously. Our first four to five years as a child, we absorb all what our parents, grandparents, and environment talk about. Their concerns about us, our future, their beliefs about life, and how do they react to us. Our subconscious mind accepts everything. As a result, the beliefs of our nearest surroundings became ours. As an adult person, we have strong feelings to be loyal to our environment even in the most cases it doesn't serve us at all.

Because of the unpleasant experiences of my mother's and my own young life, my self-esteem was very low. I packed myself in the relationship, which only proved how low I treated myself. I had debts from the very beginning when I started adult life. Even though I dreamed about something better, I didn't get it because deep, deep in my subconscious mind, I believed that I didn't deserve and I was not good enough to reach for what I wanted. All these thoughts and feelings were sent to the universe. When the feelings are radiating from the body, the universe matches to us people and situations that are reflection of the frequency of our beliefs about ourselves and life. People showed me exactly, as mirrors, my beliefs about myself. I always needed to ask about small things. I needed to deserve attention. I always needed to choose between two things. I couldn't have both. As a kid, if my behavior wasn't accepted, I was punished physically or blackmailed. My stepfather wanted me to be obedient and quiet. He repeated very often a Polish proverb: "A humble calf sucks from two mothers." I wasn't the one who was quiet, and I didn't care. I liked myself the way I was, and I wanted to be loved and accepted that way. Mostly, I wanted to get attention from my mother, to spend time with me, but she didn't understand it, and that's why we were always fighting.

What I have learned is that children are teachers for the parents in that they need to evolve. Also, children are the mirrors to their parents' unexpressed feelings. When we hide our feelings of what hurt us, the children reflect the need to express them very loudly. I was very loud and emotional. Another thing that I have learned was that we cannot receive love from others like we want because they don't know how to love us. That's why it is important to learn how to love and appreciate ourselves first. Then we will attract people who will reflect this love and appreciation back to us, never the other way around. We all have wounds from our childhood, and because of that, our hearts are closed. We keep resentments, guilt, shame, blame, or even hate. When we say that we love somebody, we don't mean it. Our behaviors are different than our words. We cannot show our affection to another person or even to our child completely because we were brought up that way. We couldn't speak about our emotions, our feelings. We weren't listened to as children, so we are not able to listen to others unconditionally. We always assume we know better what the other person wants to say without really listening to them. Our behavior is either in defensive or offensive mode. Also, we behave as though we don't care, and we disregard what the person says, which is what matters. Very often we manipulate the interlocutor and take over the whole conversation to prove that the person was wrong, and in extreme cases in conversations, people will request to be apologized to because the interlocutor started asking for the rights to be listened to. Most women become victims of that kind of manipulation, and as a domino effect, we (both parents) do the same to our children.

Our love is in our minds, and our minds cannot love. The mind doesn't feel, only logically process data based on past experiences—what we had learned and what information we receive through our senses right now. Our minds are cold and very often cruel toward our bodies and others. The mind is the kingdom of our ego where there is wanting, warring, lusting, separation, and need—need for love, need for a new husband or wife, need for children, need for money, need for a new car, need for a new house, need for the new clothes even if we have plenty in our wardrobes. When our needs are fulfilled, we feel peace and happiness for a short while until something unexpected happens, which can be the next day. If we cannot afford something, we become angry and feel less about ourselves. We blame others and life for our unhappiness. We deny the facts, we cheat ourselves, we get depressed, and we envy others because they are happy. Because of that, we deprive ourselves of our happiness. We have internal dialogues that we don't deserve and we are worse than others. We cut off friends by saying and pretending that everything is all right with us and with our lives. We stop being open and trustful. We feel internal pain, and we do not allow ourselves or others to heal the pain by opening the wounds because they hurt too much.

To bring our life into harmony, we need to first heal ourselves from all the wounds. We need to open them again, and it brings healing to our bodies and minds. Our hearts start being more open, and the past stops hurting us. We start living more in the present moment with greater optimism. We start creating and planning our new future with joy and confidence, and we truly start feeling real love again, the love that is eternal. We feel whole again.

When I was a young kid, I shared my dreams with the nearest family, when I had chance to be listened, I was ridiculed. I was told that they were impossible. The effect was that I forgot what the dreams were. I only remember that I liked drawing a lot. When I was a teenager, I loved watching fashion shows on TV. But it turned out that fashion wasn't the reason I came here. My assignment was to bring the truth to the world by sharing with tools that I found and to use them to help everyone do the same steps. It is a fearful step, because it will show us how we were programmed unconsciously our lives. But also, this step will release us from all delusive beliefs. We will become completely free.

When I was a child, my mother used to say that my grandmother would always repeat that I believed that I could get everything like the touch of a magic wand. And it turned out that I was right. We can get everything that we want with ease and joy. We only need to believe that everything is possible. We also need to have the willingness to come back home to our hearts, where all possibilities exist. The magic wand is the *law of love*, which attracts everything in our lives. I had known since I was a small girl, and I forgot it. All love is in us and surrounds us. When we start living with the truth, every door will open for us and we would share our uniqueness with love in the world. We will stop feeling being condemned, which was taught by the churches. We would really find the true kingdom, the kingdom of our Father, which is Spirit. We all have inherited unlimited supply of all good: all ideas, all money, all love, all joy, all time, and all health and youth for our bodies.

During the karma workshop, we wrote letters to our parents, then burned them. We put our resentments on the paper and then burned it. For the first time, I let go of resentment toward my father, and also I wanted to try to forgive my mother for the way she was when I started making my own choices based on my inner guidance instead of my society beliefs. It wasn't so easy because she thought that she had the right to tell me what I should do or not do. I knew she had good intentions, but I stopped being that small girl who needed to be quiet and just listen to the people who brought her up. I was a grown woman as she was. My mother wanted to stay in her comfort zone, and I wanted to grow. She was afraid, and I was not. She didn't understand that when we want to grow, we need to listen only to ourselves, because our guidance system is within, not outside us. I was over forty years old and acted strange, according her and others' understanding. I was a puzzle for them. They made assumptions that I was escaping from my obligations and didn't know what I was doing. I knew that I was being called to something else in my life. With little understanding and an open heart, I wanted to experience it. At that time, I could count only on myself and nobody else to understand me.

Letting go of my father was easier because he didn't interfere with my life. After burning the letters, I received a thought coming up from the heart that all these were planned. I felt joy and peace and shared this with my friend in the workshop. Right away, I remembered about the pamphlet from the book *Before You Were Born—Your Soul's Plan* by Robert Schwartz that I had read a few months before. So I started feeling relief.

I understood that it was planned that, after my mother had gotten pregnant with me, my parents' pathways would split. We all had issues to work out. My issue was of abandonment and following the path of love to understand, let go of all burdens, and share the truth and tools with others so they will use them to be able to understand their lives. One of my parents' issues is letting go of all resentment and unforgiveness toward themselves and life and let others support them in this process so they would not repeat it again in the next incarnation. Until they work on this, they will repeat it in another life time in a different situation. We better let go of this now to be free and move forward to the next topic, which is really only one, love. I was born as the eldest in these two families. Thanks to my parent's splitting, I have two half brothers from my mother's and my father's side. Between Bartosz and Michal are few months' difference. The same goes with Pawel and Piotr. I am the person who can connect them.

Being with my mother's family, they didn't listen to me. They had vision of me as a regular person that shares impossible ideas. It was sad that everything I had discovered and shared was judged and put in a space of disbelief. This knowledge would help members of my family look into their lives differently, release their own pain, and start life anew with a different consciousness and purpose. They didn't see what I saw, and they didn't understand why I was doing this. On the other hand, being here, I mostly met people who knew the truth and looked at life the same way I do—that life is filled with discovery, unfoldment, joy, and love. We all understood that life has meaning and purpose till the end of our existence, beyond the age of the body and the place of birth. There is no other way. But a lot of people are still living in delusion, and they are afraid of looking at life differently from how they used to. It is too scary for them and sad the same time because they don't know how beautiful they are and what they are capable of. There is a Universal law that says we all are equal.

We have right to our own choices, and we can choose what to do with things that do and don't serve us. It depends on what we are listening to: our limited minds or open hearts. We cannot push anyone to do their own work because we all have free will, which is given by God, and we need to learn how to respect their own choices. We can share the knowledge how life works and who we are, and let them choose. This includes our children also. We have no right to control and manipulate them even they are small. We can only communicate with them and respect their will. They will listen to us when we stop pushing them; just let them grow in their own pace.

All the time since I started the new process of thinking and being, I was alone, without support from anybody. My family didn't understand me. They cared by judging me. They thought like most people in the world. They think mostly of what they don't want than what they want and that to get something, you need to deserve it and work hard. Their belief is that good experiences happen by luck and bad experiences by fate. They complain about their government. They point toward what they do or don't do. But they are not aware that the government is a mirror of the nation's consciousness.

When I said to one of my uncles, when he was complaining on the officials from the Polish government, that he was giving them more power and that complaining would not change anything, he said I was stupid. I omitted what he said, but people don't want to listen to others who have a different point of view. Their minds and hearts are closed. They really suffer from the wounds of the past. They show love this way and forget that life is diverse. If we don't allow ourselves to listen to others' points of view, we cut off ourselves from learning and exploring life. We are all Life.

Most societies listen to those who speak louder; judge them by their appearance; and very often envy these people for being better educated, well-connected, or better situated. Those who have a university diploma and a PhD degree are the most respected. People think that only a person with a university degree knows more. They know a lot but mostly in the field of their professional interests, and we need to accept it and appreciate that. But we all have knowledge within us to rediscover. We see on TV like leaders or scientists wanting to prove their own right. They argue with one another; they devalue one another in front of millions of curious viewers. Some of them show very poor manners. They don't know how to listen and don't respect the point of view of their interlocutor. When the person is very certain in their beliefs and expresses it in a very confident way, most of society, whose awareness is on the same level of understanding, supports his or her beliefs by accepting them as their own. Their behaviors and actions are reflected in how the society lives in communication with others. That's why people are attracted to that kind of entertainment. People's consciousness determines what kind of programs we have on TV. When we look deeply, there are many manipulative commercials. A lot of channels have the same shows with the same topics, and only the actors and names are different. There are a lot of disasters and a lot of violence, and there is a low sense of humor. Yet people buy it and identify with this kind of entertainment and these beliefs, thinking that life looks this way. So how can our lives look different if we belief in violence, division, diseases, and disasters and if we disrespect each other?

Most people who are looking for the recognition from others feel very poor inside. By shouting, cheating, and expressing violently, they want to cover their own insecurity and they are afraid of showing their true feelings. Most of society agree with that kind of behavior. We all are afraid of being exposed. We have so much insecurity, pain, and unhealed wounds that run our lives. Most people are not aware of that. We make ourselves so busy and don't have time to sit in the peaceful place to watch our creations and thoughts. The Universe always catches what is inside you, not what you show outside. You can cheat people, but you cannot cheat yourself and the laws created by God. He created you, and according to the one of laws, what you give, you will receive. It is the law of cause and effect.

In the spiritual world, this is called karma. Because of karma, we incarnate many times on Earth to work it out. Even when you feel good about yourself but your behavior toward others is to manipulate them by cheating, lying, gossiping, stealing, disrespecting, bulling, looking for benefits only for yourself, it stays with you. Our low actions toward either an adult or a child are equal to God and are against universal laws. We cannot control and be disrespectful of others. What we do, we receive the same in the different ways, for example, losing our health, jobs, money, meaningful relationships, joy, trust, or support from others. Life gives us all the time information through people, situations, and from our body's health. You cannot cheat God. He created you and gave you the power to create your life by using laws that are in harmony with Him, and you cannot do them by yourself. Trust me, I tried. We need to come back to our Source to become innocent and start enjoying life again.

When you are offended by the nearest family member, it is not easy to be on your own journey. Everybody you have known is against you. In my case, my mother, some of her siblings, and my own son. At that time my mother's concern was about Martin her only grandson. She took my behavior as irresponsible. My mother and my son judged me as careless because I left my job and he was still studying at the university. When I sold the apartment, my mother's thoughts were what her grandson would get in the future. Everything that I did was always wrong in their view of point. It was a little sad that your own mother is against you and thinks only one way. She wasn't able to help me financially, and she also didn't help me feel good, having her worries about her grandson. I was by myself. The funniest thing was that, all I did I had my son in mind. I wanted the best for him. The kind of mental, emotional, and financial support that he got from me, I didn't get from my mother or others. I was on my own all the time.

I had a bank loan and bills to pay. I took a loan to support my son financially during his studies. I wanted him to feel comfortable and be able to focus on his studies instead of worrying about money. I gave my son encouragement when he doubted himself. I supported him in everything that he was able to see more of the world and to be more open for the better.

Once, my mother said that I had given him too much. But really? I was his parent, and I wanted him to thrive and believe in himself. Most importantly, I shared with him the knowledge how life works. He used the knowledge from time to time, but what I noticed, he preferred to think like others to fit in. I took a lot on myself at that time, but I trusted that everything would work out. I was positive, grateful, and open. I always had money to cover all my financial obligations. All the time I found the way that money came to me. It was magical.

My mother's awareness was like most people: you need to think about others and put your dreams down. Regarding my and other people's diseases, including her own, the tablet was an antidote. Doctors know better. They finished schools. They studied so many years, and they knew the body. For sure they know the anatomy of the body, but the cause is not in the body, and most of them don't know that. The cause is our thinking and unexpressed emotional blocks from childhood. By holding to the past, we keep creating more blockages, and energy cannot flow smoothly. The illness in our body is the effect. When our minds are healed by our harmonious thinking and emotional charges from childhood will be integrated, we would enjoy living in a healthy body for many, many years.

Also, I grew in a society where men and women were treated differently. The man was always first, and he could behave disrespectfully toward his wife and children. The society kept to the man's side. He had the right to learn, to get full support when he wants to achieve something. As a woman, we forgot about ourselves and a lot of us gave up on ourselves. We started believing that our role was about taking care of our children and husbands. We accepted the belief that the fulfillment of a woman is having a husband and children. We lost ourselves in the duties for our nearest family members instead of fulfilling our being here. Mostly people believe that there is only one opportunity to be fulfilled: to get a degree and good education. This is when we were young and without responsibilities toward our families. When the family comes, it is over. You need to be a mother and a wife and go to a less-paid work, and when you come back from work, you have another work called family.

We believe that we had to do everything by ourselves. Our husbands or children cannot do anything. The truth is, they can but they don't have to. We took from them their part of commitment to the family. What do most husbands do when they come back home from work? They rest. They have time for themselves to watch TV, to read, to have a nap. They wait for their wives unless they come back home with grocery shopping, to prepare the meal and serve them. We grew in societies where the woman needs to do all, and we do without rest and protect our partners because we think that he works so hard. We don't see how hard we work. Because of that, we don't let our husbands take responsibility for teaching our children or cooking for us because he cannot cook or he doesn't want. Really? They can do the same what we do.

I remember when I was forced by my husband to cook. He loved to eat and cook, but his wife had to do that. At the beginning, when we came back to Poland from Spain, our fights were about cooking. My husband did not enjoy cooking while he saw me sitting and doing nothing. One day I gave up fighting, and I started cooking for my family even though I didn't like it. I loved baking from time to time. I used to do it at home, but my pastries weren't appreciated because, according my partner, his mother baked the best two kinds of cakes, and it was enough. So I stopped baking and performed duties I didn't enjoy at all. In my case, it was my husband who tamed me and forced me to do things that I didn't like instead of appreciating what I really did want to give to our family. In other homes, mothers pushed their daughters to cooking with the words, "You need to learn how to cook to serve your family in the future." When our partner wants to spare us from cooking, he mostly invites us to the restaurant to spend a nice time there and doesn't bother about money. He wants to be far away from the kitchen. Are you able to invite your husband and children to the restaurant without any reason in the middle of the week? Probably none of us would suggest it even if we wanted to. Some of us would think, *Why should I?* I can cook, so we will eat at home; and then I will do dishes, washing, and other things. I will not spend money in the restaurant if I can do it by myself, and my family loves how I cook. We are so proud of ourselves and needy to please everybody. Because of that, we are so tired. We are so attached to our duties that they are our second nature. We even don't notice that we are in a vicious cycle. When our bodies have enough, they get ill and we are not aware that our behavior had caused it. We don't give our bodies the right to have a rest and do nothing after work.

In our minds, we have the belief that we can do it better. But the truth is that only then do we feel more appreciation for ourselves. Our self-esteem is so low that we don't let ourselves rest, then we lose control and do nothing. Our minds plan all the time, thinking about our family's needs. We don't know how to relax. We don't let our husbands or partners learn how to cook, serve us, and take some more responsibilities from us. They are better cooks than we are. They love to eat, so they know how a dish is supposed to look and taste. Our children are their children, and they can be great fathers when we let them. A lot of us see ourselves as the saviors of our small world, which is the family. We have a feeling that if it wasn't for us, the world of our children or husbands would be destroyed. What we do is giving our children the wrong impression about life, and instead of saving them right now, we teach them the same patterns that we were taught by our mothers. We are not helping the family by taking all the responsibilities on our shoulders to protect them. Our sacrifice takes out from us time for a good rest, energy, and health of our bodies. We are destroying our bodies step by step. Because of this behavior, we are taking away the opportunity for our loved ones to grow. This is one of the reasons they came to this planet again. We cut in the higher plan of their existence here. We are so in the world of others that when we have free time, the quiet time kills us. We don't know what to do. Some of stressful mothers cannot find peace at night, so they take the night pills to have a decent sleep. These pills are poison to our organs. When our bodies are withdrawn from the energy, we start noticing wrinkles, feel the pains, and start comparing ourselves with our younger version, and another lie comes in: beliefs from the society such as aging.

Because of this kind of believing, we don't give the universe the opportunity to help us. The Universal Mind called God can really do everything easier and faster way, when we only ask and relax. When we are relaxed, we become in the state of receiving, then we get wiser solutions to our problems or challenges. Life has bigger plan for us than we think. It wants us to be happy and fulfilled before we leave this planet. The most important for God is that time and aging doesn't exist. It was made up by our limited human minds. Let's do a favor to ourselves and forget about it *now*! We are not our bodies. God is eternal and lives in each of us. Eternity is our birthright.

There was a time that I was in so big progress that I stopped caring what others who surrounded me thought about me. It wasn't easy, but thanks to that, I grew and became stronger. And I encouraged others who wanted to listen, who were open for a new idea.

People are interested in people's laws. I have started to be interested in God's laws that creates and governs the Earth and all the galaxies and, most importantly, gives breath to our bodies.

God gave us many universal laws with which He sustains all of creation, such as (as we know from science) gravity, flotation, and many other physical laws, but also, there is the law of attraction, which is not taught in schools. None of these laws are seen, and they operate perfectly. They are neutral and work to our advantage. The most important law to know is *the law of attraction*, called *the law of love*, which I mentioned before to be the magic wand. The reason is that through this law, we attract all the experiences in our lives, including diseases or the recovery of our bodies, bad or good relationships, poverty or abundance—all these through vibratory thoughts in our minds and feelings in our bodies. Not knowing that we are like small children playing on the playground our parents or guardians chose for us, we have no freedom to explore by ourselves. We really don't know what life is about and what kind of experiences we want to have, and we base them only on the knowledge and experiences of others, who mostly don't know how to live their lives. Where our attention is, our energy goes. Behind this is a belief that creation is born from the experiences in our life. When we focus on love and start dreaming, we use the law correctly and start flowing harmoniously with the whole Life. That's why the law of attraction is called *the law of love*. Having this knowledge and using it is the best gift we can give ourselves. We then start growing and evolving. We then become more joyful, and our lives will start having meaning because, at the end, we will find our calling, the purpose of our existence here—to serve others through the creativity and gifts we have.

The law of attraction works in every situation—when we want to solve the problem, find solution to our income, or have decided to change our lives for the better. There are three basic steps to receive what we desire: *ask, believe, and receive.*

When we dream, we grow and become a different person. The old personality disappears one day, and we even didn't notice when it happened. This is a process of peeling away the layers and go to the core of who we really are and why we are here. There is a process of changing the paradigm of our old beliefs, which limited us and covered our true nature. It is required from us to be conscious of our thoughts, words, and actions. It must fit with our dream. Feeling good and love for our dream makes us passionate about it. When we receive our dreams, we need to be passionate about it. When we receive our dreams, we feel very good. We feel overjoyed and powerful. We are simply happy and grateful. The requirement is to remember to speak in present moment like it is happening *now*. Why? Everything in the universe is happening simultaneously. We need to send vibrations of our thoughts, *feel* like we have it right now. You will be amazed at how fast and flawless the solution will come without any worry or without controlling the outcome or the how. Allow the universe to match you vibrationally with the right people and energies, those that serve your desire. Through our human senses, we see the past, present, and future—linear time. Our true nature, as soul, lives in the *now*. Our feelings and thoughts exist only in the present moment. We can recognize them by only being in the present moment. These three ingredients bring experiences what we call future. We cannot think or feel in the past. We cannot feel or think in the future either. We cannot breathe yesterday or tomorrow. We breathe *now*. Tomorrow will be another *now* when we will think and feel our emotions. Our feelings tell us when we are aligned with our solution or dream by making us feel good. When we are out of alignment, we feel bad about ourselves and the situation we are in; we doubt and worry.

If we feel bad, it shows us that we are unconscious of our thoughts and we are drifting in negative emotions. (Emotions are thoughts in motion. The other words energy in motion. Thought is energy.) When we feel good, we know that our thoughts are on the higher frequency and we need to continue deliberately by choosing good thoughts to align with what we desire. *Gratitude is the best way to feel good.*

We also need to remember that when we create our dreams and solve any problems through the law of attraction, it is suggested to stop looking at the current circumstances. This will pass when we are aligned with what we desire. These circumstances were brought by our previous way of thinking and understanding life. To create what we desire, we need to see and, most importantly, feel that we are the person we want to be or have something right now beyond our present conditions. Then the universe will meet us with what we want in magical, flawless ways. Visualization is very useful tool in creating the best outcome that we want in our lives; we need to feel like we have it right now. After that, we can put in the pink babble and send it to the ether. Pink babble is creation that comes from the heart. After that, to emphasize it, we can say thank you, feel joy, and release it. When we know what to do, we can start taking actions aligned with what we want. In my case, when I was visualizing selling my apartment, I started packing and tidying up everything, and I packed unnecessary things and moved them to my mother's basement. When you don't know what to do and your solution or desire is beyond your ability, then allow yourself feel good, and it will be solved or delivered in a miraculous way for all involved. Such was an experience I had with the London Eye.

Nikola Tesla, the inventor of all times, created all his inventors in his mind by visualizing things. He assembled and dismantled in his mind. When everything worked out during visualization process, then he started building the devices in his laboratory.

To ease the way and keep us in the frequency of our desire, we need to answer this question for ourselves: *Why do we want this or that?*

The manifestation of our desire takes place in "the future." But it depends on which consciousness we are on and the dream would come faster or slower. If we create from the ego state and we put some limiting thoughts on it as "how" or "if we deserve," the desire can come to us later. When we put our desire in the space that we are a child of God, then miracles happen very fast, even in a few days. For God, there is nothing impossible. Only believe, and it makes it so.

We need to become the masters of our thoughts and feelings. A mindset is very important. We need to be aware what we think about, how we speak, and how we feel; and then our actions need to be in alignment with what we want. It can be scary at the beginning and a lot of doubt if it is true. It is okay if only we allow ourselves to change our beliefs, Life give us strength and guidance to overcome it. At the beginning, it can be very challenging, doing it by ourselves and having people around whose beliefs are different. But we cannot give up. In the whole process, we will receive all the support and love from others who we would never imagine that they would do that.

How to master our minds? By observing our thoughts and behaviors. First, we will notice that our mind is very scattered. We don't remember if we locked the door, turned off the light, or closed the windows when we left our house. We don't know what the code is to the intercom. We pushed the buttons automatically. When we stop suddenly in the present moment and want to remember the numbers to decode the intercom, we don't know. It takes a time to remember. Even driving, we do automatically. Why? Once remembered, the subconscious mind takes it over. We don't think what we are supposed to do when driving or doing other chores. Our focus loosens up, and we are lost in our thoughts that we don't see anything around. We drove hundreds of miles and we don't know when it happened. Our lives are on the autopilot. We are not aware of our thoughts, feelings, or our behaviors and reactions. Everything is coded in our subconscious mind. It is a vulnerable mind, and it doesn't know jokes. She takes everything seriously. The thoughts we let in through our consciousness mind, they become our life experiences. We need to filter our thoughts and choose them deliberately. What words do we use about ourselves? What kind of life do we want to experience? We are cocreators with the Great Universal Mind of God. Also, it is very important what we think about five minutes before we fall asleep. When we sleep, our subconscious mind starts working on our daily experiences. That's why it is so important to think good thoughts before we sleep. We will not change our life experiences and our way of being unless we start reprogramming our subconscious mind and face the false beliefs about life. These beliefs are imprinted from generation to generation by families, schools, society, churches, governments, and by media. Also, our past lives have a huge role in our way of thinking. Our subconscious mind was programmed from the very beginning when we were children. We didn't understand what the adults said, but our subconscious mind was poisoned by society's beliefs. That's why when we grew up, those beliefs became ours, even if they were false.

To start reprogramming our subconscious mind, the best way is to be grateful. Minds focused on gratitude attract more thoughts about gratitude and bring us to a different dimension. We start seeing our lives from a different perspective. We respect ourselves more and others. We become more open. Gratitude will bring us to the better places and circumstances even we cannot imagine. Gratitude brings us to our life's destiny. It is good to be fulfilled and be aligned with the assignment that was chosen by our soul in this lifetime.

> God is good, therefore Life is good. *Absolute Goodness is the substance, the source and the supply of all existence. This aspect of the Godhead is always in integrity with itself, which means that it cannot contradict its own laws, nature, and relationship to its creation. The nature of God is life enhancing, positive, upward spiraling—good in every way.*
>
> —*Agape Spiritual Principles and Practices*

CHAPTER 4

Who Are We?

Ye shall know the truth, and the truth shall make you free.

—John 8:32

I have told you that I AM.

—John 18:8

Before we know who we are, we need to lean on faith. "*Faith is your fortune,*" as Neville states in his book of the same title.

Sometimes we try to reach our goal of abundance, prosperity, or love from another person, but we don't receive it. You ask, "Why didn't I get what I desired the most if I had done what I was taught about law of attraction, visualization, or development books?" The answer is that, we receive what we believe and our beliefs are in our subconscious mind. As I mentioned before, we are deeply programmed by society to feel unworthy, not good enough, to feel guilty. We blame ourselves and others for our unhappiness. Those beliefs were imprinted by the surrounding from which we grew. We cannot receive what contradicts with our subconscious beliefs. Subconscious mind gives us the same or similar experiences over and over until we let go of the old beliefs about ourselves and change them little by little. It will create a new person, who we will become by following our path that was unfolded for each of us.

We need to trust in the process that the Universe wants to give us the best. At the beginning our desires are mostly based on the society's beliefs and our needs. We worry about our bills, our belongings, so we focus to manifest material independence. But when we let go of our worries and ask "What do I really need to grow?" and "Who am I?" these questions will move the whole Universe to bring the answers. We will feel the impulse to change something that we were afraid of. We will act differently, unreasonable. We will become closer to our Source. When we don't get what we want, it means that something better is waiting for us around the corner or in a different place. Because of that trust, we will become more alive and courageous. Sometimes we need to move to another country or continent to grow in a different environment for our dream for a better and fulfilled life come true. Mostly, what we expect from life is very small and limited. We want to change, but we are afraid of it. We think that the change will come by itself. It will, but it will come mostly in a painful way. Life wants us to expand and push us to our limits, but very often we are so stubborn and attached to our environment that we don't even try to cause the change in our life and our way of thinking. We are stuck in our unhealthy relationships or in our jobs that we cannot grow or we are so stressed that our bodies have enough and get ill. The body gives us the signals to stop. It says, "Give me more space to relax, take care of me. I am here to serve you longer than you think. You are consuming me." When disease comes, then nothing is more important than health and we are pushed to let go of what was not nourishing to us. Doesn't matter if we want to or not, life will do it for us when we are not willing to do it ourselves.

September 25, 2017, from Wroclaw, I went to Warsaw and flew to New York City the next day. I stayed at my aunt and uncle's place for one night.

September 26, 2017, the whole journey to find myself started. Everything was so flawless. In Kiev, where I was transferred to New York City, I started to meet people from different nationalities who were heading to NYC like I was.

When we landed at JFK airport, we needed to stand in long, long lines to get the immigration officer to let us in. It was very hot there. At that time in NYC, it was twenty-eight degrees Celsius, eighty-two Fahrenheit. When we were standing in our lines, it was the first time that I noticed a lot of divisions. There were two different lines for citizens and the guests. It was a very nervous atmosphere. The officers who guided us to the passport check in the machines made that kind of atmosphere. The officers were women. They were kind but nervous and loud at the same time. I felt relaxed and happy, but in the air, I sensed a lot of fear and insecurity. After checking passports in the machines, we were guided to the immigration officers. When it was my turn, I was welcomed very warmly by the person. We chatted a little. At the end of our talk, he wished me happy birthday, because he noticed in the passport that my birthday was in twelve days. It was a very nice and warm welcome to the new land. I was appreciative of it. It was a very good sign for me.

I stayed for four days at my friend's house. She was the only person that I knew at that time in the US. The next day she took me for sightseeing to downtown NYC. We were in the place where the World Trade Center, or Twin Towers, stood. Now there is only one tower and a memorial place for those whose lives were lost on September 11, 2001. Then we went to Brooklyn Bridge and some other places. All the time when we were sightseeing, I couldn't believe that I was in NYC. My mind couldn't catch it. It was a very strange feeling.

The next day I went to the upper town to see Central Park, Fifth Avenue, Times Square, and Rockefeller Center by myself. It was fun learning by myself and being able to move from place by place in New York City. I have very good orientation, and I found each place easily.

My body had three days to adjust to the six-hour time difference. On the fourth day, I flew to San Diego where an additional time difference of three hours was added. I felt very well all the time. A lot of people have jet leg after changing time zones, but my body was fine. I felt fresh and happy all the time. I used affirmations to feel like that, and I was grateful.

The flight from New York City to San Diego lasted six hours. The sightseeing was beautiful. I had the window seat, and I could see mountains and ranches. The view was breathtaking for me.

When we landed, I was taken to the Western Best Hotel by shuttle, which I booked back in Poland, and the new experiences were ahead of me. The hotel was located at the beautiful bay filled with sailing boats. After I checked in, I went to my room and I had some time to be by myself in the new place and to adjust before my roommate arrived. Her name was Meri. We got along very well from the very beginning.

At the end of the training, we took a picture with our name tags. It came up Meri Magdalena. Now I understand that it was another sign from Life which path was chosen for me in this lifetime.

We started the training the same day that we arrived. There were nineteen participants including me. Most of the participants were from the US, one person was from Canada, I was from Poland, one girl was from Brazil (whose heart I admired), and one person was from Argentina. There were only two men, and the rest of the participants were women. The facilitators turned out a very warm couple with whom we felt very safe during the whole process of releasing emotions and become more healthy than we had arrived. They had two wonderful, full-of-joy, and compassionate women to assist them: Sandra and Catherine. Christy was the administrative support. We all trusted them, and thankfully, we trusted one another. The cost of our training covered seven days of activities, full exclusive stay at the hotel, and one day on the facilitators' ranch. The weather was always for us. We were in California at last.

Every day we implemented something new from Louise's teachings. During the three to four days, I felt very well. I was cherished, but I didn't understand about all the emotional bursting from some of us. We worked in couples, and with every exercise, we changed our partners. It was a powerful exercise because we could know one another better, and we were very open and trustful. There was one exercise where we would hit the pillows. We needed to close our eyes, and when we started to hit the pillow, our biggest emotional pain came out. Before that training, I didn't know that body healing was an emotional one. We all were wounded. What came out from me in this exercise I noticed that it had a very powerful impact in my whole life: "*I just wanted be understood.*" That's all. I didn't know that the lack of understanding by the nearest people in my environment, such as family and ex-partner, can hurt so much. I wasn't understood as a child, as a teenager, and as a wife. But the most painful was when I wasn't understood during my process of developing a new way of thinking and acting, when I really wanted to do something with my life for a very first time. At the end of the training, Rick Nichols gave me his small book *Who Do You Think You Are?* I really felt like the hero of his book, a small eagle called Eagerlet, during my whole journey. Eagerlet was born in the turkey family in the barnyard, but he didn't fit in. He started melding with other barn's creatures and still couldn't fit in anywhere. That was until he found a family of eagles who showed him the way. Thanks to that, he was able to see his own greatness at the end. I was on my journey to myself, to my true essence. On the fifth day, we had a presentation of what we had learned. We were divided in groups, and each group was in a different room. Every person chose a topic that he or she would like to teach us about. After that we were certificated as leaders of the Heal Your Life training.

    I chose the prosperity topic, and I chose to be the last who would present the teachings in our group. Before me was my new friend, and his topic was about relationships. He asked us to look at the mirror, to look in our eyes, and say "*I love you.*" Louise Hay emphasized that looking into your eyes in the mirror and saying to yourself something nice is very important. It builds up love, self-esteem, and respect for yourself. You start taking care of yourself more, your health. You start seeing more consciously people who surround you and noticing their wrong behavior toward you. You stop putting up with it. You act differently, not hurting yourself anymore. You start listening to your inner guidance, which always starts with awareness. At the beginning, when we are saying this, we feel a lot of resistance in our bodies. We were taught that looking at our reflection and being happy with what we see is vain and shallow. Because of that, we stopped admiring the person that was in the mirror, and instead of that, we started judging ourselves. When we look into our reflection, all we see are negative things about our bodies, avoiding looking up into our eyes to really find who we are. They say that "the eyes are the window to the soul." Your soul is divine and capable of everything that is the best for and connected with your heart. When we again start loving and accepting ourselves, we would look at our reflection with appreciation of the person who we are. We speak warmly and with affection and encouragement. We deserve the most to be kind to ourselves. Many people suffer from mental illnesses because of a lack of love and respect for themselves. They have a habit of thinking negatively all the time, based on feedback from other people and their past experiences. When we had the same exercise on the second day of our training, I felt so good. But that time, when we were asked by our friend to look into our eyes in the mirror and saying something nice, I burst into tears and said that my childhood sucked. Meri, who sat at my right, said that something beyond me moved this outburst. It was my first breakdown with exception to hitting the pillows. After that, I cried on every meditation that we had till the end of our training. These meditations were with healing music. They were powerful. I loved those sounds.

I didn't remember my childhood at all. I denied it all the time. I lived only adult life. When I started to be more open to the idea that our childhood had a lot to do with our adult life and the decisions that we make, I started remembering more and more. It wasn't a nice feeling, but thanks to that, I was healing. Even I wasn't aware of that. Every illness has an emotional foundation. Our bodies were created to be healthy all the time, not accepting the body's age.

When we were a child and we got cold, we had more attention from our parents, especially our mothers. Some children got wet during the night. Some children also got ill because the environment in their house was not easy to bear, so their reaction was to be sick. Then the parents acted in more loving ways. They stopped arguing with each other. They were more understanding of their child and wanted them to recover. I remember when I was in primary school I had earaches very often. It was very easy for me to get otitis. Also, sore throat was an issue. Once, my vocal cords were so infected that I wasn't able to speak over three weeks.

The ears have the capacity to hear the truth in metaphysics. When there are problems with the ears, it means that we are not happy with what we are hearing. There can be two metaphysical causes behind why children get earaches: when there are arguments between parents all the time or when they hear a lot of times the word *no*. In the home where I grew up, there were arguments, and the word *no* was like mantra to me from my parents. So I was shutting myself off by getting earaches. And as a result, as an adult person, many times I told myself, "No, because you cannot"—the same words that my parents told me as a child.

The throat is the avenue of verbal expression. This is where our creativity flows. In the throat, we have a chakra center where change takes place by a declaration words such us "I am," "I will," "I have," and "I want." When we feel that we don't have right to speak up for ourselves or express emotions (among others, anger), we often have problems with our throat. I had all the time as a kid.

Also, another reason to get sick was when we want to avoid something and get stressed. When we become adults, we react the same way. For things that overwhelm us, we resist or we want to get loving attention from somebody else. This is our reaction that we learned in our childhood. When we got sick, we can avoid things and we receive more attention and compassion from others. We stop feeling lonely, they give us support, they are more loving, they ask us to relax, and they even feel guilty because they were the cause of our suffering (physical violence). But when we feel better and everything comes back to normal, our relationships with others go back to the same state that was before. Our relationships weren't transformed because of our illness and recovering. We again start feeling alone, not loved, and misunderstood. When we have to go back to work that we don't like, we start complaining again and feel stressful. We can only transform this with changing our thoughts and start appreciating every moment. We also need to appreciate ourselves instead of looking for approval from the outside world. We can make changes by letting go of the old belief that our happiness depends on an outside outcome. Illnesses in our bodies are created by disharmony in our lives more than the body being exposed and infected by a virus or bacteria.

We need to understand that air gives our bodies life. We are breathing because of that. The air cannot kill us unless we believe in it. There is a lot of smoke, but that is not the air's fault, only by people who don't care about their health. Others have contributed to this, and we repeat their mistakes. Also, the air is not contagious like advertisements say to sell more drugs. Our thoughts are programmed with that kind of marketing. That's why people get cold during winter, fall, or any other season. It depends on what kind of illness is on our TV. We started believing people on the screen that we can get ill because there is a season to get ill. All this stuff was made up by the pharmacological industry to sell more drugs or vaccinations for flu, which are more dangerous for our health than helpful. People believe in it, and they get sick every season. Their mantra when talking with others is, now we have flu season, cold season, allergy season, etc. All these thoughts are given from mother to daughter, and in the present times, it has escalated and created new diseases through media. That's why the pharmacology industry has grown and still growing all over the world. Please think about it. If it really was a season for illness or allergy, then every person would be ill. The truth is that, only people who believe in it get the cold or have an allergic response to something. Maybe they got the flu once, then they listened to the surroundings—now is season for this or that—then they get the cold again. Instead of listening to false beliefs, we need to think of what we did that made our bodies get sick. Maybe we worked too much; maybe our work was very stressful; maybe we were worried too much, maybe we talked to ourselves false mantra that we will get cold; maybe we acted as having an allergy to people or situations in our lives, having feeling of being persecuted; or maybe we rejected our bodies by saying old stories from the past.

On the sixth day of our training in San Diego, we were taken to the facilitators' ranch by bus, which was rented by them. The sightseeing on the ranch was breathtaking. There were a lot of trees and mountains.

We were invited to the ranch to go through a labyrinth. First, in my imagination, there were big, dark walls in a labyrinth. This was what was imprinted in my subconscious mind after reading the myth of the Minotaur in primary school. Second, I didn't know what a labyrinth had in common with healing our lives.

When the ceremony started, we were asked to take one small stone from the square pot, which was the statue of Quan Yin. It was under a long oblong bell. Above the bell was an inscription, "Peace." Everyone put their own intention for the path in the labyrinth and hit the bell. My intention was to follow the path of love and my heart. At that time I didn't know that I chose path of self-realization.

When I was brought to the US, I thought about success all the time, but that day I chose the path of my heart. When all of us have put our intention, we were asked to go down the labyrinth. We went down a pathway where statues of angels welcomed us. There were a few benches to seat after ceremony and to take notes if somebody chose to do this. When we came to the labyrinth, it was a place surrounded by trees. The labyrinth was made from small stones on the sand. It was a beautiful place. We were asked to put the stone that we took from the pot and add to the labyrinth circle while we were walking and to take a crystal from the pot that was in the center of the labyrinth. We could only reach it when we finished our path one way. It was a very wonderful experience.

We all walked step by step only, being centered in ourselves. Real magic happened, and a lot of us had tears in our eyes. Some of us were crying. By walking in the labyrinth, we had possibility to be with ourselves. It was very powerful emotional healing tool. It allows us to connect with our true nature and calling. When I reached the center of the labyrinth, I wanted to move closer to the pot with the crystals to pick up, I noticed that my friend also wanted reach the pot. I stepped back and let her reach it first. She took out a pink crystal. Later, I found out after the ceremony, when we all shared our experiences from the labyrinth, the word "success" was written on her rock. Thankful that I let her reach first because I could see a fragment of a beautiful blue crystal. When I picked it up, I hold in my hand a crystal in the shape of a *pure* heart. I was astonished and so happy.

All the time I thought that everything good that was happening to me was by chance, but it wasn't true. Every intention that I put in my life was given to me because I asked for it. Whether it was a "good" or "bad" experience, it was given to me through my intention, through my belief in it.

When I picked up the heart, I came back to the exit of the labyrinth the same way how I got in. We all did the same. When we were at the exit, our facilitators embraced each of us one by one and everybody could choose the place to be with themselves. As I mentioned before, some of us chose the benches on the pathway. Other found places near to house. I went straight to the house, on the first floor. I used the restroom before the ceremony, so I knew where I was heading. There was an altar. There were statues and pictures of ancient masters who taught about Truth, like Buddha, Quin Yian, Jesus Christ, and others.

When I saw the picture of Jesus Christ, I sat on the floor and started crying. I couldn't stop. The labyrinth moved something in me that my tears were falling continuously. I wasn't able to stop, and honestly, I didn't want to. I wanted to cry out the whole misunderstanding that was given by the church about Jesus Christ, that he was only equal to God, and that's why I didn't follow his teachings. He was a guru who mastered his path of self-realization to one with God and taught us the Truth of who we are. His path was love, joy, forgiveness, and faith. He said, "*It is done unto you as you believe.*" In human consciousness, "faith" is connected to churches and religions, what they grew up and practiced. Faith has nothing in common with religion. There is only one God beyond all religions. He lives in everyone. The commandment "*You will not have other gods before me*" was misinterpreted by churches to keep people in fear.

The only God is in you, and you need to come to Him to get guidance from within, as Jesus Christ had or others saints who found God in themselves. We all are one in Christ consciousness. That's why it was said in the Bible, "*His only son.*" It was about us all. The pictures and statues of saints and the cross of Jesus Christ became objects to pray for salvation. Churches didn't teach us that Jesus Christ and every person that was elevated as a saint was an ordinary man or woman at the beginning. These people's communion with True Self transformed them, and they transformed the lives of others. Their thoughts, words, and actions were expression of True God in the man, not the false God in the clouds who punishes. That kind of God was made up by people, by churches, to have power over other people. A lot of saints had an opposition in the churches at the beginning. The unwavering faith in themselves, in the Power bigger than they were as a human being, gave them strength and pushed them forward. Mother Teresa, who was elevated as a saint by the Catholic Church, was an ordinary woman. Her awakening and faith gave her power to establish the Missionaries of Charity in 133 countries, and she did it in one lifetime. Do you believe that she would be able to achieve it without communion with the True God, the Power within her, the True Christ, God's beloved son? Christ speaks through our hearts and receives guidance through intuition third eye. Jesus told us that we can do the same miracles that he did or even bigger by saying, "*Seek ye first the kingdom of God, and his righteousness; and all these things shell be added unto you.*"

We can use our creative Power for the highest good for all of us, or we can use it to destroy us. The Power listens to our thoughts and our beliefs and creates the experiences in our lives. Faith is not religion; faith is in what we believe. When we believe that we can achieve something, we are right, and when we say that it is impossible, we are right also. *Faith is trust*, strong belief in something that is not proven. On the other hand, we have *beliefs, which are our conviction* of the truth of some statement or reality of some people, especially when it is presented on someone's experience. Faith is knowing that whatever we claim as our will, will find manifestation in our experience. ("It is done unto you as you believe.") We are always creating, and when by wrong thinking, we believe that we cannot do, have something, or be someone, we have that kind of experience in our lives. True faith can bring us closer to ourselves, to see the abilities that we have in us and how we can evolve in them, to become in our consciousness more than merely a human being. Being by myself in the room and after crying on the floor, I wrote down an intention that I didn't know how it would manifest, but I asked for a connection with my master, angels and guides. I asked for guidance for the fulfillment of my purpose, that I would be able to help others to find their own way to themselves and heal their lives by having them follow their hearts.

When our Heal Your Life training was ending, I was wondering what was next. We were offered a coaching Heal Your Life training after this one, which would start in three to four days later, but I knew if I paid for the coaching program, I would leave with no money.

I decided that the life coaching needed to wait, and I asked a new friend from the training if I could stay at her and her husband's house. They both were on the training with me. She said *yes*. We sat at the facilitators ranch on the swing after the labyrinth ceremony and our quiet time. When she stood up, I saw the image of the white wolf in her posture. The protector of a household.

Saturday, October 7, was the last day of our activities. We all said goodbye to ourselves, and we were connected on Facebook and WhatsApp, and we had scheduled once a month zoom meetings with Patricia and Rick on Wednesdays.

On October 8, my birthday, I started my new adventure throughout California. Looking few months back, when I received guidance about Louise Hay and knew nothing about her, only following the sign of our mutual date of birth, I was on the right path to my soul's destiny in this lifetime.

On my birthday, I was invited to breakfast by my new friend from Brazil, the one I shared the room with on our last night. I moved to her bedroom, because most of the participants checked out the day before, including my roommate Meri. We both saved money this way. After breakfast, I took the train to Santa Fe. There was a beautiful train station. I was picked up by my friend whom I had asked to stay in her house, and we went to her and her husband's ranch. Her husband was the man whose presentation made me burst into tears for the first time during the training. I was privileged to be on a second ranch in one week. It was a wonderful experience. When I saw ranches from the plane the week before, even I didn't dream that I would visit two of them.

On the ranch, I met the employees of my hosts. There was one beautiful girl who baked a birthday cake for me, and when I came into the house, "Happy Birthday" decorations and balloons were on the wall. That was magic. Thank you for all the blessings that I received from the people in this journey. For their love, kindness, trust, thank you.

I was on this ranch for four days and came back to San Diego. I was asked by my host to leave on the phone. She was in San Diego at that time for a Heal Your Life coaching program. The phone call was after her meditation. She got the message then. She was a household keeper and protector. Whatever she saw, it showed that I would eventually put her business in danger or other reasons. That's why she asked me to leave. I believe our intentions were different. I wanted to stay for a short time as a guest to figure out my next step, and she probably thought that I would like to stay longer to work for her. I am thankful that our paths were split so fast and in a harmonious way. Also I knew that she was only God's tool to push me forward, because I was hiding. I was afraid of my next move, and I needed to go. I came back to San Diego, and I had opportunities to see more of the city on my own and the small towns near to it like Calsbard, Oceanside. To get there, I took the Amtrak to Calsbard. The view was stunning. The railway trucks were next to the beach. I had view on the Pacific Ocean along the way. The towns had a very nice ambiance.

I liked the good energy of San Diego and the nice people there. But I also noticed another thing while I was there. One night when I was walking along the streets, I noticed a lot of people lying on the sidewalks, minding their own business. I didn't know what was happening. Why were these people lying on the streets? Later I found out that the United States, especially California, had been dealing with homelessness issue for years. I spent four nights in San Diego. I had to make another decision where my next step would be. I decided that I would go to Los Angeles. I knew that there was one place where I could go and maybe get help. It was Agape International Spiritual Center. I knew about this place because its founder, Rev. Michael Bernard Beckwith, was in *The Secret,* and being in Poland,

I sometimes listened to him on YouTube, like "The Answer Is You," but I had never felt the need to go to the Agape website and listen to his sermons. I wasn't interested in Agape's life because, being in my small Polish town, it was impossible for me to go there. I didn't even try to imagine it. It was too big for my mind. I had Rhonda Byrne's books in which I really believed.

In the US, Doreen Virtue's book *Angelic Numbers*, which I bought in Poland, had become my guide to ask if my steps were right. I still have this book, and I consult it if I like to know where I am at, in the sense of vibration to my current life. Good to have assurance that everything is all right and I am protected all the time. If I wasn't sure what to do because the situation was overwhelming, I would look at the numbers that the Universe had given to me at this moment and follow them or felt peace if I was in the right place.

Taking the first steps on my own in a different country with a different culture that was so far from my European one was scary for me because I didn't believe that I would be able to settle down here by myself and teach what I have learned. Whatever I had tried, it was like against me. I knew that I was safe wherever I went, but I didn't see the reason I was here. My dream was to become a spiritual teacher, but how could I become one in a foreign country? My English was only communicative, I didn't have place to live, and I didn't have the experience in the Heal Your Life teachings even though I was certified. Being in the program, I asked coaches who were assisting there if I could be with one of them and be an assistant to learn more, but my request was omitted. I was on my own again.

You can ask why I didn't go back to Poland. One thing I was sure was that in Poland, I closed everything and I was brought here to start my new life. My purpose wasn't to earn money and come back to Poland with them. I wanted learn and be of service to people. I didn't have any plans like other people had; I only followed my intuition and the signs given to me from outside. Many times my mind went crazy of what I was doing, but I kept the faith.

On the Amtrak ticket to Los Angeles, I had the number 573. It meant that I followed the guidance of Ascendant Masters, and I made extraordinary progress. It was good sign and encouragement for me and my fearful mind.

When I arrived in Los Angeles by train, I had the opportunity see for the first time the Los Angeles Union Station. It was a beautiful place, which I knew from watching *The Big Bang Theory*, my favorite TV series. Later I found out that in the LA Union Station, a pianist plays when people wait for their trains to make a nice ambiance.

I had booked a room in Downtown Los Angeles. It turned out that a lot of people from Latin America lived there. The same day I went by Uber to Agape International Spiritual Center. It was a Monday and turned out that the place was closed. But angels brought me an employee of the community. She was going out of the building. Thank you that she appeared there. If it wasn't for her, I wouldn't be still here. We started talking, and I asked her if I could see Rev. Michael Beckwith. She said that to see Reverend Michael, I needed to make an appointment through his assistant and he was unavailable that time because the following night he was flying to South Korea. She asked me to come next day when the office would open and the receptionist would help me find an accommodation.

I did what she said, and the next day, with my suitcase, I went to Agape Spiritual International Center again. An awesome thing had happened to me. Riding Uber and heading to Agape, I was taken a different way than the day before, and I saw a small blue building, and not far away was an arch with ivy leaves on it. It was the place that I saw during my transcendent breathwork session in Poland. The building was called Iglesia de Jesus. It was amazing to me that Los Angeles was the place where I was heading from the very beginning.

When I arrived in Agape, I spent the whole morning with the receptionist. His name was Victor Dickerson. He helped me find a hotel room near the Agape International Spiritual Center and booked me for two nights.

While in the reception area and talking to Victor, I noticed Rev. Michael Bernard Beckwith was heading to the reception area. It was a wonderful encounter, and I didn't have to make an appointment to see him. He opened his arms, and I really felt love and caring. Agape from Ancient Greek means unconditional love. The welcome was really unconditional as the organization meaning is and I am grateful for this. After telling him a shortcut of my story of how I got there from Poland, he asked me if I was going to take his class. It was enough for me to consider it as a sign to focus my attention to what kinds of classes Agape International Spiritual Center has. Also, Reverend Michael asked Victor to ask an Agape practitioner to say a prayer with me, about the right place to live, and everything that I needed at that time. I also received a leaflet to the Share House to find a cheaper accommodation. From that day, for a while, Reverend Michael became my indicator in knowing the next step to take when I didn't know what to do. I felt like being home in Agape community for a while.

The prayers there are different than those in Catholic churches. They are called affirmative prayers. You don't plead like a beggar. You affirm that what you need, you have it or have received right now. It means that when you pray for solution, you accept that the solution is given to you right now. Because you are connected with the Universal Mind and you will be guided to the right people and places. As I mentioned before, in Jesus's quote "Ask and you have received," He didn't tell you to get down on your knees and plead because you are a sinner and unworthy of that you want and need to live. He said you only need to ask, and it will be given to you. We were taught by our religions to kneel and plead our own Father for our birthright. As a result, we lost our divine origin and felt less and less in our own eyes, not in our Father's. He always loves us unconditionally and gives us the support and tools to rise up and start our lives anew in harmony with Him. But because we were brought up in societies that believe in condemnation and guilt, we have become the beggars instead of eagles and masters of our lives. My book and message have the title *Life Speaks to You* thanks to my friend, Ania Krzywda, who omitted the guidance for her given through words on the radio. She shared this with me years ago when I started crawling on this wisdom and didn't have any proof at that time, only faith. That's why I didn't know how to explain to her that life really communicates with us, that it encourages us, supports us, wants us to grow, tells us everything is all right, and gives us guidance as well as shows us our disharmonious way of being when we put up with what doesn't serve us, which most commonly appears as illnesses in our bodies or worsens them—when we feel exhaustion, resignation, and a lot of emotional pain. Because, at that time, I wasn't able explain to my best friend that life communicated with her, it became my mission to find the Truth and spread this to everyone who is ready for change, and this book is my contribution to each of you, telling you that life really speaks to you all the time. Be aware and receptive of its guidance, and you will not have to be worried anymore. In Agape International Spiritual Center and other communities that remind people about the hidden Truth, they call God with different names, like Father, Mother, or Friend. Why? Because Divine Energy is without gender. He manifests Itself us a woman or a man on Earth. All creation on this planet has feminine and masculine aspect to life was complete. Yin and Yang. Feminine allowing, masculine acting.

When I got to the hotel, Victor gave me a lift. For two days I had the opportunity to walk around and see the Inglewood area of Los Angeles. The following day, I called to the Share House, and I received an accommodation in Long Beach. I was told that women and men are not in the same houses, and because of that, the only place for a woman was in Long Beach. I noticed division again. But I was grateful that I had a place to stay. When I wasn't sure if I was supposed to leave the Culver City area for Long Beach, I got the massage at once through "the angelic number" book. I checked the numbers of the house where I was headed, and the answer was that "it was a part of the plan." Whether I liked it or not, I had stopped doubting about my decision. Also, ahead of me was a wonderful evening because I was headed to Agape International Spiritual Center for their service. There was a lot of joy, singing, and fun.

After the sermon, when I left the building, a man approached me, and he started complimenting me. It was nice, but there was something in his eyes that made me uncomfortable. He was devoted to his job working for Reverend Michael, but I started learning that not all people in the Agape community were on the same stage of awareness as their leader. It was a long lesson.

Next morning I got to Long Beach by metro train. I was astonished because I thought that all subways go only underground, like in NYC, but not here. It was another opportunity to see the countryside. The distance between Los Angeles and Long Beach is over twenty-four miles (over thirty-eight kilometers).

When I got to the place, the person that managed Share House gave me an accommodation next to main house, and I shared the room with a lovely elder woman. There were two rooms in the bungalow where we lived. The second room was occupied by two younger girls. One of them told me that my name Magdalena has a meaning and it means *tower* because Mary Magdalena came from the city called Magdala, which means *tower*. I was surprised that my name had any meaning.

The rooms were clean, and the kitchen was big and bright. It was a clean place. I always was given the best in the possible ways.

I am grateful for my roommate who shared with me her experiences in life and how beautiful she spoke about her jobs and about Australia. She used to live there also. I am thankful that she was willing to listen to me and tried understanding my English. Later it turned out that Americans do not always understand UK English. We Europeans are taught Imperial English, but Americans have their own language. I was blessed that I was open-minded and had started learning about this country and its people by my own experiences and not listen to other people's opinions. Because of that, I had nice experiences with people of different awareness, and I really felt safe. I always received help or direction from others. I always meet an angel in human body to guide me.

Being in Long Beach, I had mixed feelings, but I remembered that I promised myself to put intention before the labyrinth a few weeks before. I chose the path of heart and love. The Share Houses are for people who were under government benefits, who didn't have enough money to live in their own houses, because they had problems with mental health or other additions before and they aren't capable to stand on their own feet for a long time. I decided that I would see in every man or woman my equal. I stopped judging others regarding their circumstances. I treated everybody with the same kindness and respect. Really, I felt like my heart was opening. I had nice feedback also. There was something in me that when I was walking along Long Beach, people needed to talk to me. It was another good experience. At that time it was late October, and one day the temperature was 105 degrees Fahrenheit (over 40 degrees Celsius). On that day I was walking, I needed to be by myself, and I noticed a girl who wore a pair of nice new boots. It was a very hot fall season. I was wearing shorts and flip-flops all the time. For me it was a little funny, because I noticed how we all are attached to something, like changing of seasons and following what fashion has to say in the area where we live. We want to always fit in.

Another day when I was walking, I saw a woman who was at the train station and was looking for change in the ticket machines. I could see that she didn't have any money, and she had to look for them in the machines. I took out my wallet. I had a lot of quarters, dimes, and nickels in it. I put the whole content on her palm. I saw her face. She was astonished. She felt abundance, and I did. It was a wonderful exchange. I was generous everywhere I was. The reason was that I was taught by the book *The Magic* that we need to first give to receive. That way, we acknowledge that the source of our supply is not human but inexhaustible energy. That's why I was not afraid to leave jobs that served their purpose for a certain time and moved forward with trust. I knew that I would be always supplied.

Being around Rev. Michael Beckwith's teachings, I noticed that he influenced Rhonda Byrne through his knowledge. Thanks to that, she was able to put in her books his thought by practicing and understanding it. That's why her books have had a big influence on me and others who wanted change their lives. Because of that, we all were practicing the principles of life given in her writings even though we didn't know it at that time.

As I mentioned before, the distance between Long Beach and Los Angeles was over twenty-four miles. Agape International Spiritual Center was in Culver City. To get there it took me over two hours by train and buses. One day I took an adventure to the center because I wanted to be around those people whom I met during my first days in Los Angeles. I reached there early afternoon. Then I was invited to volunteering by the first angel that I met when I arrived in Agape International Spiritual Center when the building was closed. She invited me to help her and other people with the packing of pamphlets for the Sunday service. It was late afternoon. I knew that I should get back to Long Beach before night, but it was stronger for me to know these people and be around them. I was so grateful for the help I received at the beginning, and I wanted to return their kindness. Because of that, I was given a lift to the train station from where I could get back to Long Beach. It wasn't the end of my adventure.

At the beginning, some names of towns were difficult for me to remember and some names were so similar that being at night in the train, I wasn't sure if I was getting off at the right train station. Hesitantly, I moved back to the train. I felt a little scared that night; and another angel, as a human being, appeared in my life. He asked me where I wanted to get off, and it turned out that we both were getting off at the same Metro train station. He invited me to the restaurant near he lived. It happened half way to my place where I stayed. We spent a nice hour there. After that, he gave me a lift, and I was able to return safely to the place where I was staying.

Being in the restaurant, I received a beautiful red velvet rose from the owner of the restaurant. He had a gesture to give roses away to every woman in his restaurant that night. I found out from the person who invited me for a small meal in the restaurant that he was a psychologist in a Los Angeles hospital, and every day he would travel from Long Beach to Los Angeles and back. A lot of people chose to live on the suburbs of Los Angeles and get to work by public transportation because Los Angeles is crowded with cars. I am grateful for this meeting. The rose that I got in the restaurant stayed in my place in Long Beach. The petals were so thick, and the color was so juicy red. It was an alluring, rich flower. Long Beach had beautiful, vast beaches and lots of attractions. I was blessed being there, and also I knew that I needed to move forward.

I wanted to stay near the Agape International Spiritual Center in Culver City because I registered for the first class there in person. The name of the class was Universal Laws Governing Spiritual Living.

The accommodation prices were very high at that time, so I decided take the class online and asked my friend Agnieszka if she could host me in New York City for a while so I could figure out what was next. She agreed. She was a lifeboat every time when I was on my life crosswords.

Also the same time I contacted my new friend from the Heal Your Life training who lived near San Francisco. She was my first partner in our Heal Your Life exercises. Her name was Paula.

It is amazing that people connected by the Universe become friends for the rest of their lives. When we met on the Heal Your Life training, she had an accident the day before. She told me that she fell down from the stairs. The words that came up through me wasn't Magdalena's, it was someone's more wiser. I said, "When you fall down, you can only rise up, and now move forward." When we reach rock bottom, we can only go higher if we know that we have this possibility. In Paula's case, it was a metaphor but very visible. I love her to the core. She is so loving and such a caring person.

She invited me to her home. We agreed that I would buy a bus ticket to San Jose, and she picked me up there. Paula is a nurse teacher, and she had some classes twenty minutes from San Jose that day, in a hospital in Mountain View. Later I found out that the Google headquarters was also there and that the whole Silicon Valley region is situated in the southern part of the San Francisco Bay Area, which serves as a global center for high technology and innovation. And San Jose is the biggest city of the Silicon Valley region.

I stayed in Long Beach for two weeks. I waited for Reverend Michael to come back from South Korea to be on his Sunday service, and the time came. The service was powerful. The energy was different than the first time. It was higher. My heart was bumping, and I felt happy. My soul was happy. I felt like I was home at the right place and the right time. It was a wonderful experience. It was beautiful end of my stay in Los Angeles area. I felt so blessed.

My friend Victor came to Long Beach to see me before I left, and we spent a nice afternoon together.

On Tuesday morning, heading to the Pacific train station in Long Beach, unknown people bid farewell to me by saying "Good morning" to me all the way to the train station. It was an extraordinary experience.

When I got to Union Station in Los Angeles and boarded the bus, I didn't know that they were waiting ahead of me over five hours of breathtaking scenery.

Traveling by Amtrak train from San Diego to Los Angeles, I saw beaches on the left and admired them. When I was traveling from Los Angeles to San Jose, I saw mountains, lakes, and some farmlands. I was astonished. I didn't know that in the middle of the land I could see all these things.

I always knew what a type of transport to choose. I never check what the countryside would be like when I traveled. That's why I was amazed because I didn't plan it, and I got to see so beautiful sceneries. I am so grateful for getting to know places by myself. It was blessing that I didn't have anybody who would impose or direct me in any way, that I should be here or there. At the end, when I spoke with someone about my experiences, it turned out that I went to the places where tourists visit most.

I am always at the right time and the right place and do what is right. Affirmation works all the time and everywhere.

When bus reached San Jose, it was dark and I didn't have opportunity to see the city during daylight. My friend Paula picked me up and took me to her workplace, at a hospital in Mountain View. When we walked inside, I felt like I entered a library, not hospital. There was light wood mixed with glass. It was quiet. I really felt like it was an exclusive library. It was a good experience. When my friend went to take care of her business there, I began observing the people who worked there and the machines. The cleaner had a machine that was following him automatically. It was amazing.

When my friend was done, she took me to her home, which was between San Jose and San Francisco. I was introduced to her family.

I had a dream that night. It was about our Heal Your Life training. We all were pushed to start our workshops, and I didn't feel it at all. I told to Paula about that dream, and she just said, "Magdalena, you are not ready, that's all." When she said that, I felt relieved. I stopped pushing myself and released the guilt about not willing to do this at that time.

I was learning that the part of spiritual growth is also letting go of guilt and other low energies, which happened to be my boulders. I have chosen seven years ago my own path, and I still felt guilty about doing this. I felt guilt toward my son, my mother, and people around me. Even though the decisions that I made that time turned out the best for all of us, there was still guilt inside that I chose myself. Nobody thought or acted like me. It was for me like going for something unprovable and elusive. That kind of guilt was caused by my loyalty toward the people that I loved, but they weren't supportive to my dreams. I was attached to their opinions about me, and I was looking for approval from them if what I was doing was right. My guilt was dragging me down all the time. I dreamed about fulfillment, but this kind of low energy kept me in the tone of being unworthy to be what I was dreaming about. It was a cycle.

On the same day we had our first Zoom meeting with our Heal Your Life facilitators. After my night revelation that I was not ready to do what I had come to learn, I felt very relaxed. After our Zoom meeting, Paula took me to San Francisco. We spent all day there, and we also went to Sausalito. To get there, we drove through the Golden Gate Bridge. The next day we spent in her home area. I saw the campus where her family lived and worked, which was nearby. The weather was beautiful, and I could see part of San Francisco from a distance.

I spent three lovely days with Paula and her family, then it was time to move forward. Paula took me to the airport in San Francisco, and from there, I flew to New York City. I remember how I was scared going back to NYC because honestly, I didn't know what I would do there. I just believed that I would know. Most importantly, I was about to start an Agape International Spiritual class online. This thought kept me in positive mode, and I trusted.

When I landed in NYC, my friend Agnieszka picked me up. I was given her older daughter's room. I spent over one month with Agnieszka's family. I had full exclusive stay there. I am thankful for this. At that time I was able to finish my Zoom classes; and I recognized that I was on the third stage of my spiritual growth. That's why my mind was so confused when I came to the US. Now I understand. My life vision was much higher than I could imagine. Spirit took over my life, and there was no way back. I stopped controlling my life. I surrendered myself with gratitude to my higher guidance. That's why I ended up in the United States. I read about it in Rev. Michael Bernard Beckwith's book *Life Visioning*. We have four stages of spiritual growth when we allow:

• Life does to us, we feel like victims of people, events, and circumstances.

• When we find out that we are creators of our lives, then we do a vision boards and we govern what we want to have from life. We feel like we control our lives. We feel like gods. These two first stages are led by our ego.

• On third stage, we lose our control. When we surrender to it, then in this stage, our Higher Self leads us to the places where we belong. Our mind is so confused, and we feel like we are losing control of our lives. We need to surrender to that chaos. Thanks to that, we evolve as a human being.

• On the fourth stage, we are *one* with God. Our thoughts, speech, and actions are in harmony with our Higher Self. Ego dies. We see everything as One. There is no separation between us, only unity and love of our hearts move us to actions, which serve everyone.

Then the family is the whole world, not only people whom we were brought up with or people we are familiar with. But some of us want to stay on the first level of our ego consciousness, the victim one. Because of that, we don't give ourselves the opportunity to let our Spirit take over our paths and bring love and harmony to our lives and to others'.

During these classes, I also figured out who I wanted to become at the time. I remember it was our last Zoom pod when I said, "I am an Agape licensed practitioner." The same day I went to the NYC center. I got on the subway, and I noticed a poster. The description said in bold capital letters, "YOU HAVE YOUR FUTURE FIGURED OUT. NOW PURSUE IT." Also, there was no coincidence that on that poster was Afro-American man. I received all the confirmation that I needed, but what about the second part of the inscription? How can I pursue it? I was in New York City, and my savings were running out. It was the same dilemma, *How*? when I received thought about Louise Hay being in my apartment in Poland and now about coming back to Los Angeles. I didn't have a place to live, I had savings to use about $2,000–$3,000, and I really didn't think about going back to California because I just came from there. I wanted fit in with the environment where I was. What I had learned during the Universal Laws Governing Spiritual Living online class was that what we are afraid of most is what we need to do because only then we can find out what blessings are waiting for us.

When I was in New York City, I went to the First Church of Religious Science, which was founded by Ernest Holmes in 1927. Louise Hay started her journey to greatness with this church. She was invited to the lecture "Change Your Thinking, Change Your Life." After that, she started changing her life by taking classes there, implementing what she was taught, and as a result, she became a licensed practitioner there. Also Agape International Spiritual Center was based on his teachings. Being in New York City, I was looking for signs. That's why I started following Louise's steps. It was Wednesday, and the first event was a service, and after the service was a meeting about Louise's teachings from her book *You Can Heal Your Life*. The same pastor led the service and the class. He asked us to introduce ourselves and what brought us there. When it was my turn, I just said that I was brought to the US for a Heal Your Life training. There wasn't any coincidence. The pastor said that Louise Hay connected a lot of people. For those who knew and loved her, memories were very fresh. She made the transition in August 30, 2017. It had passed only three months since she passed away when I met a pastor and the community of First Church of Religious Science.

After the class, one of the church practitioners came to me and said that the pastor invited me to participate in their meeting, which would be next Tuesday. That week I had one foot in Poland.

Honestly, I didn't know what to do. I couldn't occupy my friend's room for eternity, and we agreed that I would release it to her daughter in one week. I didn't have place to go. Also, I knew as I mentioned before that I closed everything in Poland, so there was no point going back to the old life.

The practitioner's words gave me the power and hope that something good would come out from that. When I heard this, I knew that I needed to give myself one week more, but where can I go? Being in New York City, I connected with my old neighbors Maria and Tadeusz. They won green cards in the lottery twenty-five years before and immigrated to the US with their small children. They have been living in New Jersey state since then. They invited me to a weekend activity. They showed me the beautiful Ramapo Mountain State Forest. We were walking around the lake. We had a good time together. So I called Maria with question, asking if I could stay with them for one week more to find out why I was invited by the pastor. She said *yes*. But I didn't know what would come next after that week. Meanwhile I was working with Ernest Holmes's book *This Thing Called You* while I was taking online classes. I bought this book in Agape International Spiritual Center, and I was using the affirmation:

> *New conditions are being created for me—conditions of harmony, happiness, peace and joy.*
> *All circumstances and situations are being harmonized.*
> *Wherever I go I shall meet peace, joy and happiness.*
> *Whatever I do shall be done with reason and intelligence.*
> *I shall be surrounded by friendship, by beauty, by right action.*
> *My whole being responds to this conviction.*
> *Simply, with complete conviction, I accept my freedom.*

When the day came that I was about to move to Elmwood Park, New Jersey, I got a text massage from my uncle in the morning. He texted that his friend Andrew who lived in the New York area was open to help me and he would contact me. When I read this, I was so happy and I responded to my uncle, asking for the phone number. He reminded me that I already had his friend's phone number. He gave it to me in Warsaw before my flight to the US.

I called Andrew, and he said that he would help me and pick me up from New York City the next day. So I asked Agnieszka if I could stay one more night, and next day I would be taken to Spring Valley, New York. She said *yes*. I canceled visit at Maria's and Tadeusz's and thanked them that they wanted me to help. After a phone call with Andrew, I felt wanted. It was first time since I came to the US that somebody said, "I will take care of you." Since the Heal Your Life training finished, I had been asking all the time about a place to stay. I didn't feel good asking for accommodation all the time, but I didn't have choice, if I wanted survive here and find my own way. I was deeply grateful to all the people who have reached out to help me. Thank you.

In Spring Valley, I was taken care of by Andrew and his very warm wife, Krystyna. From their place, I went to the meeting in the First Church of Religious Science in New York City. It took me about two or more hours to get there, but it didn't matter. I loved exploring routes. I was very curious to see my new surroundings. The meeting that I got invited to was about Ernest Holmes's teachings. I bought the book *The Science of Mind* by Ernest Holmes, and I was thankful for the invitation, because if it wasn't for this invitation, I wouldn't be in the place where I am right now.

On December 9, 2017, the Agape Spiritual Center had their thirty-first anniversary. When I was at Agape International Spiritual Center, I heard the announcements and I wanted to be there, but when I flew to New York City, I thought that it was over. As I mentioned before, Reverend Michael had become a guide for me for a while. I remember it like it was today. I touched my phone display, and out of the blue, the YouTube application opened itself with Rev. Michael saying, "*You must be here.*" I felt like he spoke to me. I heard the message. My heart wanted to go there, but the fear of not having enough money to pursue it appeared in my mind again. I had only four days to buy a ticket for a one-night trip, and I had only about $1,800 in my bank account then. But my heart wanted to go there.

On Wednesday, December 6, I bought a round-trip ticket to Los Angeles for one night. I received a discount of $194 by buying a packet. The round-trip airline ticket with a good-quality hotel room in it. I stayed in Four Points by Sheraton by one night. Every number that I noticed during the process of purchasing I checked with Doureen Virtue's book *Angel Numbers*. All the signs showed me that I was doing right. Then I stopped being afraid about money, and I knew that everything would work out for me. I flew from Newark airport, New Jersey, to LAX one in Los Angeles, California. I asked Tadeusz if he could give me a ride to the Newark Airport. He said *yes*. It turned out that the trip from Elmwood Park, New Jersey, to the airport was about fifteen minutes by car. I was grateful that everything was so flawless, and I really felt very good. I spent a night at Maria and Tadeusz's. On the next day, he dropped me off at the airport, and I flew to Los Angeles. It was Saturday, one week after seeing Reverend Michael on my phone.

When we landed in Los Angeles and I went out from the LAX airport, I felt grounded, happy, and in the right place. It was a wonderful feeling. When I got to the hotel using the hotel's shuttle, I checked in and went to my room. When I sat on the bed, my heart was thumping. I never felt this before. It was like my heart wanted to jumped out from my chest with joy.

I was in California, looking out of the window and saw a beautiful sunset. The weather was warm. Because of that, I had only a sleeveless blouse, skirt, and a pair of sandals. It was December 9, a hot evening.

I reached Agape International Spiritual Center by Uber. My pool mate was a woman with a name Mary. Again, Mary Magdalena appeared in my spiritual space.

The evening was very inspirational with invited guests who shared their own journey on the stage. After was a buffet. Victor, my very first friend from Agape community, introduced me to a Polish woman who flew from the New York area also to attend the event in Agape International Spiritual Center and to spend a few days in California. I saw the next sign that a good connection was made. She had the same designer purse that I had, and the color was the same.

I have never really felt so much connection with other Polish women than with Beata. Life brought us to each other. We spoke awhile, and we promised to be in touch. Later on, I understood that I flew to the event only to meet Beata and have connection with her. I left the event to get to my hotel because I had to fly back to New York City. This time I was landing at JFK airport early morning. The funniest thing that I didn't do when I arrived in Los Angeles was that I didn't set my watch three hours back. I noticed that after I glanced to the hotel's wall clock when I was waiting for a shuttle to the airport, and a few minutes after, I had checked out from the room hotel. There was no way to go back to bed. When I was dropped off at LAX airport, it was so early that I waited about one or two hours at the airport before checking in and for the other services to open.

When I came back to Spring Valley, I needed to make another decision. Christmastime was coming, and the room that I occupied was needed to be released. Andrew and Kristina had visitors to spend Christmas together. Kristina's closest family was arriving from Brooklyn, New York City. I had again two choices: Poland or Los Angeles. I wrote on a piece of paper what I needed to do and what I was afraid of the most. I stated Los Angeles. That's why I was very close to making a right decision. To assure myself that I was doing right, I asked a question during meditation and I listened for the answer. I didn't receive any answer, but I got up, took my laptop, and bought a one-way Greyhound bus ticket from New York City to Los Angeles. I had decided that if I was going to Los Angeles, I had onetime opportunity to see the countryside in a wider picture, and I really needed these three days not to worry about what next.

A week or two before my leaving for Los Angeles, I contacted Beata, and since then we have been on the phone all the time.

Being on the East Coast, I was judged and misunderstood by some people. I felt like I was in Poland. It was the same way of thinking. Everybody knew better how my life should look like. They said that what I wanted was too big or impossible to reach out and for what reason was I doing that?

I don't blame them because they were mirroring my doubts, fears, and belief that people didn't understand what I was doing. But

I knew that I need to move forward, because I promised myself a few years before that I would trust and listen only to my inner guidance. This was what pushed me through, and everything worked out.

Another one of my favorite affirmations that I listened to very often, channeled through Ester Hicks by the Higher Spirit family called Itself Abraham:

> Everything is always working out for me, everything is always working out for me, everything is always working out for me.

Then my body started relaxing, and my mind started being quiet and peaceful.

I left for Los Angeles on December 18, 2017, and the journey lasted over sixty-nine hours.

I had about $700 on my bank account. That was the time when my faith was the strongest ever. When I boarded the Greyhound bus, my heart started thumping again. My heart was ready for the adventure and my mind, a little less. I heard a scary voice in my head saying, "What are you doing?" but I trusted the signals from my heart. When I let myself make that choice without reasoning or judgment for what I was doing, I realized that a central command is in my heart and that intuition is the most important tool to follow. At the same moment, in my own journey, I have started on the path to find the Truth of our existence. Once again, intuitive guidance has nothing in common with listing cons and pros; it only leads us to fulfillment and guides us safely in every situation.

The same day Beata started calling me and kept my spirit high. On the third day, in the morning, I arrived in Los Angeles. I had booked room in Motel 6, near to LAX airport. I knew that motel from San Diego when I stayed four nights there. They had very clean and comfortable rooms. They had wide beds, and the price was lower than a three- or four-star hotel.

I liked walking to know the area; and one evening, when I was walking back to the motel, a man approached me and showed me the sky. I turned back, and I noticed a cloud in the shape of dragon.

I was amazed. It turned out that the man was a homeless person who just got the documents that would allow him get a job. When I spoke to the man, I knew that life was giving me another sign, where my focus should to be. I needed to be involved in homelessness. That day was very special day for me, according to the Mayan sacred calendar. It was the Day of Freedom. We all have a solar family in Tzolkin, and everybody has four themes to evolve in their lifetime. Mine were truth, intuition, harmony, and freedom. Throughout my whole life, I needed to evolve my intuitive guidance to be free, live the truth, and share with others. Also, to evolve in self-control, to achieve harmony, and to be surrounded by beauty.

I shared with Beata the encounter. I was so grateful to her for being there for me on the phone during the entire travel. She also called me when I was in the motel for six nights.

On the third day, she told me, "Magdalena, it is time to go somewhere. Go to a Polish church."

I knew that a Polish church wouldn't be the answer, but I went there. I spoke with the current Polish pastor at that time. He was replaced at the end of 2020 with a new, more communicative, attentive, and loving person. He was not interested in what I was talking. His attention was focused to the gardener, and I felt like I was speaking to the air. He told me to hang the announcement on the board, which people passed by very rarely, and that was it. Only the person can act like that, who takes his function for granted instead of being of service to others. When I left the Polish church, I noticed a small building next door. It was a Polish retirement house. I went to the building, and I met a person who gave me the direction to the manager of the place. And he said something like, "He will help you."

For me, it was another good sign. When I found the manager, I asked him about a room to live in the retirement home, but he said that there is no place. I felt a little disappointment, but he asked me to keep in touch with him. In two days, I called him, and it turned out that he was the owner of the house and I could stay there. On the seventh night, I slept in my new room. The whole house was to my disposition at that time. There were three bedrooms, a swimming pool, and a guesthouse on the backyard. I was amazed. I just wanted a place to stay, and I got from Life a whole house with a swimming pool. Thank you, God.

I borrowed some money from my friends and family in Poland, which helped me pay the rent, and registered for another class in Agape Spiritual Center, which was a meditation class with Reverend Michael and Rev. Cheryl Ward. At that time I thought that I was on the ride to become a practitioner on behalf of Agape International Spiritual Center. There were ten prerequisite classes to take before registering for the Agape University and receiving a license. Then a person becomes an active member of Agape community as a licensed practitioner. The whole journey to be licensed takes three to four years.

On January 21, 2018, it was a big event in Agape International Spiritual Center—the Thirty-Second Annual National Hugging Day. It was a huge venture for those who were preparing it. The idea was to break the Guinness World Record in the hug group. They needed over fifty or even more people with their national passports to break this record. I found out about this event from Beata, who registered herself, but she wasn't able to participate. I was the one who represented Poland. They had a really fresh Polish girl. The rest of the participants were residents of the United States for years. The record wasn't broken, but there were hundreds of people who enjoyed and connected with one another with hugs and love. There were very high vibrations.

Meanwhile, I was asked to take care of a small boy. I knew that it was given to me to overwork the past experience as mother. The boy resembled my own son in the same age. I was grateful that Life gave me the privilege to take care of the boy. I was cleaning the past by releasing the guilt that I didn't have enough opportunity to take care of my son as I really wanted. Being with this boy, I was able to put 100 percent of my attention without worrying about money because I was compensated for being only with him. We had a lot of fun. I reconnected myself with my joyous nature, my inner child. We laughed, sang, danced, and learn Spanish through songs on YouTube. At that time, we both started learning about the place where we lived. For the boy, the whole experience connected with the planet Earth was a new, but we were on the same knowledge about everything in America. It was wonderful to learn a new place through a child's eyes.

I remember once when I was heading to the house where the boy lived, I noticed two pigeons on the lamp. It looked like a couple communicating with each other in caring way. I didn't see connection with me at that moment, so I put it in the frame of a nice image. Later I found out that it was a sign of what would happen the same day.

I was sitting with the boy in the dining room while he was eating, when his uncle sat at the opposite side of the table and we started chatting. Then I noticed the face of the small less-than-two-year-old boy. He was so proud of himself and had an all-knowing attitude. It was so funny to watch him so uplifted. At the same time I received the image of two pigeons from the morning. That's why I knew why he felt so good about himself. The reason was that he made his uncle sit at the table and start a conversation with me.

Later on, I had an experience with another child, a girl that confirmed how all the children are connected intuitively to their source. As I mentioned before, we don't have to say anything to children, they simply knew what is going around. They catch everything and follow their inner guidance. As adults, we lose that kind of vulnerability. Thanks to this small boy, I received an inspirational idea to write the series of books for children, which is waiting for me in the near future.

Meanwhile, I started serving in Hand in Hand through Agape International Spiritual Center community. I served food to homeless people in Santa Monica on Saturdays. My heart was bumping from joy. But also I was asking myself why people that knew the principles of life weren't helping these people through the knowledge that they had. I was new there, and I was in the process of understanding and learning about homelessness. Also, I judged by appearances. The truth was that those people committed their free time every Saturday morning and Christmas to serve food and good word to people who were experiencing homelessness. These people needed to be appreciated and not judged.

Being in Agape's classes, I started be more aware of myself. I had ups and downs in knowing myself, but what kept me on the track was gratitude.

I met some new friends in Agape International Spiritual Center. I met another Polish young man, Krzysztof, who came from Krakow for three months to take classes in Agape community. He shared with me that he healed himself from back pain in three days after watching *The Secret* by releasing all the emotions from the body. Also when he came to Los Angeles, he wanted to have a free place to stay and he manifested that. I was amazed with his understanding of *The Secret* regarding health in his body and easiness with other manifestations in his young life.

When I had decided that it was a time to extend my tourist visa, Life gave me a person who helped me to do this. First, I considered applying for a student visa, and I even found a sponsor, but in the end, I chose that I would extend my tourist visa. I didn't want to commit myself to the work which would require me to stay as if I received a sponsorship. At the end, it turned out that I did the right decision for all involved. The person who helped me with the application to extend my legal status found out where to send it. I didn't get that information on my own when I was at the Federal Building in Downtown Los Angeles. I am grateful for her and her help. I met her on one of the Agape classes, Oath of Manifestation. She flew from Denver to be in the energy of Agape International Spiritual Center. She stayed with me for a while. At the time she was wondering if she would move to the City of Angels. We helped each other. When we lived together for a while, I started feeling not being myself. Again, I started giving my own energy and putting others over me. When I noticed that, Life gave me a surprise. When I was on the bus coming back home from Santa Monica, the girl called me, and she said that she was on her way to visit her friend in the different state. I was grateful for that. I was able to feel like home again. We always meet people on our way who need to teach us about ourselves, what our values are, how much important self-confidence is, and not to take on ourselves any guilt that we didn't meet their expectations.

I felt insecure being in the new environment, and I had mostly English-speaking people around me, like I wanted, but I gave them my own power away because I thought that they knew more than I did and they lived in their own country. That's why they felt more confident.

In the Oath of Manifestation class, we had a final project. I remember how my body was shaking when I started sharing my story briefly, how it appeared that I started living in Los Angeles. We were split into five groups called pods. Our group decided that each of us would read the excerpt from the Oath of Manifestation created by Rev. Micheal Bernard Beckwith and Rev. Cheryl Ward. Every person chose a fragment which resonated with them at that time. Below is my part of the statement:

> Through this Oath of Manifestation *all* things are possible! I declare, absolutely that I live in a *friendly Universe* that is always providing for me. I feel it powerfully happening now!

My body was shaking, not because of fear that I was speaking in front of people, but it was releasing all the stress that it had been carried during five months of trying to figure out what my next step would be and where I was heading. The above phrase was the truth for me, no doubt.

I am thankful that I answered the call when my soul started calling. Some people have similar experiences to be awakened, but they deny it. They don't want to wake up. For them, it is more important what other people say than their own soul's calling. Many times they'd say, "I don't need it," and they doom themselves to silent suffering in solitude. They show the mask of a contented person on the outside, but inside, they suffer and are afraid of what would happen next. Our soul started knocking first time when we were twenty-six years old, but for most of us, we gave up the calling and we continued with our ego choices. We become more and more attached to what we want (material possessions). Some of us climbed the career ladder, which was far away from our true calling. Others gave their power away by listening to others what they should do or not do. We all are afraid and believe in lack. There are addictions and feelings of dissatisfaction with life and lack of fulfillment. All these are ego programs. We take our lives in our hands to gain material security, forgetting that Spirit always supports us in small things and big ones. When we allow ourselves answer the inner call, we will be led safely to healthy and fulfilled life.

Thanks to my willingness to hear my inner voice, I started being more aware of my behaviors that didn't serve me, and I knew that I always have a choice to change it. And when I see something old in me, I asked the Universe to help me let go of it by saying affirmation from Louise Hay's book: "I am willing to let go of the pattern which creates this condition in my life" and the pattern in me was released in a short time." Later I used also the words: "God please change me that I will be able to be a change to others." Thank you for my teachers who came when I was ready, even if it was in a form of a book.

I sent my application form to extend my tourist visa to Texas two days before my legal stay would end. I sent it by FedEx, and it was delivered on the second day. Nobody around me at that time believed that I would get the extension. I knew that I would receive it because I was in alignment with my soul's purpose here. After one month, I got a positive answer.

I was grateful for this because I could still be here to learn how to be of service to others.

When I was on Oath of Manifestation class in Agape International Spiritual Center, I met Thelma Chichester. She was our group facilitator. I loved her for her openness and attitude to be helpful to all of us. She was an Agape chief administrative officer, and because of that, we as a group had nice surprises from her. For example, we were visioning our final project in the room where the Agape board had their meetings and visioning regarding to the whole Agape International Spiritual Center mission. It was really fun to be in her group and in her presence.

As a group, we bought gifts to Rev. Cheryl Ward, who led the class, and to Thelma, our pod leader. Thelma made another surprise for all of us. She also gave us gifts. All the members of our pod got

Reverend Michael's book with his signature except me. I got another book that was perfect for me: *I Am the Word* by Paul Selig. Thanks to that, my awareness started to immediately grow, and I was able to start merging with my own Christ Self. I appreciated that gift very much.

One day I was watching an Agape service online, and I saw Rev. Michael Bernard Beckwith giving an award to Greg Johnson, the founder of L.O.V.E. Foundation, a foundation that helps homeless youth in Hollywood area. I knew that I needed to take another step if I would like to learn more about homelessness in Los Angeles and may be a help for them in the near future.

I received Greg's telephone number from Thelma, and I waited for the right moment. My mind was adjusting to everything what I was learning and experiencing at that time, and I have learned that there was a right time for everything. When something is for me, it will come to me organically, flawlessly, and I will be ready for a new experience.

It turned out that at some point Thelma and I became friends, and we became wonderful mirrors for each other.

I remember it like it happened today; it was one of these days when we received help from cosmic energy to look into our lives. At that day, it was a mirror one. I received a huge insight about how I treated myself and my time.

That morning, I was waiting for about five or more minutes at the door of the boy's grandmother's home. It never happened before. When I noticed it, I didn't bother with that. I thought there is nothing wrong with it.

That same evening I had an appointment with Thelma at the Agape International Spiritual Center. I was to be a volunteer for the Revelation Event 2018. I was assigned to support the parking lot. I was waiting for her. When I reached the Agape community, I was asked to wait for Thelma. When she came back to her office, we started talking about my volunteering at the event. But during our conversation, Thelma was receiving text messages and responded to them the whole time. I didn't feel listened to, and there were a lot of distractions around. Thelma's coworkers started coming into her office with questions regarding the revelation event. Instead of spending a few minutes in Thelma's office, I spent much more time. I got used to the turmoil of Thelma's work environment because I knew that she had a lot of responsiblities there. But on that day, I was heading straight from Santa Monica after work, which took me two hours to get there instead of going home and having a good rest. And even then, I didn't recognize there was something wrong in my behavior toward myself. But when I left the Agape building and went to my one of favorites grocery stores, Trader Joe's, I was able to notice it at last thanks to a young cashier. In Trader Joe's, the staff is very well trained, and the ambience is very nice. There's a lot of light. The cashiers are always polite and talkative, and they stay focused on the client.

But that day was different. The cashier, while waiting for my money, had his head turned in the opposite way. He was focused on something else. When I took out the money to pay for my food, I was waiting for a while. He was looking somewhere unseen to me. I didn't want to disturb him, and it looked like time stopped. When he turned back to me to take the money, I suddenly got it. In one second, I received images of these three experiences through which I saw the picture of my current life and how I treated myself and my time. I was so grateful for this insight and the people who played beautifully their roles to wake me up. I released the intention to the ether that I was willing to let go of the pattern that was not working for me. I started taking care of myself and my needs more. At that time, I was on the third class in Agape International Spiritual Center. It was the Self-Awareness and the Evolving Consciousness class with Rev. Cheryl and Rev. Ronald D. Blair.

> To know oneself, at the deepest level, is simultaneously to know God: this is the secret of gnosis… Self-knowledge is knowledge of God; the self and the divine are identical. (A text taken from the Nag Hammadi Library)

> When you afraid of God you are afraid of yourself. (*A Course in Miracles*)

Thanks to this ten-week class, I received a lot of insights about my old beliefs. Some of them were mine as a result of my past experiences, and some of them were not. They were implanted by others in my subconscious mind.

Also I became aware that I was still attached energetically to my mother. Awareness gave me possibility to release it. I stopped feeling guilty that I didn't do what she wanted me to do. I have my own life. We both needed to learn to love each other the way we were without any expectations from one another.

Through this class, I learned how important a leadership is. The leader can connect people or make a chaos. In every class, we were split into pods and we had the pod facilitators. In the Self-Awareness and the Evolving Consciousness class, most of us knew each other because we spent ten weeks in the Oath of Manifestation class together. As participants, we were very cooperative during our pod arrangements, like finding a name for our pod and other things, but it wasn't easy to settle, because our pod facilitator implemented a lot of confusion. I observed that our facilitator had a controlling issue. I was grateful for this insight because I had the same issue before in everything and I released a lot during my journey. I remember that day and how chaos arose, I pointed with my pointer finger to my friend who said that what was happening in Brazil was not his to consider.

That day I understood that using gratitude to improve our lives doesn't guarantee that we would feel connection with All. I saw myself in my friends as a mirror very clearly. It was the exact attitude I had before. For sure thanks to gratitude, we evolve, become aware, and life is opened for us. I am an example. Also, I was shocked of my behavior, because I had stopped pointing out others many years before. I apologized to him later. I knew that all the behaviors appeared because of our facilitator's leadership. I remember DeAnna, another person whom I met at the Oath of Manifestation class. I admired her from the very beginning, I looked at her and I noticed like she hid herself to feel safe. She didn't want to be involved in this turmoil. Other people from our pod did something else. It was fun observing myself and others during the chaos that appeared. Our facilitator was a wonderful person, and she was in the process of learning how to become a good pod leader in the near future.

That day was very important for me as a subsequent one with energy of freedom according to Tzolkin. When we are aware of ourselves, our behaviors, and our thoughts, we are free to make choices in accordance to our way of being instead of reacting to others' behavior toward us. It also gives us freedom to leave people and situations that stop serving us, our evolution as a human being, and our soul. There are two ways of being: acting from a space of love or yearning for love. Another topic that I need to evolve in this lifetime is freedom of choice.

When Agape Revelation event came at the end of April 2018, I sat on Dr. Joe Dispenza's lecture. My body started reacting. It was like some kind of energy was releasing from my body and was rising up. Dr. Joe Dispenza said, "Even we are in the future with our mind but our bodies are still in the past. Then our bodies hold us back." They have memory cells, where all our past thoughts and experiences are kept. Because of that, we are not able to change anything in our bodies unless we give back the willpower to our minds. Then the old thinking and behaviors can be changed, and our bodies become more healthy and alive. What helps to achieve this process is to focus more in the present moment. Meanwhile, we will be guided to release all the past emotions from the body, which were held because of negative past experiences in our lives. We will take back control of our thoughts to heal our minds, and wisdom will be introduced to us. Otherwise, we will have the same experiences in the future over and over again unless we learn this. There is a requirement to be present and have brighter thoughts about ourselves, our bodies, and our lives to heal our past and have a new future.

When we become masters of our minds, we become mindful and then we will live in the present moment instead of living in the past or in the future. Being in *now*, the thoughts of spirit start to flow to our minds, where there is guidance, right actions, and the transformation of the person will occur.

In May 2018, I had another personal revelation. I was sitting at the table eating breakfast, and suddenly, a thought came to me: *What is my origin?* And a big flow of energy went from my soral plexus chakra along the way to my head. I felt it and saw it. The answer came at once: *Byra*. I knew what I needed to do. The whole day I was amazed with this experience.

The next month I filed, through the Polish consulate, in Los Angeles to council town of Jozefow, where I was born, to change my last name. All started there, and I returned to the beginning. After one and a half month, I received directly the decision from Poland that my family name was changed from Ferens to Byra. Then I applied for a new passport, paying half price because my current passport was still valid.

In June, Agape International Spiritual Center community organized a volunteering day. There were sixteen nonprofit organizations that we could choose from. The person who guided me to the enrollment stand was Debra, whom I met in the Agape's bookstore after participating in my first service there. She was like an angel, and she chose for me Ernest Holme's book *This Thing Called You* at that time, which turned out that I needed for my first class, "Foundations of Universal Laws Governing Spiritual Living," in Agape. She was blessing then for me, and she appeared as a blessing this time also. She invited people for enroll for volunteering day.

I knew what organization I would choose. It was obvious: L.O.V.E. Foundation. Debra also enrolled herself to volunteer there.

I wondered why there were dots between the letters *L. O. V. E.* Later, I learned that this was an abbreviation of "Living Our Vision Everyday." Greg told me that it came to him after he was asked by a facilitator who led his life-visioning class: "What would you do with your license as the Agape licensed practitioner?"

Life visioning was used by Rev. Michael Bernard Beckwith when he was in the process of establishing Agape International Spiritual Center in 1986, and he still uses the process with the board members to make decisions regarding the organization. I remember when I first read *Life Visioning* by Rev. Michael B. Beckwith in Poland, I didn't understand a lot of it. When I was learning in Los Angeles, I started understanding more and more.

When the volunteering day came, we met at Agape's building, and after a welcome speech, we split into our groups and we had a carpool to reach our destinations of volunteering. I volunteered in Hollywood. It was my first time being in that area. Till then I wasn't interested to explore Los Angeles. My life was centered around the Agape community, and the classes there. It was the most important for me at that time. Whatever I needed to learn about or see something, I received through Agape International Spiritual Center activities such as classes or volunteering programs where I met a lot of new people for me to find the new friends at the time.

When we arrived to Hollywood, we prepared the tables and the stage. The truck with burgers and french fries arrived. The event was held at the Walk of Fame. It was the first time that I was able to see the golden stars on the sidewalk with the renowned names of actresses, actors, and movie-industry personalities. We invited people who walked by to have some food and listen to music. There were a lot of people who experienced homelessness. They had an opportunity to eat something and be around other people to chat. It was a lot of fun. I wasn't prepared for that kind experience. I thought that it would be like in "hand in hand" organization in Santa Monica where I only served food. I was caught by surprise. Thank you for this experience. I met new people from other communities. The girl whom I was cooperating with in dismantling the stage resembled my best friend from high school. That girl came from Sweden ten years before to be a part of scientology community.

During this event, there was a lot of love. We all cooperated and had fun.

Two months later (in August) I was a part of another event organized by L.O.V.E Foundation. We were preparing the event for the people who experienced homelessness wherein they would be able to get a shower and haircut. Some food and music were in program also. We brought some clothes that we didn't use to share with homeless people. Also, new socks and underwear were supplied. There was a person from another homeless organization who provided hygiene kits for the homeless people. This event was aired on ABC7 national TV.

In July, I was on a *ayahuasca* ceremony. I found out about ayahuasca through Agape International Spiritual Center as usual. In January, when I was at the service, there were free books given to the Agape community from Gerard Powell, the owner of Rythmia in Costa Rica, and he described his journey to himself. His salvation was ayahuasca. He received a lot of answers for himself through drinking plant medicine. Ayahuasca is called respectfully "Mother Earth medicine" by many indigenous people and medicine women and men of South and Central America. In some ancient scripts, there were pictures that indicated that Jesus drank this magical brew and gave to his disciples. A lot of people had been healed through drinking ayahuasca by releasing their own blockages and finding themselves that they are more than the human body by seeing Reality. I couldn't go to Costa Rica even if I badly wanted to. I tried to find the way, but I also knew that I needed to stay in the USA. I was brought here for the reason. As the law of attraction says, when we do something to happen, then we strive with it and nothing happens. I let go of it, and I knew that someday I will be on ayahuasca ceremony by releasing attachment to the place. I didn't wait too long because it happened in six months. Life knows what is better for us. *Ask, believe, receive* in the way that you would not imagine. As I indicated before, what comes to me easy is mine and I am safe. The way I found out about the ceremony was very spontaneous.

I went to Agape International Spiritual Center for service to meet my Polish friend Krzysztof, and with him was our mutual friend who said that he just came back from ayahuasca ceremony. He invited me to the ceremony as a friend, and after a few weeks, I ended up near to Los Angeles county for my first and last ayahuasca healing weekend with my friend and I met a lot of wonderful people. The price was enough that I could afford for it, and I was 100 percent sure that I would be safe, and it was true. I am grateful for this experience and the people. My mantra was always, "*I meet people who I can trust.*" One week before the ayahuasca ceremony we needed to be on a diet without caffeine. I love to drink coffee latte because of its taste. The caffeine doesn't make my body more energetic. After drinking coffee at night, I can fall asleep easily. To feel energetic every day, I used affirmation, like "*I am whole, perfect strong, powerful, loving, harmonious, and happy*," from Charles Haanel book, or I put out an intention before falling asleep that the next day I would be full of energy, healthy, and happy. It worked every time. We need only the affirmation that resonates with us. Believe in it, and it becomes the truth for us.

Being on detoxication from caffeine, I realized that after drinking coffee, the caffeine went down to my legs as I felt muscle pain in my legs. The first night after I stopped drinking my latte, I wasn't able to asleep. I felt this pain for three days. At that time I decided that I would not drink coffee at all. After three to four weeks, I bought a cup of latte only to check if I can feel the coffee would go down to my legs. It really went. I felt like the drink stopped on my ankles. I was amazed at how I was able to feel it. It was fun. At that time, I had stopped drinking coffee for many months. A few weeks later a thought came to me about cacao. I started drinking it instead of my latte. The best thing about cacao is that it has magnesium, which the body absorbs. On the other hand, coffee rinses away magnesium from our bodies. The body cells need to have magnesium to absorb all knowledge we learn through the experiences or to remember things by our minds.

I learned after the ayahuasca ceremony that the best way to apply magnesium is through the skin. We can spray it on our forearms, feet, and calves. I found out that cacao was a Mayan drink and it has caffeine. With that first revelation, I was amazed. Everything was about the Mayans. I was open to know more and adopted it, but with the second part, I was surprised because cacao is given to small kids in Poland. I drank cacao for breakfast, and I loved it. Mayans used cacao in ceremonies to open the heart chakra. I found out about it from my friend three years later, who uses cacao before the crystal bowl soundbath for healing.

On the ayahuasca ceremony we wore white clothes. We were informed that dark clothes keep light away.

The ceremony lasted for two nights. During the ceremony, there were three servings of the plant medicine. Each serving had special name. I took two servings of the plant medicine. It was enough for me.

The first night was wonderful. When I laid my head on the cushion, I felt like smiling. I saw a lot of colors, mostly purple and green, and formed in shapes that resembled angels. There was a lot of light, and I repeated the mantra, "I am healthy." Also my intention was to stay in the body.

I learned later that after drinking ayahuasca, we should purge because the body is releasing emotions. People would take *hoppe* sometimes to help them release stuck emotions, and they throw up. So the next night, we all put another intention, and I invited the jaguar to this ceremony because I started to notice his presence that day. I didn't take a tablet, and the jaguar took me to the darkness. After taking ayahuasca, I remember thinking that I didn't want any medicine in my body anymore. I wanted to throw up, but I wasn't able to. The person who assisted me asked me to drink water so I would vomit. I knew he was right, but I couldn't do that, and I also knew that I would not force my body by putting two fingers to my mouth as I was taught and did in the past. I felt that the body and mind are two different things. And my body didn't deserve to be violated as it was in the past by myself and from letting others be disrespectful to my body. That's why, at the end, I listened to the person and drank water. When I did it, I started purging, and I kept vomiting for the rest of the night. I rested in another room for the rest of the ceremony. The healer came to give the energy treatment to restore my body. I took my tablet, and my body felt like it was renewed. The dose that I used was a really small one. It was still in my mind that my body cannot live without a tablet. I believe that one day, my body will recover fully and that I will be safe to function completely and perfectly without any medication, as I did when was a child and teenager. I believe in it, and I know that it is done in the realm of Spirit. Now I was guided to having the manifestation appear in my physical body. The person who assisted me told me that he saw two of my projects that were imprinted in my soul. He also said that I was very sensitive to the energy. I didn't ask him about these visions. I wanted find out by myself. At that time I didn't feel that I was able to implement any project. I was thankful for the help and assistance that I got from these people. I let go full of emotions during these hours.

The next day after the ceremony, I sat outside on the grass, and suddenly, tears started falling down. My eyes were closed and only felt the grass, peace, and tears. Suddenly, I received straight from my heart the name Mary Magdalene. I knew that I needed to find out more about her. I went into the house, and I asked one of the people who assisted us during the ceremony. I told him about my experience outside, about the name, and he told me that I received the name, Mary Magdalene. There was no coincidence that from the very beginning, when I came to San Diego, my roommate's name was Meri. Then when I came back to Los Angeles from the East Coast for only one night, the passenger next to me in the Uber was a woman called Mary, and now I received this name as an initiation to my role in this world. He told me that he had a friend, and she was very interested in the Mary Magdalene topic. He contacted her, and she gave me the titles of trilogy by Kathleen McGowan: *The Expected One*, *The Book of Love*, and *The Poet Prince*. I was ready to read them three months later. They were fiction books but based on information from the Gnostic scriptures found and given to the public information in the early midst of twentieth century in Egypt. All saved demiurgical traditions texts about early Christian are kept at the Nag Hammadi Library. The author did a lot of research on her own to put important information that were hidden by ages for the readers. In the first book were fragments from the gospel of Mary Magdalene. Her gospel is the only existing early Christian text written under the name of a woman. And it turned out that she was a very important disciple to whom Jesus's male disciples turn for advice and wisdom. The most important massage is that after the death of Jesus Christ, she was the one who continued his teachings as a woman apostle, often called Mary of Magdala. And the view that Mary Magdalene was a prostitute is a piece of theological fiction; it is used to paint women as sinners, penitents, and a cause of men's violent behavior and disrespect toward a person. The beauty of a woman was based only on her body, which should bear more male descendants. From being a very important woman and the person who had a huge part in evolving Christianity, Mary Magdalene was announced by the church to be a prostitute. She was a spiritual teacher, a priestess in the early Christianity age. After the crucifixion of Jesus Christ, she escaped to France to continue his legacy. In the second book were the teachings of Jesus. After my revelation on the ranch during the Heal Your Life training, when I was crying, sitting on the floor, and looking at the picture of Jesus Christ, I knew that I was on the path to discover more. His path was love, joy, forgiveness, and faith. He lived this way and taught others to do the same. But most importantly, he wanted us to understand and showed us who we really are by resurrection. Christ walks on the earth, and we forget that we all are him.

After the ayahuasca ceremony, my body adapted that experience, and the following week, I went onto the Queen Up Your Act event in Temsecal Park organized by the ex-wife of Reverend Michael and her friend. I had a break from Agape International Spiritual Center, and I wanted be around her energy because I loved her freedom of expression and childlike joy. She seemed to be a wonderful woman. Her music has power. I remember one Sunday when Reverend Michael asked her to finished his speech with the playing on the piano, my body felt it in every cell. It was powerful experience.

My soul was at home when I came to Agape International Spiritual Center, and I was on the first service with Reverend Michael in 2017. But my body experienced powerful healing and joy when his ex-wife's music was on.

Being in Agape International Spiritual Center, I received a lot: I learned about myself, I met new friends, I started be more and more aware, but also, I had a time when I needed rest from this community. I started feeling like I lost a lot of my energy being with the people there.

I remember the words of my new met friend Rodolfo A. Esteves. We met during serving food to the homeless people in Santa Monica in November. A few months after Queen Up Your Act event, he said to me, after I had shared with him my experience of losing energy in Agape community, "Energy cannot be wasted because energy is everywhere, just poorly invested." His spiritual journey brought him to Agape International Center also but many years before me. He had his own awakening as a young man, over twenty years ago.

I met Rodolfo a few days before I left Los Angeles for the East Coast again. Life gave me another person to become my guide and spiritual brother when I needed one the most.

Coming back to Tamascal Park and the Queen Your Act weekend, which was held in July, it was a wonderful experience. There were two hundred women. We stayed in cabin houses where we slept for three nights and had a lot of joy. It was my first time to do vasana yoga. I danced in a row with the American girls to old American hits. We all had a good time there. They were really three joyous days. I bought a lapis lazuli stone at that time. Lapis lazuli helps with self-expression and activates a throat chakra. It is responsible for speech. I can only thank my friend Dana who gave me a lift to Tamascal Park and brought to the gemstone stand. She shared with me that her grandma was Polish and she brought her up. That's why she felt connection with me.

In August, I got an offer to move to Santa Monica for two and half months. I was asked to stay with a Polish teenager who wanted to study in a Santa Monica high school for a year. Her mother, who was in Poland, needed to have an annual leave from the university where she lectured to join her. That's why she asked me to stay with her daughter until she would be able to finish up in her job and come to Santa Monica for ten months. It was a mutual favor.

Staying in Santa Monica, I had everything close by. I worked there. I had the Pacific Ocean, more trees, and shops. Temescal Park was in Santa Monica, and Malibu was twenty-five minutes by bus. I went to Malibu once. The road was along the beach. Malibu beach is more beautiful for me than any other place in the area. I fell in love with this place.

I also visited Getty Villa, which was in Malibu. It was a gift to the community by billionaire J. Paul Getty. He left there his private collection of coins and statues from ancient Greece and Rome. The place was on the hill in the woods and the view from the Getty terraces was the ocean. There was an amphitheater where performances were played. Getty Villa was free for tourists. J. Paul Getty left also Getty Museum, which was in Los Angeles. He left his heritage to others. He was operating from London, and he passed away before Getty Villa was ready.

In Santa Monica, I started speaking about writing a book but I didn't know how to write. My time was very limited, and I was in the moving mode all the time. I didn't have one place to live where I could unpack and focus on one thing that I really wanted. Then the realization came to me that it was time for me to move forward and manifest more time for myself and find out how to write.

I knew that I needed to move out from Santa Monica in the middle of November. I decided to talk to the boy's mother, and I told her that I would terminate the job in one month. It would be the end of October. In the end, I extended my work one week longer. What I loved about the boy's mother was her purity and how she was torn between her own professional obligations and love to her son. I saw in her a pure, loving person and full of joy. I was grateful for the love that I gave and received from this small boy and the warmness from the boy's whole family. Thanks to the boy's grandmother, I learned a lot about food and other stuff in California. I appreciated their kindness.

When I decided to leave my job, I had no idea where I would live. I chose to live in trust. I knew that I would know when the time came.

On my birthday, October 8, I took a trip to Anaheim and spent all day in Disneyland to have some fun. There are two amusement parks, and to see all the attractions, you need about three straight days.

That day was a bank holiday. There were a lot of people, mostly families with children. Because of that, there were a lot of lines. I had the opportunity to ride in the most attended attractions, and the rest of the day I spent walking through the Disneyland streets eating delicious ice creams and churros. Also I had opportunity to be on the parade, which closes the day in Disneyland. The ticket was for the whole day, so when I got out of Disneyland and suddenly wanted have a ride on the fast train that takes the visitors from very main entrance to the area of Tomorrowland, I was able to do that. Thanks to that I saw all the attractions in Disneyland from different perspective.

Meanwhile, I bought one-day ticket to Dr. Joe Dispenza's lecture organized by Hay House, which was held on November 3. I left all my worries about my accommodation and flew to Las Vegas on November 2. I arrived Friday morning. I had a wonderful day of sightseeing. Also I felt energy flowing through my solar plexus chakra. I felt present. It turned out that Las Vegas has a train where it stops at all the main attractions. So I was in London, Paris, Bellagio Hotel, MGM hotel, and others places where tourists visit. I was at the Caesars Palace and I had opportunity see the place where *The Hangover* movie was made. The hotel made impression on me, and I thought that nothing else can compare until I saw Bellagio's fall exhibition. Later that night I went back to Bellagio to see the fountain show. The lights, music, water, and plenty of people—it was beautiful and fun.

The next day, all day, I was in the ballroom listening to Dr. Joe Dispenza. It was very interesting day acquiring new knowledge. Dr. Joe Dispsenza connected spiritual knowledge with the newest science discoveries. His latest book title was *Becoming Supernatural.*

The new technology inventions are more and more advanced, and thanks to that, science can rediscover the Truth of what spiritual teachers and gurus taught through ages. That the matter is created from atoms and electrons, and those are created from biophotons, which in Greek means "life" and "light." When we had a break, we were able to look around. I stopped at the stand with the intentions jewelry (you will find them among others on Instagram @intentionsjewelry). I was attracted to a new Thot bracelet, a patron of writers, teachers, and healers—all three that I desired to become. These bracelets are very powerful and elegant. A mother and daughter are running the business, Shareane and Adrienne Baff. Shareane makes the bracelets with intention so every bead is filled with Divine Energy to serve a new owner, have a good life. The process lasts up to three weeks. Adrienne is the designer of each bracelet. They are made from Swarovski beads. Being at their stand in Las Vegas, I wasn't aware how strong the vibrations they have had until I checked their website two years later and was able to feel the healing energy from each bracelet.

I also met Sandra J. Filer, who was as an assistant in Heal Your Life training the year before, and she leads this work for many years. She became the main Heal Your Life coach and trainer from the USA because Patricia Crane, PhD, and Rick Nicolas decided to finish their work as the workshop trainers. They did this work all over the world for more than twenty-two years. Their first Heal You Life overseas workshop was in Poland. Patricia is an author of the book *Ordering from the Cosmic Kitchen*, and Rick is the author of a beautiful small book on the inner child, which I mentioned in the previous chapter. He is also a photographer and a beautiful human being. Both with Patricia compiled the book *Pearls of Wisdom*.

On Dr. Joe Dispenza's lecture, also I met a Polish girl, Ania, who was a model in New York City for many years. A beautiful girl full of joy and heart. She was there with her partner, and I received from him the link to Anita Morjooni's audiobook, *Dying to be Me*.

When I was in the airplane, going back to Los Angeles, I asked for a juice. The stewardess gave me the juice and a napkin. When I turned the napkin, I saw an inscription: *New York City*. I knew that this wasn't a coincidence. I wasn't happy about the sign, but I knew that somehow I would be there.

When I came back to Los Angeles, I needed to figure out my next move. Time was running out for me. Few weeks earlier, my friend from my younger years contacted me. He lived in Linden, New Jersey. When I was thinking where I could move, I texted a few people in Los Angeles and also him. He offered me to come to Linden and have the time to figure out my next move. I believed that we both had some kind of expectations about our meeting, and I noticed after two or three days that we both were on different levels of understanding. Our ideals were on two opposite poles. From good friends, we became more like acquaintances. I let myself be me and him to be himself, and it gave me a glimpse of how we were different. In his attitude, with what he dealt with at that time, what was missing was the most important ingredient, which was faith—the faith that everything would work out for him and the highest good for his family.

I saw all the signs that East Coast was not for me. The day when I was leaving Los Angeles, it started snowing in Newark, New Jersey. I paid overweight fee for an additional two overweight luggages. I took two suitcases because I thought that I was staying for a longer time. To feel better, I got a thought with affirmation that paying this $100, I would become a millionaire. I felt better and started smiling. At that time for a first time my carry-on bag was checked thoroughly. When I reached the gate, it turned out that boarding would be cancelled because of the snow. We didn't know if the plane would take off. I was grateful for this because I had opportunity to stay longer in Los Angeles' atmosphere and look out the window at the LAX airport to see a sunny day. I didn't feel good about leaving the city. Because of the delay, we received a voucher to buy something care of the airline. Once we were boarded, we were asked to get off the plane. After five hours of delay, we took off for Newark, New Jersey. When we landed at the Newark airport, we waited over two hours in the airplane to get to the gate. Everything was delayed due to the snow. All these signs were vivid. That's why after three days being in Linden, I pulled out a card from the oracle card deck, which I had with me, and on it was written "Be honest with yourself." After this message, I stopped pretending that everything would be all right, and I started asking myself, "What is my next step?"

Rodolfo was in contact with me every day since I was at the LAX airport and flying to New Jersey area. I am so thankful for his checking up on me all the time. Thanks to him, I kept myself high, and my heart was open. I knew that I needed to experience East Coast again to understand where my place is.

When speaking to Rodolfo, I always felt more myself. When he spoke to me, he spoke to my soul, to who really I am. At that time, I didn't understand totally, but I felt it. It was a wonderful feeling. I felt more powerful, more free, and joyous. I started being awakened by Life and receiving soul mates as a personal teachers or coaches.

Rodolfo was one of them. He is the author of *The Power of Thank You: A Story of Gratitude, Love, and Self-Realization*.

The first night in Linden suddenly I started repeating to myself, "*I am spirit having human incarnation. I am spirit having human incarnation. I am spirit having human incarnation.*" Then I felt energy move up my body, and the body started being longer. I felt a warm, beautiful feeling around my heart. It helped me be in the awareness of Truth and love.

Staying in Santa Monica I bought a DreamBuilder program that I received a link through Agape International Spiritual Center and another course, which was a Hay House writer's course. Both were online.

Thanks to DreamBuilder program, I started rebuild my dreams. I needed this because I started doubting what I had dreamed of. Being on East Coast, I was again in the situation where people believed in hard work, diseases, and were focused on disasters and money. Instead of really appreciating every moment of their lives and stop doubting that life was always for them.

In the online writer's course, I received information on how to become a writer and also some useful tools such as tapping to release tension from the body and how to stop listening to my small ego, which can sabotage myself, for example, "I don't want to pursue my new adventure to become a writer." When we start doing something new, we have a lot of thoughts of doubt. Tapping gives freedom to release that. The person who helped me in this course wrote a book about this technique. His name was Nick Ortner, and the book title was *The Tapping Solution*. Also I saw him on YouTube. He helped kids release all the tension at an elementary school.

In the US, some schools really take care of the kids and help them to go through all the stress that scholar programs can do. They look for solution from other sources to let the children become complete adult persons. There is no only one way. The academic education has brought a lot of smart people but emphasizes only memorizing things instead of what the student had learned to pass the exams and prove how knowledgeable the person is on the topic, which cuts them off from their own Source. And they assess themselves and other people based on their knowledge from the books. Their explanations are given from the head. Everything that they use to support expressing themselves is logic. The more we read academic books and know more, the more we chase diplomas, which proves that we are good at our field. Our mind becomes a library, and we have the impulse that we need to know more and more. We study to get a jobs because we doubt that we know enough to get that job. We get more certificates, and they are never enough. We become more and more disconnected from our own Source of Creation. It doesn't give us peace of mind and the feeling of being fulfilled and complete.

There are some of people who show off their acquired knowledge to cover their own belief about themselves, that they are not so smart like they wanted to be. In the most cases, they are not aware of that. Being in the space of the academic learning gives us only opportunity to create more opinions on how life should be and what is wrong or right. Laughing at others because they are not educated, not smart enough, or are not interested in this kind of learning only proves how the ego rules our behaviors. There is lack of tolerance. Diplomas don't bring us what we are truly looking for, which is peace and the inner knowing that we are safe, supported, and loved. Diploma is needed mostly for an employment purpose to prove that we are good enough to be hired, nothing else. But this fact does not always bring fulfillment and balance in our lives.

In this stage of our world, our worthiness has been rated through numbers and how much we are qualified through the certificates we had gained. Some of the kids were born to become a singer, a dancer, a painter, a writer, a sculptor, etc. Do you think that they need so much information about numbers or science, where every few years there is a new discovery or a new theory? We need to have general knowledge about how to move in this world. What needs to be emphasized in education is our creativity and how to be loving and tolerant toward our peers. We need to be taught about imagination and how important it is to be connected to our hearts, where love and fulfillment is. But most schools demand from us to learn things that we would not use in our adult life at all. Connected to our Wisdom within, we don't really need to know a lot. We are guided. I am the example. My whole journey in the US is through inner guidance. I didn't know anything about the places where I was heading or where I was supposed to be and what I needed to learn to become what is meant for me. My first step was a Heal Your Life training in San Diego, but it lasted only one week. My school was Life, connection to it, to follow step by step. And because of that, I saw beautiful landscapes, I met wonderful people, I was always in the right time, I learned a lot, and I was safe.

As a kid we really know who we want to be. Every child knows what they love and don't like. This is a guidance. As an adult, we forgot what we love. We were taught that we need to do what we have to not what we love to. Love is everything, and through love, we can only expand and feel alive. Going to schools where everyone is put in the same box, we forgot who we wanted become and feel less and less when we cannot catch up with our peers. We are pushed by teachers and our parents who love us, but they stop having their own common sense. They put their own ambitions in their children that they become sometimes worse than the teachers instead of being loving and understanding parents. We start to compare ourselves to others, and because of that, we lose our uniqueness of being. We learn something that we were not interested in. It was, and still is, a waste of our time. Instead we should spend time on our passions and evolve in it and be a true gift to the world as a human being. When we are in harmony with our inner being, we feel connected with everything and everyone. Money comes easily and it is impossible to be poor. Our creative nature takes over our limited minds and we flow with Life, which is abundant, and we are abundant. We have this inner knowing. We were born with it.

We play many roles during our lifetime on this planet, but our true state of being is changeless. We need to go back and be connected to this Source, to be fulfilled and start to live our life with passion, without fear. Our way of being needs to be in service to others, not only see our playground.

While staying in Linden, I went to New York City a few times. I visited the First Church of Religious Science and met some new people. I began to see New York City a little differently. I saw the Lincoln

Filming Center. I had lunch there with newly met friend. I learned from the person that the Lincoln Filming Center was the place were the First Church of Religious Science held services in their golden years. There were services for three thousand or more people. At that time Louise Hay and Dr. Wayne Dyer started their careers in this community. Thanks to meeting the person who gave me that tour, I saw New York as a friendlier place than a year before. I knew that it was my perspective, that I felt more confident in moving throughout the United States. New York City was the same. I also visited my friend Agnieszka and her family for a few hours, but most of the time, I was in New Jersey area. I reconnected with another friend from high school. I appreciated his kindness and believing in me when I shared what I was up to.

When I was traveling from Linden to New York City, I listened to the book *The Untethered Soul* by Michael A. Singer.

Once, I spotted a poster on the train station. The inscription read:

>   BE FEARLESS
>   HAVE FAITH
>   BE READY

I knew that I was preparing to the next step, which was going back to Los Angeles.

At that time, I also wanted to meet with Beata, but our schedules were different. So I dedicated my free time to listen to Hay House online writer's course and do the homework from the DreamBuilder program.

Once, I took a notebook and I started make notes, like I was starting to write. It was a new experience for me, and I loved it. But I really started writing this book when I came back to Los Angeles.

From the DreamBuilder program, I received a free session with a coach, where we would work on my dream. It was a wonderful feeling when I spoke aloud about my dream and the person only encouraged me and helped me to rediscover this dream. It was imprinted into my subconsciousness mind. When she asked me, "What if you would not do any move toward your dream?" Suddenly I started feeling cold and my body was shaking. I felt like I would kill my dream if I didn't make any move. After this session, I went to my laptop and bought one-way ticket to Los Angeles. The price was lower, and it turned out later that this airline had a higher standard than the previous one that flew me to Newark.

I contacted Edward, the landlord, of the house where I used to stay at the beginning when I first came to Los Angeles, and he said that there was place for me. I contacted friend who I met when we lived together in this house for a while to pick me up from the airport. She was to give a lift to her sister to LAX airport the same day I would arrive, so she could picked me up. It was magic. Everything was flawless.

When I started being afraid of coming back to Los Angeles, I received a thought, *Trust God who is within you.* And again, I started trusting.

After three weeks in Linden, New Jersey, I went back to Los Angeles.

At the Newark airport, everything went smoothly. My one luggage was overweight, but it turned out that was in the range and I didn't pay any excess luggage. I was relieved. When I got to the gate, I had time to have breakfast, and when boarding started everything was flawless and on time. Before we took off, the captain said that we would land earlier than was scheduled.

When we landed in Los Angeles, I took my luggage and went off the LAX airport. I felt grounded again, and it felt like home. It was for me a vivid sign that I must start my new life here in the City of Angels. The whole journey to Linden was for me to be clear that my home was in Los Angeles. Being in Los Angeles, I felt protected and safe. Even when I spent a lot of time by myself, I didn't feel alone. When I was on the East Coast, I felt cold inside every time. I did my best to lift myself up and help others to do the same. When I interacted with others, I would look for people who are interested in spirituality as I did, but it was all temporary. People who I stayed with didn't know anything about trusting Life and growing with it. Some of them wanted to help me, but when I didn't fulfill their expectations by listening to their pieces of advice, they stop being interested in me and I became a strange person to them. For example, I was warned that traveling by myself in the USA is dangerous and other limiting beliefs were implemented to my consciousness. My friend, whose hospitality I appreciated, wanted to "rescue" me by putting loud music or watching TV showing world disasters when I wanted talk to him or spend quiet time with myself learning online courses and preparing myself for the next step. When we believe in the world of disasters, we live in it and we attract more and more things to confirm our beliefs about it. Our relationships don't work, and we see our life as a catastrophy. Why are we so determined to kill ourselves inside instead of living fully and be connected? The newspapers and TV only help us to believe in this kind of world.

I chose live in the world where there is peace, love, abundance, and freedom to express itself in creative ways. My new friends in Los Angeles are these kinds of people. They believe that this world can be a better place for everyone.

I am thankful for this encounter because I had realized more how we react when our expectations are not met. Our attitude is changing toward another person, and we become cold. My friend was the mirror for me, how I was treated others in the past when they didn't meet my imaginations about them. Life is a learning process of yourself through other people. At that time I had opportunity to regain the savings that I invested when I sold my apartment in Poland, and because of that, I was covered for a while. I met new people in New York City. I received guidance to where my focus should be when I go back to Los Angeles from a person I met in NYC during Thanksgiving Day. I met him in the place where food was served to people experiencing homelessness in Brooklyn. I got the address to the headquarters of Self-Realization Fellowship in Los Angeles. It turned out later that this contact was a blessing for my future growing. I was heading to a master who was waiting for me to teach me how find and communion with God.

The people I stayed with in the East Coast didn't understand what I was talking about. They thought that I was from a different planet and I was naive. They couldn't understand that I was on a path that none of them have taken, or they were ones who had given up shortly when they didn't see any results. I used to live an unconscious life like they do. I was on the path of awakening and Truth. I made a choice to start trusting Life at the age of thirty-seven. When we are in our heads focusing on our everyday to-do list and see the circumstances of the outside world, we lose ourselves by identifying with the body, which is only 1 percent of the whole entity. Where is the 99 percent?

It cannot be seen through the five senses. We can only feel it. It is our true essence who came to this world to express Itself on planet Earth. How can we be connected to it? By being aware of our emotions, thoughts, feelings, longings, and discontent. We need to take responsibility for this inner world. We are not our thoughts, emotions, or feelings; but they become our guiding system of what works or doesn't work in our lives. Due to lack of the knowledge, we are not taking responsibility for our behaviors and lives. Life supposed to be harmonious, and it starts with our inner world. Our thoughts are causing our emotions, either bad or good feelings. All thoughts, emotions, feelings are vibration and sends information to the Universal Mind-Spirit. We need to be aware of that. Good feelings will bring more good feelings by receiving good news, promotion, health, and love—whatever we wish. But the most important is peace of mind, that everything is all right. Bad feelings bring us experiences that we don't like. Then we feel more down and less. We always are free to choose our thoughts. Let's do that deliberately.

What are our values of life? What really matters to each of us? We have our inner guidance. We need to make choices on its foundation. It will serve us much better than listening to others what we should do or have. Our true world is within. The outside world only mirrors what we have within. Our relationships are in disharmony; marriages end; a lot of inequality, disharmony between wealth and poverty. Looking at our inner world is the answer to all the problems that we have on planet Earth. By being disconnected from ourselves, we see only mess in the outside world. Most of us act like victims and say that life is bad and all bad things are happening to me, and because of that, I need to protect myself. Because of this attitude, our planet is being destroyed by people and governments that wants to protect its country against other countries. That's why there are borders, homelessness, and diseases. We can see how our global ego plays the first role on our planet and disconnects us all. We all are responsible for that but don't play our own part as a Spirit and do internal work to feel a connection with everything and everyone. Then we will rise the whole consciousness on planet Earth, and the governments will be replaced automatically with people who see unity, peace, commonwealth and global health—people who stop using media to program our subconscious minds in the name of good will with diseases, unfairness, fear and death; people who stop protecting us from things we all created out of ignorance individually and globally; people who show the way to love, natural health, unity, and peace. This is our future if only we take responsibility for our part in this world. That's why we came here again in these transformational times. We didn't come here to live for a while and die; we came to make a difference in this world.

There is no such thing like nationality or boundaries in our inner world. We come from one Source that creates all—our planet Earth, galaxies, all the cosmos. We all are created the same. So who are we truly? *We are souls, a radiating ray of the infinite Universal Spirit, our Father. A soul takes on individuality, a 100 percent of entity, by embodying itself first in causal body made of bliss and pure intuitive consciousness, then in astral body composed of mind and prana—indestructible light and life energy, which is covered with physical body of perishable matter.* As a human, we only identify ourselves with the physical body made of different frequency of atoms' vibration. The life force in Hindu scripture is called *prana*; in Chinese, *qi*; and in Japanese, *Reiki*. And the science calls it a biofield energy. We forgot that within and around our familiar physical frame is the wondrous astral body of light and divine life.

We are so attached to our physical form that we identify ourselves and others through culture, nationality, different color of skin, different traits (ego), family, where we grew up, and the religion that we used to live and believe.

We are so focused on and identify with the body that we explore it all the time, from *A* to *Z*. I am fat; I am slim; I am hungry; I am not capable; I cannot do that because I am too small, too tired, or too old; I don't know how to do that; etc. "I am" consciousness is very limited, attached to our five body senses. There is so many books on how our body should function, how our body should be fed, how our body should be exercised, how our body should rest, etc. There are so many diets about losing the weight, but none is good. People who diet lose their weight but later return back to their previous weight or even gain more weight when they stop using them. We need to start using the Power that is within us, our divinity which is a healer. Most of people are afraid of something that is new. Their minds are very close and resistant. They deny everything that doesn't fit in to their world of belief system. They are afraid of losing all their identities, what they had built up throughout their adult life. They do that to protect themselves from the wounds they experienced in the past. They are afraid of themselves, their own better version.

We really need to lose our small self to regain our True Self. It requires starting being aware again. We are called human beings, not human doings. We can act or do when we are aware of the motives behind our actions. We can stop and ask ourselves, "Do I do something on autopilot because I was brought up that way? Or do I use my free will to create my life more consciously by watching for behaviors and habits that don't serve me at all and eliminate them?" There is so much love for us from the Spirit that we cannot be afraid of making changes in our awareness. We are protected and supported by Life. The change can only bring peace to our own individual world and on a global level. The first step is watching our thoughts, emotions, and feelings. We could start replacing our negative old beliefs about ourselves by affirmations based on the Truth of who we are, start being grateful for life, and connect with our Source of Creation through meditation. All this will help us widen our awareness, see the Truth, and again connect our soul with the inner guidance called intuition. We need to sit in a quiet place and start listening to our soul, which is waiting to be heard. It is the soul journeying on the planet Earth, not our small ego, which will stop existing when the soul lets go of its physical body one day. The ego doesn't know anything; it only sees the past, current circumstances, and builds future base on it. Its understanding of the world is what it sees through the body's eyes, what was learned and experienced. That's why our lives are the same over and over. We repeat the same scenario. We listen to our ego, and we are afraid because of our experiences in the past, and we are afraid of the future. People very often say, "I don't need this or that." For example, I dream about traveling but I don't have enough money. I had bad experiences with it, so I would stay at home and do nothing, or I am too old for traveling or to have a new life. Saying I am okay with what I have and in the place where I am or I am okay without freedom to do what I really want to do—you are not being true to yourself. Deep in your heart you would love to experience more life. It is our true nature. But we don't do anything about that because we listen to the ego, which is afraid of everything. The ego sees only walls and has a lot of reasons to stop us. Behind these is nothing else, like the fear of unknown. What would your life look like if you stopped listening to illusive fear instead of having faith that life is for you and wants you to evolve? How would you act and think? By being okay with what is, we deprive ourselves of what was given to us from the very beginning before we were born.

After landing in Los Angeles and meeting my friend at LAX airport, she took me for dinner and we both came back home. For the next few weekends, we shared one room together.

The day I arrived, according to Mayan sacred calendar, was the Day of Believing in Yourself. It was December 8, 2018. I knew that I needed to start writing to spread the message to others about what I have experienced and found out and how I transformed by using the principles of life to live by the Truth about us and Life itself.

My dream is for all of us to see ourselves in a True Light as unlimited souls, spirits having a human incarnation being here for a while to bring heaven on earth, which we have both in us.

Next day after arriving, I went to Agape International Spiritual Center. It was wonderful to interact again with people I knew. Another surprise was waiting for me. When I was at a service, I saw on display a picture of Mary Morrissey, the founder of Life Solution

Institute. She invented the DreamBuilder program. When I enrolled to the online course, there was an offer of two free tickets to a live DreamBuilder event on January 2019 in Los Angeles. There were a condition: I needed to pay $200 for a ticket to reserve a seat and the money would be 100 percent refundable when I come to the event. I wanted be there, but honestly, I didn't know if I would be in Los Angeles at that time. I couldn't let myself freeze the money because it was in the program offer as a "free" gift. To my understanding, if someone offers something for free, it means there are no conditions. If there are some conditions, it is not unconditional and only serves to protect its own business. It is understandable, but there can be some loses from one or both sides. I am thankful that I grew up with the understanding of free products having no conditions because the illusion of "free" offerings in the United States by businesses are many times abused. If we are afraid of loss, we're supposed to state the price that we want to receive for the service or the product or specify the offer differently, not state as free because, at the end, it can turn out otherwise. People will pay for it if they are capable and interested in it. Unnecessarily, we manipulate people in the name of goodwill for others. A free gift is "the free one" without expectations or attachments to the outcome. Thanks to that, we can evolve in trust that all the bills will be paid and income will be abundant. That's why we do our work. Life doesn't cheat us and doesn't ask us to pay for the air. But we can pay a price if we go against its laws, such as when we manipulate. Sometimes we need to deal with the consequences later.

So what happened when I saw on display Mary Morrissey during Sunday service in Agape? Mary Morrissey announced that anybody who would register through Agape International Spiritual Center to the live three-day event would pay $97. I was amazed. I knew that I will be on that event. I didn't know how, but I put my intention to be there, and it worked out.

That same day, after service, a friend of mine that I met in the Agape community asked me to stay with her granddaughter for two days and I said *yes*. Because of that, to show her appreciation, she gave me $100. Thanks to that, I paid for the live DreamBuilder event.

Being in Los Angeles I always meet people who take care about me. I felt warmth from them and kindness and selflessness. But to meet this kind of people, we need to be like them inside. Like attracts like. That's why in Los Angeles I had mirrors of my true nature and I was able to be open and my help was accepted with joy. What I needed to learn during my journey to the United States is to ask for help from other people. It was a huge lesson for me. To live in harmony, we need to understand the circle of giving and receiving. We need to learn to accept other's help and ask for it and be grateful for it, because then there is harmony in our environment.

Good to be home.

The Universe, being infinite, is in a constant state of evolutionary expansion. We live in a non-static, ever-evolving Universe, which is the source of our individual evolutionary impulse and our capacity to expand into our fullest potential (which is infinite). Each individual's expansion contributes to the evolutionary progress of the whole.

—Agape Spiritual Principles and Practices

CHAPTER 5

Can We Be More Surrendered to Life?

On the ground where I now stand, I declare my aliveness, my sensitivity to the Good that surrounds and infiltrates me. I live authentically, ever attuned to intuitive guidance from within that expresses through me as originality, creativity, harmony, and wholeness.

—Rev. Michael B. Beckwith

Coming back to Los Angeles and moving to the place where I used to live, I knew I was starting my life anew. I started writing. Everything that I learned from the Hay House online writing course I implemented when I felt something needed to be done. I received a lot of precious information. Also I received information that didn't serve me at all. How did I know? I started feeling less and compared myself to those who were there as the mentors of the course. When I noticed it, I released it and stopped putting attention to it. I wanted to enjoy writing my first book. Stop comparing myself to others here was long-term lesson. We all are unique, and each of us has our own unique journey to true Self. During the first few days, I wrote four chapters. I felt joy doing this.

Then came the first day of the three-day DreamBuilder event in Los Angeles. From there, I learned other tools to bring people to awareness that we are luminous beings and our bodies are created from energy. The simple and basic way is to rub your hands for twenty to thirty seconds, when you feel the warmth start, move them away and bring them back. You can feel energy between them.

Being in the field of creative energy, we started dreaming more and more. We had exercises where we shared our dream with our new partner. Every time when we had this exercise, our dream expanded. It was wonderful feeling how it could grow. I started seeing and feeling more and more of my dream. After every break, we were asked to change places. It was very liberating idea because we all had the possibility of meeting new people and be a part of our mutual growth.

On second day, my partner was a Polish girl whom I met on a break that same day. It turned out that she came with her thirty-year-old son to the event. They were from Canada. We both shared our dreams, and when she shared her dream, which I would call a mission, I saw blue colors of her sanctuary where healing and unity will be held. I saw this place in the shape of pyramid, and I told her about that, and she told me, "Oh, yes, I need to remember about this shape." When we are in the field of seeing and trust, what we can foresee can only help others. I was amazed with it, because I was able to help her by trusting the picture that I saw in my mind and told her about it. My inner-seeing abilities grew. People want us to help by seeing us as an outside source of the role by giving us advices on how we should act or react or run our life. This kind of help is very limited, judgmental, and not true. In the most cases, they want us to fit in to their understanding of life and be in their service for their own wants. We need to tune into our True Being within to harmonize our lives in every domain and help others to do the same. Then we can support another person, bringing their vision to the world, the unique expression of Itself in this world. On the live event, money was collected from these who wanted to donate to a wonderful cause. The nonprofit organization in Africa. There are created villages for children there that they can learn, have good food, water, clothing and a better future. The organization was founded by Mary Morrissey's friend. She discovered her soul's calling during private coaching session with Mary.

I started developing myself as more than a human being. I started experiencing and getting to know my self in the way I was created, not what I and other people used to think about me. By being born in a physical body, we all have similar ideas about ourselves and the world: be born, go to school, get a degree, get a good job, earn good money, get family, get old, and die. And between that, getting ill because the world is full of "dangerous" diseases. We see the world as not perfect; dangerous; full of hate, fear, and doubt. We all have ideas what is possible or not. It depends on our point of view, which is determined by our place of birth, gender, and the family we were born to. Poor and rich families, each has their own beliefs and limits. And when any harm happens to us, we are so attached to it that we let our life run around that and create stories about that. We are full of emotional pain. This is a very shallow and scary way of seeing and living. We all live in this kind of narrow ways of perception. But when we put intention that we want to really know the Truth, what is the True Source of All, and who we really are, our hearts and minds start being more open. We start seeing more possibilities and trust that Life is for us, not against us. Our perception starts changing. We become more happy and more joyful and trustful toward others. Most importantly, we start trusting ourselves and be more open and in tune with the intuitive guidance from within. The outside world is an illusion. That's why it changes all the time.

So Life gave me time and ideas, which I followed, and I started growing in the direction of where I was dreaming to become.

Then I got an idea to start writing affirmative prayers that were based on fundamental Truth as I am one with God. The idea came out when my friend Donata from Poland had some kind of financial problem and I let myself put in a short affirmative prayer for her. She had goose bumps. What happened after two or three short months, she started becoming more prosperous by doing what she loved to do. The possibilities had started overflowing to her. What was the reason? Most importantly, she started loving and accepting herself, and because of that, she started loving and accepting others. After that, the Universe only confirmed the truth that was included in the prayer. She always thanks me for suggesting she open a Facebook account because word of her custom-made earrings were spread through this social media application better than Instagram (@palo-manegra.bijou).

Other opportunities came also: her earrings were introduced in fashion shows. She texted me once, "The Universe has fame for me," and she laughed. This is the Truth. She used to uplift herself through different spiritual teachings, among them *A Course in Miracles*. This was only her inner individual work that let her experience happiness and prosperity. Her mind was open for something else. I love her to the core of my being. We have always supported each other. When we felt down, we lifted each other up. Once when I doubted and worried, she reminded me what I told her when she needed my support. She is a great teacher and friend to me.

Once I told her a story I read from one of Osho's books. It was a parable in which an adviser of the king, a wise man, wrote a sentence for his king when he and his kingdom were in trouble: "*Everything will pass.*" After reading the sentence, the king stopped being worried and regained his kingdom back. When he was greeted by his subjects, he was so proud and pompous because of his success. Then the wise man asked the king to look into the inscription, which he kept safe in his royal ring. When the king read again, "*Everything will pass,*" in a state of victory, he understood that this glory will pass and he stopped pumping up his ego and started being humble and happy for the moment. He was brought to the present moment. We need to remember that our ego is very scared or very pumped up. It happens when we identify with the situation or become attached to the outcome. When we feel uncertain in need or worry, we can say to ourselves: "*Everything will pass. I know, God, that you are in charge and everything will work out for my highest good. I am asking about the best way. Thank you.*" And let go of all worry. You will see the magic as all circumstances will start to change for better. When we experience triumphs, we need to be happy and excited about them but also say, "*God, I know that you are Source of my success and well-being. Thank you, I love you.*" You can call God in the name that is closest for you, for example, Heavenly Father, Divine Mother, Life, Spirit, Friend, Universe, Source of All, etc.

Being in Los Angeles, I met a lot of people who experienced a lot of—let's call them bad things, including homelessness, but now they are successful, full of light, and in service of others. My experiences showed me all the time that I don't have to worry because I am always, always safe and supported by my Source of Life. There is always a way out, which we can see or hear when we are peaceful and trustful.

Donata also introduced me to the social media. One day I texted her with the question asking for ideas on how to generate income, and she gave me an idea of posting videos on YouTube and to be visible in Instagram. I was grateful to her, because she was like the ignition for me to act. I knew that I have a story to tell, but I didn't know how to start. Then it happened. One day my friend Rodolfo called me, and suddenly, he started speaking about Eagle Rock. My whole body started shaking like I was cold. I knew that I needed to be there. The first time I heard about Eagle Rock was a year before, but I didn't have the opportunity to go there. After the call, I spoke to my new Polish friend, and he offered me a ride to the Topanga Park State where Eagle Rock was. It was a wonderful news, and it was flawless. I knew that it would be my first recording to inspire and help others to understand who we are. The idea that Donata gave me and my first recording happened in only one week. On that day we had beautiful weather even when it had been raining all week and the weather forecast for next week was also rain. Only one day was sunny, the day we were planning go to the Eagle Rock. As I mentioned before, I always have beautiful weather wherever I go somewhere.

It was January 9, 2019, only a month after I came back from the East Coast. That day it was meaningful for me according to the Mayan sacred calendar (TZOLKIN). The day's energy was called Warrior. It means to be courageous and connected with the power of intuitive intelligence. The assignment of this energy is raising awareness. I was born in the Warrior wave. My assignment is to be courageous and act upon my inner guidance to become independent. I remember when I started following TZOLKIN, even if I had a positive attitude, in this particular day of energy, I felt fear in my chest. I was afraid of my future. My mind was worried and felt separation. When we think that we are alone, we feel fear and our mind is fixating. When we are peaceful, we can see that we are protected. I stopped having that kind of fixations on days with this kind of energy. I started to even more trust Life and listen to my intuition.

Tzolkin is metaphysical, not from planet Earth. The code to read the Mayan sacred calendar was discovered by Dr. Jose Arguelles, whose father was a native Mayan. The Mayan called themselves time navigators. They said, "We are Masters of Time and Masters of Illusion." The Mayan knew that a human being was created in the image and likeness of the Creator. They called him Hunab Ku. That's why the code of life is the code of a human being, 13:20. This code we can find in our bodies. There are thirteen numbers defining the movement and are reflected as our thirteen main joints. The number 20 defines twenty excellent aspects of our Creator, which means the material from which life is woven. It is reflected in twenty basic amino acids. Also our fingers and toes all together we have twenty in our bodies. Everything that lives is saturated with our Creator's consciousness. The uniqueness of the sacred Mayan calendar is versatility. It does not measure time only in the linear way: from-to. *Time* also exists as a specific energy program, with specific quality and content. Unlike Western calendars, which had a linear measure, the Mayan had a vector technique of measuring time, in which there was always a starting point and a point of destination, which is why time never ended. The end of one cycle meant beginning the next one. Tzolkin creates possibility of full insight into the incarnation potential. Every human action produces a strictly defined effect, and Tzolkin immediately indicates the causal. Every day, one of the 260 archetypes (9 months) affects the field of human awareness, which is why every day for each person is a personal diagnosis. Good or bad mood swings are information whether the person consciousness is in resonance or in dissonance with universal energy.[1] Every person as a member of the earthly community is included in this sacred calendar, and its incarnation code is recorded as an energy program in the spiritual dimen-

---

[1] Hanna Kotwicka, *Code of Incarnation, Vol. 1.*

sion, where all past and future is happening *now*. Therefore, the task of each of us is to attract this program to our daily lives and implement it in the physical world. This is the meaning of the proverb, "To bring Heaven to the Earth." Every action what we do has become the past right away. We live in eternal *now*, where everything is alive and connected. All 260 archetypes are *now*. Jose Arguelles, based on the ancient Mayan, founded common algorithm and synchronized the 260 days Tzolkin with the 365 days Gregorian calendar. That's why we see expanding in time. He called it the Calendar of 13 Moons/28 days + 1 (13 months, 28 days plus 1 outside the time where the potential exchange of the year takes place). Included every month are energetic waves with the topic of the wave (every wave has 13 days). Every 9 months with 260 universal Tzolkin archetypes, we can see how our awareness is. Are we more aware of our behaviors? Do we know when to stop pushing ourselves or forcing others? Are we more happy and trustful to Life? Are our lives harmonized in every aspect of our existence like health, work, relationships, time, money? Are we free to express Itself fully? Do we feel connected to the whole Life like people, animals, stones, rivers, whole nature? Are we connected with our inner guidance, intuition, and act upon it? Are we letting go with ease jobs, people, material things that don't serve us to move forward with our lives, or are we still are attached to them? How is our growing as an aspect of the Creator? Can we respect ourselves more and others? Do we care about our bodies, or do we eat junk food and abuse our bodies through sex, alcohol, or drugs? Are we more open and even childlike and forgiving? Are we really free and looking for connection with our Creator to be free from illusion?

The sacred Mayan calendar is created for 104 years. So our bodies can live 104 years with ease. We received it from our Creator. As we know in the world of illusion, bodies live shorter and with diseases. The reason is our ignorance to the Truth. All physical world is based on the atom with dual pole and is assigned to the mind. Those who deal with the Time or want to know their destiny always meet Mayan and their sacred calendar. When we meet with Tzolkin, we have fifty-two years to understand our incarnation destiny as an individual. Also those who are advanced in the Tzolkin reading understand everything what is going on in the world. They can read through Tzolkin archetypes. These entities are really advanced spiritual beings, and they keep themselves calm. TV or newspapers propaganda has no influence on them. Whatever is happening in the world right now, it is clearing what will not serve to humanity in the future. The collective awareness that has been evolving stays in the universal bank for future generations.

Tzolkin is four-dimensional galactic matrix. Someone who wants to feel it needs to eliminate linear thinking. These are indicators for us to grow and evolve as a person and soul. As I mention above, the journey on planet Earth is the journey of the soul. A spirit who incarnated as a human being and wears a body with all its characteristics needs to be evolved and transformed. We are not mortal beings attached to its three-dimensional body and fearful ego and, because of that, limited mind. We need to come back to our hearts. We will find peace there and our True Nature. In our hearts, feelings, dreams, and answers exist. Our soul connects with us through the heart. Heart is an indicator for our direction to follow. Only then as a human being life can be fulfilled. We again will start enjoying our lives for this short time when we are here. We become more open and alive like we were as the children. We start being less attached with what we have or don't have, and because of that, we stop being so afraid of moving forward and celebrate things, which are only illusions. Really, we are evolving beings. We didn't come here for having, getting old, and wait when body makes the transition for our soul to be fully free. We came to explore life, love, and be joyful. Really, we have a choice to live differently than society taught us. We were taught that life is difficult, that we need to cheat and take advantage of others to succeed, that we need to be afraid of those who we don't know and protect ourselves and our future to survive, and that life gives us only problems and cannot support us. Diseases are natural state of the body instead of good health, and we are consumers instead of givers. We give our consciousness to our planet Earth all the time, in which we need to evolve who we are. Everything that we were taught is a big lie made up by low-consciousness people and their own greedy goals. Only Truth can set us free. Master Jesus said, *"Ye shall know the truth, and the truth shall make you free."*

Can you imagine the world in peace, without borders, where everybody is safe; has place to live, food to eat, clean water to drink; has freedom to express itself truly and fully; and bodies in complete health? In a world where people stop believing in aging? All this exist in unseen world *now*. To experience that kind of world, each of us needs to take responsibility for our behaviors and take individual journey to heal themselves from experiences from their past and reconnect to its own inner self, True Essence of being, loving, compassionate, free from material attachments, and fear. Pure Light is who we truly are, and our existence is always *now*. What we do now we will harvest in the future. Every day is *now*; tomorrow always will be *now*. There is eternal *now*.

Being in Topanga Canyon was an extraordinary experience. The sightseeing was breathtaking. There was a cave as an eagle head where everybody can seat and enjoy a view. I made my first video, which was in Polish. I called it "Moving Our Thought Limits to Become Self." Later, I needed to learn how to edit videos and upload them on YouTube. I added English subtitles at the beginning. When I started recording, I had no idea how I would lead the viewers to their inner self step by step. But a few days later the idea popped up: *A Course in Miracles*. It was great because I was able give the message in Polish and English, which was my intention at the beginning. The whole intention is to spread love and understanding to the world in three languages English, Polish, and Spanish. I have spoken in these three languages on different levels of knowledge throughout my life. Before I came to the United States, I didn't know that there were two main languages: English and Spanish. It was another exciting surprise for me from Life. Giving message in Polish is always easier for me because it is my native language. However, my English, which I had learned, was on intermediate level, and it was the European one. In Europe, we were taught English from the Oxford manuals. American English and culture is very different. I understood easily this language because I watched American movies, comedies, and animation movies to feel good at the beginning of my path. But

I was not always understood by Americans at the very beginning. Some people pretended that they understood and were nodding their heads, and some of them understood me perfectly. It was very confusing to my mind, and I was blaming myself, saying I was supposed to speak English better. When I started attending English classes in Evans Adult Community School and later at Santa Monica Collage, I stopped taking it personally whether other people understood me or not. The classes gave me a lot of confidence when I realized that I was in the learning process, and I really was courageous and willing to learn. And I made huge progress. As we know, not everyone chooses to learn the native language of the country they reside in. They meld with people of their culture and this is enough for them. Also English native spoken people, they can use English everywhere they go effortlessly, and some of them don't make the effort to learn more. The lazy ears of many Americans didn't want to adjust to my accent. At the beginning, my preferable way of communication was through text messages or emails, but with the time and after participating in different programs where English was the only language, I started enjoying speaking English by phone, which made it easier and easier for me. Regarding Spanish, I understood a lot and started practicing it on a daily basis through the Duolingo or Memrise applications. Later on, my friend offered to teach me Spanish, but our time schedules were different, that's why we didn't have possibility to seat together and learn.

Another surprise from Life was when I figured out that my soul's last incarnation was finished here in the United States. It was the simplest and the funniest way for me how I found out about this. At that time I was staying in Santa Monica, and I remember speaking with my friend Iwona by phone. I asked a question: "I wonder if the soul comes back to the place where last incarnation finished."

The next day I continued reading the book *Meet Your Angels* by Ella Selena, a Polish parapsychologist and a fortune reader. I read about fourteenth letter of angelic alphabet called Nun, and I realized that I was handed the ticket with the number 14 when I was at the American Embassy in Krakow waiting to receive my American tourist visa. The angel of the letter Nun represents energy, which reminds about incarnation by emergence of new things in our lives, often taking us to other places related to our new home and even to a different time.

After my first short prayer for Donata, it took me two months to write a first prayer for myself. It was longer and more detailed. Two days before the written prayer, I received the thought *It would be good to start taking moringa again.* The answer came in the form of the Zija multilevel marketing company, which had one of the best *moringa oleifera* in the world. They took care of moringa plantations; the trees grew up in the Himalayas, where there was no pollution and the soil was clean. The drying process of the ingredients was also implemented very carefully and naturally without rushing or adding something artificial to the whole process. The company was sold to another multilevel marketing industry when the owner decided to retired for good. He had other businesses and was very well known in the supplemental world before. At that time, I started being involved in the process of multilevel marketing. Thanks to that, I have learned a lot about the *moringa oleifera* tree and other natural products that Zija was producing and selling. After three or four months, I decided to use products that resonated with me and stop focusing on things that hinder me from doing what I really wanted to do in my life. I know that we can heal ourselves and rejuvenate our bodies by knowing the core of our issue and healing it through understanding, and we can start implementing this in our lives to stop suffering. Good-quality food can help our bodies function well, but formulas cannot keep the body healthy if our minds are still focusing on disasters, worries, and protecting ourselves from others by implementing unhealthy behavior toward them and ourselves. *Moringa oleifera* appeared in my life through the Agape community. I heard about this tree for the first time there. I checked the internet, and it popped up that *moringa oleifera* was used by Egyptians to heal the body from many diseases. And epilepsy appeared as a first in the article. That's why I knew that it is the right plant for me. Another thing that I found out that good-quality moringa is 100 percent food. It has everything that our bodies need—all the vitamins, minerals, enzymes, amino acids, proteins, etc. *Moringa oleifera* can support and restore health, healing three hundred aliments. The ancient Egyptians knew that and used it as well as the indigenous people of Africa. And in other continents where *moringa oleifera* grows, people use it in their cuisine every day.

There are many moringa supplements in the stores in the United States, but the quality is very different. And I noticed it right away. In the sachet were mixed only leaves, seeds, and fruits without the bark of the *moringa oleifera* tree. It was composed that way. The one sachet was giving to the body all the ingredients required, according to current dietary indications, for the whole day. Thanks to the purity of the product, pregnant or nursing women could use it. Also, babies from two months old could receive a little dose of this supplement to build up their immune system and be free from colds and other viruses.

Also, Zija had very good-quality therapeutic essential oils that support the immune system, detoxify the organs, help with relaxation, can be a part of the body's healing process (which includes the nervous system, diabetes, muscle regeneration, skin problems), and alleviate all kinds of pain (including menstrual pain, migraines, and diminishing temperature). And they have many others properties too. For example, frankincense therapeutic essential oil, which is called the king of essential oils, is what I add one or two drops of to my moringa drink to strengthen its effect on my neurological issue. Later on I learned to add it to my water or juices and in the cosmetics I use on my face. Other therapeutic essential oils and their benefits are the following: eucalyptus supports nervous system, helps the respiratory system and dental issues, and takes care of the skin very well; lemon can be used on the fingernails to strengthen them and to clean the kidneys; lavender can be used when sleep cannot come; oregano is better than antibiotics and cleanses the liver; rosemary is better than insulin for diabetes and helps the body renew and heal itself from the disease; and peppermint is perfect for headaches and migraines (when a few drops are mixed with an oil base and put on the temples, at the back of the neck, and on the wrists, the relief comes in one minute).

Drivers can use it to safely get to their destination. The scent sharpens the senses and the mind preventing from falling asleep. We can use it instead of energy drinks which destroy our organs. Babies and children, when they have fever, instead of giving something artificial from pharmacy to decrease temperature, they can receive one or two drops peppermint essential therapeutic oil in the form of massaging their feet mixed with olive oil or other base, and the fever disappears in half an hour or less. All essential therapeutic oil has many applications and can be used orally; in aromatherapy; and on the skin as a cosmetic. All the properties of the essential therapeutic oils are proven by science and used in some Western clinics. Instead of going to a pharmacy for the pills for a short relief and put more toxin to the body, we have nature condensed in one drop of essential therapeutic oil that can support our bodies' and minds' well-being. They are treated as supplement in the holistic world. I loved them. After Zija had been sold, I started using therapeutic essential oils from Young Living. I love quality and simplicity. Here, there is so many cosmetics and range of supplements that a person doesn't know what to choose. In Poland I used to use cosmetics and supplements from MLM company also. Supplements labeled as healthy on the shelves of cosmetic stores or in the pharmacies, their ingredients are not always purified. Our skin is the biggest organ in the body. The fastest way the body absorbs healthy or unhealthy products is through the skin. That's why it is so important to be aware what we apply on it. I learned a lot, and I am grateful for this journey, and after a few months again with MLM, I made decision to trust Life that I will be always supported and follow my passion as a spiritual teacher and have an income from that and be in great service for others.

We can ask, what is *trust?* It is a state of surrender to the Divine Self, knowing that one is supported on one's journey toward wholeness. Trust implies the understanding that the lessons one is giving, no matter what their appearance, are serving one's highest evolution.[1]

Through this definition we can understand that we cannot judge others or ourselves by appearances. We all are on the evolutionary path. It depends on to who we listen to: our soul or our ego.

---

[1] *The Mayan Oracle, Return Path to the Stars* by Ariel Spilsbury and Michael Bryner.

I knew that all this experiences put me in position of what was really important to me and it was my choice. I wanted grow, so life gave me these kinds of experiences so that I would evolve to make my own choices. Everyone has a different journey, but what is most important is that we need to distinguish what our soul wants and what our ego is afraid of, and because of that, we make our choices in our lives. When we are choosing our soul path, we can be certain that the whole Universe supports as fully. When we choose our ego, bumps happen and we don't feel really happy and fulfilled. We need to let go of our control to let God support us in our endeavor called life.

Being on the journey with *A Course in Miracles* and DreamBuilding program, I had time to record thirteen sections in two languages: Polish and English. There was a total of twenty-six recordings, editing, and uploads. It was a wonderful experience for me. I became my own teacher, and I was able to help others understand what the *A Course in Miracles* teaches and give tools how we can reconnect ourselves with our dreams. I was able to complete four chapters of my book by adding more details. The chapters were given to editing, and one was sent as a book proposal to Hay Publishing House. I wrote a few prayers by myself, and I loved doing it.

Life gave me another opportunity to trust. Edward, the landlord of the place where I used to stay, told me that he wanted to rent the whole house to one family and we who were currently occupying the rooms needed to move out. I connected him with my friend from Agape International Spiritual Center, and he rented her the whole house, The rest of us found our new homes. One of my friend left with her husband for Poland. At that time I didn't have any income or savings, so it was very challenging for me to believe that everything would work out for me and it did. Better than I could imagine. I surrender myself to that situation and contacted some people who I met in Los Angeles. Greg connected me with a very vigorous and loving older lady in Culver City. Spirit always knows better on what we need to grow and how take care of us and others. I lived in the beautiful area, and I didn't have to pay rent. Everything that I needed was close, and I started living with people of different nationalities, and we communicated only in English. My intention was to evolve in English. Staying in Culver City, I was helping the person with cooking and doing errands for her two days every week in exchange for a room. The rest of week I had for myself. It was a perfect match at that time. We helped each other in the hard times for us. I was a person who was with her when she was releasing her old life. She was in grief because of the passing away of her dearest member of her family. I also reconnected her with her passion to help homeless people. L.O.V.E. Foundation was the perfect match for her. She started volunteering there again. Meanwhile two jobs opportunities came month after another thanks to my friend, who was leaving for Poland. She wanted to help me get a job, and she found two for me. I really appreciate her for that. One job was babysitting a young child named Victoria, and another during the weekend was with an elder person. He used to be a well-known architect here. Because of these jobs, I was able to support myself with ease and have some savings for later when an induced pandemic hit. But again, the questions of *how* (if I was booked seven days a week), *where*, and *what* I was really supposed to focus on were with me all the time. Soon, there unfolded two great surprises that Life kept for me in Culver City. One came after another.

Every person is an individualized expression of the One Spirit. *Every person is made in the image and likeness of God and is capable of awakening to this realization and giving expression to the qualities of unconditional love, compassion, wisdom, bliss, peace, and creativity.*

—*Agape Spiritual Principles and Practices*

CHAPTER 6

Can Our Hearts Be Healed?

*I am the light of the world. Forgiveness is my
function as the light of the world.
My forgiveness is the means by which the world
is healed, together with myself.
Let this help me learn what forgiveness means.
Let me, then forgive the world, that it may be healed along with me.*

—*A Course in Miracles*

One of the surprises in Culver City was Landmark Worldwide LLC, which headquarters are in San Francisco. I remember that day when my friend Fatimata Sanogo called me while I was heading to the park across to the place where I used to live with the question, "What's next?" On that day she invited me to her place for the introduction to The Landmark Forum in three weeks. I met Fatimata in Agape International Spiritual Center. She was young and a beautiful joyous soul, full of light and love for everybody. At that time, Fatimata was studying biochemistry, and later on for advanced study, she chose epidemiology. But what she was most proud of herself for was that she was able to establish a nonprofit organization for the girls, Sahel Sage, in her hometown, Dori. She comes from Burkina Faso, West Africa. The website is www.sahelsage.org. She was able to found this organization, participating in one of Landmark's programs called Self-Expression Leadership Program. All these I found out later.

I went to the introduction to the Landmark Forum three weeks later after Fatimata's call. I was late and I didn't know why the Landmark Forum appeared in my consciousness at that time, but I knew that it was the right direction.

> *All that I need to know at any given moment is revealed to me.*
> *I trust myself and I trust Life.*
> *All is well*—Louise Hay

I paid $200 deposit following week, and right away after, I received an income from my two days' work. It was $270, so I was able to buy food for a week, and I knew that I would pay the rest of the tuition because of an additional job for the weekends. Life works this way. It always supplies to let us grow and give us opportunities to meet new people, new friends who are in alignment with our growing. After registration to the Landmark Forum, I understood why Life brought me to Culver City. Where I lived was a ten-to-fifteen-minute walk to the Landmark Los Angeles Center. I was amazed. Life gave me place to live for free. The rent prices in Culver City are high. I received money to grow. And Life saved me time getting to the center, so I was able to participate in Landmark's programs and assist later on. As I mentioned before, moving from place to place in Los Angeles takes a lot of time.

Feeling out the application form when registering for the Landmark Forum, I wrote down what I wanted to accomplish through this program. My intention was to focus on one thing, which would be bringing myself fulfillment in my work and attracting to my life a loving, supportive, and joyous relationship with the right partner for me.

I took three days off from my weekend job. I had found the person to swap with me for these days, and I was able to start the Landmark Forum. It was August 2, 2020. The Landmark Forum lasted three and half days. It started on Friday morning and finished

Tuesday night. Monday is a day free from the Forum, but it is a part of transformation. By the whole weekend, we were in the space with the Landmark Forum Leader, for thirteen hours to bring awareness to our blind spots and our pain that we have produced during our whole life and realize that we run our lives because of something that we weren't aware of. I beheld wonderful breakthroughs of people in ten minutes, which benefited us all. In everyone is a part of another person. Because the people were healed from their past pain in front of our eyes, the rest of us were able to finish what we were unconscious and had opportunity to create a new possibilities in our lives by declaring a new way of being and how we want to appear in our lives. It was very releasing experience for each of us. There were over 150 people in the room, and it was the safest space to begin transformation. Our change begins with the closest family and friends. The contact is deeper and really loving. I had a lot of breakthroughs and insights during and after the Landmark Forum.

Being on a spiritual journey, we become more aware and trustful but sometimes really lonely between transformation from old life to the new one. Mostly, our life looks like me and others. Others are those who don't understand me, those who hurt me, those who don't want to live the way I live, those, those, those, etc. The truth is that we are responsible for our relationship with ourselves and others. Landmark as global community emphasizes this aspect of our lives very much. When we are open and authentic, we become a change in our nearest families and the environment where we live or used to live. It happened with every participant in the room including me. My relationship with my mother, brothers, and son is more open than ever. I know that I changed my attitude toward them, and our conversations are more loving. There is more understanding from both sides. I stopped chasing ideals regarding romantic relationships. On the second day of the Landmark Forum, during the exercise "How Identities Get Constructed," I was sitting on the chair and started seeing images of when I was three years old and my uncle spanked me, then as a teenager fighting with my stepfather, and as an adult person fighting with my partner, my ex-husband. Also, I saw the image of the person who I was interested in here at that time, and in this picture, I saw myself screaming. Automatically I stopped being interested in a person who I thought was ideal for me, and I realized why I hadn't been in a relationship since I broke up with my ex-husband. I lost trust in the men because of my past experiences. Due to them, I felt unworthy of being loved unconditionally, and I stopped trusting that I would choose the right person to be happy instead of losing myself again. It was a huge discovery for me, and I understood that I have a choice—that I can either hold myself to this faulty belief or start trusting myself and life that I can be in a loving relationship with a person who is loving and emotionally healthy. At the same time, I was free of the ballast of a social requirement—that I needed to look for relationship to be fulfilled. Life knows when we are ready, and then the right person will appear in our lives to love, support, and to grow together with us as I mentioned before.

On the fourth day of the Landmark Forum, I had another insight. At that time, I was walking with Victoria, and she was sleeping in the stroller. Suddenly I received a thought about myself as a child who was born without a father. Right away my subconscious programmed belief that something was wrong with me disappeared, and I felt like a huge boulder of energy was released from my chest. At the same time, I started feeling love in the air and started smiling to myself without reason.

Two days before, I texted my father to thank him for my life, and this allowed me to release resentment in my consciousness, which purified my heart.

A few months later, I had another profound breakthrough regarding my relationship with my father. At that time, I was in the Introduction Leaders Program.

Every boulder keeps us in the space of being disconnected resented and it creates the rim around our hearts. Unknowingly we behave in a certain way to gain something from others and life, which is not for us. We hurt ourselves very much, causing loss, emotional pain, and diseases in our bodies. As I mentioned before, beliefs about ourselves and life limit us a lot, and the worst part of it is that we agree with it. We always find reasons to put ourselves down, and we feed our fears and give them away to others including our children, which we limit ourselves and them. All these keeps us from being free and fulfilled. It dims our light and our joy from within.

Many years ago, when I walked into my own spiritual path, I asked Life to protect me from wrong choices and I could see that it does all the time. I stopped asking the question why and only started trusting and moving forward.

Because of my clearing my blind spots, I really felt that I forgave everybody in my life and transformed it by taking responsibility for my actions in the past. I cleared it with them, and because of that, I felt I have forgiven myself. Before, I repeated many times that I forgave myself even though I didn't know for what, and I forgave others, but it wasn't true. There were only words. True forgiveness is when we are open to talk honestly with those because of who we felt hurt and also admit our mistakes without blaming each other. After transformation, we see all the people as a blessing to our growing without resentment, only love. That kind of forgiveness let us start feeling free and connected with life and to self-express fully. We become a different person, more open and joyous, more authentic; and whatever is happening in our lives, we feel free to speak up and act without looking what others think. We are connected with our inner light.

Thanks to that, we are able have people in our lives back when we want them and if they want us. We cannot push anybody to like or love us because we were transformed. They haven't had opportunity to experience what we had. Because of that, they cannot resonate with us and it is okay. In the Universe is an ethical code: everyone has free will. We can become a right model, share with the Truth, and wait until people will make the decision to join us and put their contribution to the universal bank of global consciousness as One. Also they have the right to still live in illusion, separation, fear, and listen to their ego. It is every person's choice, and believe me, we all are guided to the Truth. There are many paths, teachers, and also lessons that put an individual on their path to greatness.

What I have learned through my journey that there is no such "me and those." Those are only our mirrors on how we behave, react, what limits we put on ourselves. They are great teachers for us. Sometimes, unnecessarily, we keep them longer in our lives than what was needed. There is only one reason that we do that: we are afraid of letting go and move forward.

I remember one Sunday evening in our Landmark Forum, an eighteen-year-old girl thanked the Landmark Forum Leader and shared with us how she was mad at her parents because they put her in the Landmark Forum on Friday morning. But on Sunday evening, she was so thankful to them that they gave her the opportunity to be there. She understood that her parents, even if they weren't her biological parents, stood by her all the time but she was miserable and disconnected to them because she didn't feel loved. The reason was that she kept her story of being abandoned because she was from the orphanage. When she shared, we all had tears in our eyes including the Landmark Forum Leader. These people committed their own lives to bring peace to the world, to be a space for others, to let them heal from wounds that we are unnecessarily attached to and blocked them to be able to express fully our love and uniqueness. Additionally, I found out that Landmark donated to Africa money from each Landmark Forum. So you help yourself by transforming what stops you in your life, adding to global consciousness more love. Also, part of your money helps people in the poorer countries transform their lives and live happier, so you are in the flow of abundance because of being unknowingly generous.

Another transformation that I had from the Landmark Forum was with my younger half brother, Bartosz. We were brought up together, and I was a cause of his suffering as an older sister for sure. As I mentioned before, my stepfather was unpredictable toward me, and because of that, my behavior toward my younger brother was abusive. It was some kind of paying off for all my pain. After the Landmark Forum, I wasn't able to pretend that my behavior toward my brother had explanation. What I understood that Bartosz wasn't responsible for his father's behavior at all. I remember the day when I called him to say sorry for my wrong behavior toward him. I was on the bus to my job, and I called him in the United Kingdom. He was driving back home from his work. I was sorry for everything that I did toward him when we were children and I said what those things were. We remember very well when we did something wrong toward another person, but our ego wants to pretend that nothing happened. We always find reasons not to apologize, and we feel shame and blame others for our behaviors to look clean and pretend that it has no meaning to another person at all. The ego divides a lot and has its own preferences of with whom we want to deal or not. In our closest families we see a lot of division. We deal with these who are better according to us, who has more money or have the same understanding of life that we have and they agree with us, to give them encouragement and stand for them. We judge others according their apperance instead of taking responsibility for our behaviors to bring more love and tolerance to our closest ones. This is our true nature—Christ Consciousness. During our conversation, I was crying like a beaver. At the end of our call, I noticed that Bartosz was reborn. He was shining. I was able to see how he felt lighter and more joyous. What I started feeling was unconditional love. Unconditional love to my younger brother, to myself, and everything around. Now my communication with him is more open and sincere. I was getting to know him more and more, and my heart was opening wider and wider.

By being in the state of forgiveness, we are closer to our Source. We feel more connection, and we become more sensitive, which allows us to "hear" and feel the guidance from our Higher Self.

We can heal and open our hearts to those who may have hurt us even if that person is us. We need to understand that forgiveness is a daily practice and that much of what grieves us is a result of accumulated emotions that are stored in our bodies, which in turn creates diseases.

Living so close to the Los Angeles Landmark Center, which is the biggest one in the world, I was able to be in the space of their training more often and be with people who were in their highest ideals of themselves and for others. I was in the environment of all cultures and nations. We all had the same goal: to support each other, be a better human being, and be a safe space for others during their transformation by releasing our own past and start living with fullness. Through Landmark I have learned more English than in school because we were talking about everything in English. I felt safe expressing myself fully without comparison. I lost blockage that stopped me from being fully expressed in this language. Thanks to that, it helped me evolve in it.

After the Landmark Forum, at the end of August, I took a ten-week seminar called Being Extraordinary. The seminar was included in the price of the Landmark Forum. Thanks to the seminar, I again took the wheels of my life and I said to the lady that I used to stay with that I need to move forward. It was the end of September. We agreed that I would move out in five months. During these five months, I had opportunity to participate in the Advanced Course, the Self-Expression and Leadership Program, and assisting there. By assisting I was in the space for the transformation of other participants in the Landmark Forum.

My Landmark Advanced Course started in October 11, 2019. The program was held in the same venue as the Landmark Forum. We were with the Landmark Forum Leader for three and half days to create possibilities for our future. Thanks to this, I was put to the present moment. Being in the US by myself for over two years, I didn't feel that I belong to the American community and also I didn't feel that I belong to the Polish community. I left Poland and the whole continent behind to start my adventure and life in the USA. People here see you through your own eyes where is a lot of fear and focus only on earning money. My attitude was different. I wanted to grow and understand my purpose of life, and because of that, we haven't had a lot of common. That's why I felt that I didn't belong to Polish community in the USA, even I had a real support for which I am so grateful. I knew for sure that I was brought here to expand my awareness from the national to the global one.

On the third day of the Landmark Advanced Course, I felt that I belong to these people, to the people who were in front of me. We were all in the space of a new life, and I didn't expect anything from them, only the feeling of being present and love them. Thanks to that, the next day I started talking to passersby more confidently, more open and joyful. I saw smiles and kindness everywhere again. But I didn't wait to get that from others. I was the one who was giving joy, smiles, and kindness; and I saw the reflection of myself in the others. I became the same person who left Poland, with joy and faith that everything will work out and I was in the right place to grow. I started regaining my self-confidence. I stopped waiting for others to contact me by phone, I was the one who contacted them first and reminded them that I am here. I started standing up for myself. I felt great, and the feedback was only love.

Through the Self-Expression and Leadership Program, I learned again that I needed to put myself out there. My project for the Los Angeles community was to bring spiritual workshops to every homeless organization. My idea was to let people who experience homelessness be aware that their rejection of themselves and negative thinking brought them to their situation and I wanted them to become alive and dream again. They needed to take responsibility for their lives, which start with the thoughts. I know that through dreaming, we become different person and we peel off all the shields that create the separation, and then the possibilities come. Seeing homelessness in California, or even in New York City, I knew that this is the only way that cities can be free from the homelessness issue—through different approaches of teaching those people that every thought creates our experience, that we can create our lives anew, and that it starts from gratitude for what we have, empowering them to feel good about themselves. There are plenty of homeless organizations in the United States, and they do what they can. They give these people everything that is in their power, but the people still are on the streets. According to the statistics, in 2019, there were 564,000 homeless people in the United States. Only in Los Angeles County, there were 58,936 homeless people. Reality is that, some of them are mentally ill; other have chosen it as a lifestyle.

The Self-Expression Leadership Program lasted four months. This program was created in a way that we give up leadership to the community. We as the participants needed to connect with right people, enroll them to take a step as a leader in our project, and bring to their community our idea. I felt like I was in school during most of the classes and it was okay because I witnessed how many people who participated in the program had their own breakthroughs. They shared their wisdom and love. They got back their True Being in this program.

Regarding my project, I was in contact with spiritual communities among others Self-Realization Fellowship and Agape International Spiritual Center to bring their license practitioners to homeless organizations and hold the workshops. I e-mailed and called to the homeless organizations, but I didn't have a lot of responses. Some of the employees hung up. What I found out was that there are some policies and rules in communities, both spiritual and homeless ones. The homeless organization cannot bring exact spirituality to their organizations to run the business, and spiritual communities needed to get a letter from the homeless organizations that they need their assistance. After three months of my commitment, I felt stuck because of that. I was so committed that, once, I made an effort to overcome my fear of speaking in front of the whole room of unknown American women who were native speakers of English. I went to the Downtown Women's Center in Los Angeles to share for the first time the story of my journey in the USA and my life here on suitcases like these homeless women, only my focus was different from theirs. That's why I always had a place to live: I couldn't count on any organization because I wasn't a citizen or resident here. Thanks to that, I was able to take my life in my hands and follow my dreams, even sometimes I felt that I was heading nowhere, and learn, asking friends and unknown people about places to live and paying for it. This gave me an advantage over the homeless people, who relied only on institutions. That experience was my first time speaking at the microphone and empowering women in Los Angeles.

My courage didn't help the project at that time, but I surrendered, and I decided to use the law of attraction. I thanked in advance for setting up workshops in every homeless organization to bring out the people from the streets and let go. What happened was, my coach who was assigned to me in this program connected me with another participant in the Self-Expression Leadership Program who was involved in homeless issue in Los Angeles county. She invited me to the Fourth Annual Homeless Initiative Conference, which would took place in Millennium Biltmore Hotel in Downtown Los Angeles one week before we graduated our program. What I found out from her that she attracted, through law of attraction, her own place to live when she experienced homelessness. She was on YouTube all the time watching, listening about the law of attraction and putting it in the practice. So she only confirmed what I was about. At the event, there were a lot of representatives from homeless organizations, TV stations, as well as county and state representatives. The event lasted all day. For the second part, we went to different rooms. In each of the rooms were information about different homeless programs. I was attracted to the room called Emerald. I didn't know why, maybe because the name of the program that was held there wasn't understandable for me, and I went because of curiosity? And I knew that it was something else. I walked in the room, and I found out that Los Angeles Homeless Service Authority had new approach to the homelessness. They had a trained staff to help every individual who experience homelessness connect with friends and families and negotiate prices with the landlords to take people from the streets before they would get a place to live from the county. There is a very long home waiting list. And most importantly, they guide homeless people to their dreams and empower them. I spoke with the representative, and he told me that the people become different person when they know how to achieve their goals and that LAHSA is going to train employees in every homeless organization to support those people in their lives in a new way by empowering them. They had workshops and were going to spread them in every homeless organization in the county. So my community project was done through the community. I met all parameters, including the media, which I was resisting when I was filling out my community project form. I was amazed with the outcome.

On our last class of the Self-Expression and Leadership Program, we had to speak in front of class, to acknowledge our small leadership community, and to share about our projects. My coach Keith was bantered with me. He said, "Magdalena, you also will speak at the microphone." I knew that everything would be all right. I had my first practice few weeks before. Even if I had a story in my head that my English was not good enough to speak at the microphone in front of people who had been known me for four months. In my speech, I shared with the outcome of my project, even I was joking about my clothing. It was very hot that day, and the weather forecast on the internet showed the rain. Probably I missed it a little also. There were only a few short days with rain here. So I wore rubber boots sent from Poland and raincoat then. I joked that I looked like I was coming back from fishing, and everybody laughed. I acknowledge all the participants because they truly impacted me with their openness and honesty. Those who didn't know me met me and some of us had become friends throughout the program. Each of us received something from this program, which pushed us to get out from our comfort zone and put ourselves into community. Thanks to that, a lot of us received unexpected personal benefits. I started knowing more about Los Angeles, meeting different people and communities, and I was regaining my confidence as well through speaking publictly twice at the microphone. Some of the participants evolved professionally and received a promotion or a new job, or like Fatimata, who founded her own a nonprofit organization in her leadership program. As a surprise a year later, I found out that *Dog Whisperer*, which I loved watching many years before in Ireland, was at first a small community project invented by Cesar Millan in his Self-Expression Leadership Program, and as a result, he became an internationally known personality as a dog trainer and author. And he has his own Dog Psychology Center not so far away from Los Angeles.

The Landmark Forum, the Advanced Course, and The Self-Expression and Leadership Program are called in Landmark as Curriculum of Living. After these programs, I put myself into seven-month program called Introduction Leaders Program, which is supposed to peel off everything from the participant what blocks them from the full expression and also gives opportunity to become an Introduction Leader to the Landmark Forum when the participant meets all measures required by the program. Becoming an Introduction Leader of Landmark gives opportunity to be hired in Landmark Worldwide. Also this can be a path as a first step to become the Landmark Forum Leader. It would take about eight years.

The Divine Mind of God is the creative power of the Universe. Thought creates. Every person, as an individualized expression of the Divine, thinks and creates through the power of free choice. *Through the exercise of freewill, each person is able to choose and assume responsibility for their own soul's evolution. Through this freedom of choice all things are made new, the past is transcended and infinite possibilities are at hand.*

—*Agape Spiritual Principles and Practices*

CHAPTER 7

What Makes Our Mind Peaceful and Safe?

Be still and know that I am God.

—*Psalms*

One month after moving to Culver City, I started receiving signs about the Self-Realization Fellowship. Self-Realization Fellowship/ Yogoda Satsanga Society of India was founded by Paramahansa Yogananda. He came to Boston as India's representative to an International Congress of Religious Liberals in 1920. The same year he founded Self-Realization Fellowship. His mission was to spread worldwide pure and integral Kriya Yoga teachings. In 1925, he established Self-Realization Fellowship International Headquarters at Mount Washington in Los Angeles.

The signs for Self-Realization Fellowship I received step by step. In August 2018, three months before I flew to New Jersey area, I was volunteering in Agape International Spiritual Center, which was located on Buckingham Parkway in Culver City. At that time the whole community was preparing to move the center to another place after twenty years being in one place. That day I found a picture of archangel Raphael, who is an angel responsible for healing. I started affirming and calling the energy of archangel Raphael to be healed. The next sign was in New York City. I received the address to the Self-Realization Fellowship headquarters from a photographer when we were volunteering in Brooklyn on Thanksgiving Day. I noticed that Self-Realization Fellowship's location was on San Rafael Avenue in Los Angeles. I knew that healing is there, but I didn't know how. When I was about to come back to Los Angeles from Linden, I e-mailed to Self-Realization Fellowship (SRF/YSS) if they have a place to stay. The response came after few months when I was back in Los Angeles. I found out that Self-Realization Fellowship had ashrams only for nuns and monks, so I was postponing a visit to the headquarters of Self-Realization Fellowship, called Mother Center, because I stopped seeing a connection to my healing after I found out that there was no place for me to stay. I started treating it more like a tourist visit. How many times have we lost interest in something or someone when it turned out that this was not how we thought it was supposed to serve our cause without realizing that there was the diamond, which we were looking for, and behind it was the answer to our prayers? I had done this many times in the past to myself, but not this time, and it has been so for over ten years. I knew that I needed to continue my journey, and I put out the intention that if it is mine, it would come to me in the right time. And it did.

> It may take a year,
> It may take a day,
> But what is meant to be,
> It always find its way.
> (Anonymous)

It came after seven months. It was like in a clock. I received a newsletter from Self-Realization Fellowship, which was sent to Linden, New Jersey, but before leaving that place, I redirected it to Los Angeles, to my previous address. The same time a young man was moving in to the apartment in Culver City. He was devotee of Guru Paramahansa Yogananada's teachings, and he used to volunteer at Lake Shrine, one of Self-Realization Fellowship temples.

I knew that it was my time to visit Self-Realization Fellowship. I was guided to Lake Shrine. I chose Sunday for a visit because there were services held and also some events and retreats, which I found out about later. Lake Shrine is a home for the monks. They live there, and it is located on Pacific Palisades with a breathtaking view of the Pacific Ocean on one side. The other side had a view of the hills where the private residences are located. First, what welcomed me at Lake Shrine was a monarch butterfly. The same creature that sat on my lap three years before when I was in grandparents' garden. When I attended the service, the monk spoke about a Polish man who survived II World War and moved to the US. I saw stained glass with lotuses in the temple, swans, ducks, koi fish, turtles in the lake, monarch butterflies, and hummingbirds flying in the garden that surrounds the lake. All the creatures that had accompanied me during my journey on the spiritual realm and now they were in one place. I knew that I was at my destination but I didn't understand the whole meaning of my journey. At that time I didn't know that I was in the place where True God and way for my healing would be revealed to me. I was like a tourist. After the service, I stayed for the guided meditation in the Dutch-windmill chapel. I felt like I was expanded and surrounded by light. It was a wonderful experience. I put intention to buy Self-Realization Fellowship/Yogoda Satsanga Society lessons to learn from them how to meditate, who we are and why we are here. Also I bought the book *The Autobiography of a Yogi*.

My time was very limited when I started my second work, and I wasn't able to participate in Self-Realization Fellowship community, but I applied at the translation department of SRF to translate into Polish the teachings of Paramahansa Yogananda. I purchased lessons three months later and finished reading *The Autobiography of a Yogi*. At that time, reading this book was very difficult for me because it had a new way of writing and terminology I was not aware of before. My soul understood and was very happy, but my mind asked a lot of questions, one of them being, "How it is possible that I can be healed?" At that time, I was looking for someone to do the healing for me, not realizing that I was brought to the source of my healing, and that person who can heal me would be myself. Another question

I had was this: Why I was guided to Self-Realization Fellowship, and what do I have common with the other people in the community? Later on, I asked this: How can I find God in me and self-realize? Also, how can I be a part of the SRF community to support the teachings being spread around the world to bring peace and truth to the world? At that time, my mind was all over the place, and I was looking for the answers and my purpose while I was here. And I thought that I wasn't looking for God exactly. I was looking for proof of what I have learned and practiced before—that really, life works this way. I was between faith and doubt during my difficult circumstances here and was pushed to be in action all the time. It turned out that God is the path to find the Truth, and my soul was ready to go back to the core of being. That's why I received my guru, the master who knew God by self-realization and knew how to lead other souls to ascent. This master is the one who was waiting for me to introduce me to God in me and all of the spiritual realm. When Paramahansa Yoganada passed away, his teachings became the guru for every soul looking for true fulfillment and joy in the world. God is first. Only through an enlightened and self-realized guru can the soul find freedom from the body bandage and experience Reality and also be freed from bad karma faster, which is one of the reasons we incarnate here over and over. Karma is from our past actions that were against God's laws to not hurt ourselves, others, and our planet Earth. That's why a true guru can release us from our past bad actions, like Jesus did by surrendering to be crucified. He was a guru who taught us about God and led His disciples to ascension; the same like it is done through gurus in India, they take responsibility for us as a soul and guide us straight away to be in communion with the omnipotent Spirit to find Him the unity of all. True gurus guide us to self-realization as a soul and also give us teachings on how we are supposed to behave and forgive to be able to act in harmony with our hearts and be happy on the earthy realm as a child of God instead of living unhealthy and unfulfilled lives.

After finishing the last chapter of the *Autobiography of a Yogi*, I realized that I was guided from the very beginning to be here. When I took out the stone with the jaguar on that last workshop of

TZOLKIN, it said, "The master is waiting for you." When I started my healing through Ayuverda in Stalowa Wola, Aldona had the book of Paramahansa Yoganada and deck of cards that we picked up all together. The description, which I pulled out often during our sessions, was "you are like a lotus a beautiful soul…" At that time, I didn't understand how I can find this soul and real beauty. I didn't know that it was me. Another sign was when I was in Central Park in New York City in 2017, a monk in an orange sari gave me a picture of Guan Yin (the Chinese goddess of peace, compassion, and mercy). In chapter 49 of *Autobiography of a Yogi*, it says, "A large natural lake, a blue jewel in a mountain diadem, has given the estate its name of Lake Shrine… Two marble statues from China adorn the site—a statue of Lord Buddha and one of Kwan Yin (the Chinese personification of the Divine Mother)." Being my first time in Lake Shrine, I didn't notice that. That's why I felt like a tourist. Every time when I was able to go to Lake Shrine, the monarch butterfly invited me in. Once when I was leaving the area of Lake Shrine and waited for the bus to get back to Culver City, the monarch butterfly was flying in the direction of Lake Shrine. I felt like I was missing something and wanted stay near the temple. Every time when I was around, my soul wanted to break out through my chest to stay in that place. As I mentioned above, I was brought to the Master who was waiting for me. Even I had a lot of resistance to accept the teachings because they were different from what I had been learning before. He was waiting for me patiently until I understood.

Every year, between late July and early August, the annual gathering members of Self-Realization Fellowship is held in the fabulous Westin Bonaventure Hotel, Downtown Los Angeles. It is called SRF/YSS World Convocation. The event lasts for one week. People from all over the world come to meditate and immerse in the teachings of Paramahansa Yogananda. I was able to go there in August 2019 to attend the lecture "How to Connect with the Master." At that time there were about five thousand people from all over the world in the Convocation. I remember I was sitting in the huge ballroom waiting for the lecture and I was looking at Paramahansa Yogananda's picture. I noticed that he had one eye a little narrowed like I had on my one of my pictures taken recently. It was for my mind another confirmation that I am in the right place. I was looking for similarities with Yogananda. For example, he came to the USA to bring Kriya Yoga to the world and I came to the United States to become a spiritual leader to fulfill my dream. After noticing the similarity and accepting it, I felt like a cushion of condensed energy sat on my shoulders. I knew that feeling from accessing to my Akashic records. I knew that Guruji accepted me as his disciple. It was he who was on my shoulders. It was my first initiation. Another one was to Kriya Yoga about one year later.

Being in the hotel with all these people, for the first time since I had come to the USA, I felt unity. It was like we all know one another from ages. There weren't any feelings of gaining something for each other, only mutual one goal: love for God. I learned a beautiful chant by singing with all. It was first time when I felt so much unity and condensed Unconditional Love. We all were in the Presence of God.

> *Listen, listen to my heart song,*
> *I will never forsake Thee, I will never forget Thee…*
> (Paramahansa Yogananda)

Through previous teachings and teachers, I was taught that we are here to thrive to love ourselves, use law of attraction to manifest good things in our lives, be focused on what we want, etc. It was the biggest challenge for me to accept the teachings of Paramahansa Yogananda after reading all these books and practicing what was written. These books and teachings weren't able to bring me back in the space of God realization. It didn't give me realization of my true essence. Every soul wants to experience again its divine nature. We will all leave behind the material world when soul releases the body. Soul always looks for the true connection with the Creator. None of material longings will bring soul happiness, like being in the presence of its own divinity, its own Father. All material belongings and goals are a part of our journey on planet Earth. Desires are earthy experiences and because of that, another cause that we incarnate again and again to fulfill them. Desire is a positive impulse given by soul which we follow to be fulfilled our part of creation on the planet Earth. When we don't follow it, we become stuck, getting old, resentful, and live purposeless lives. Our part of creation, which God assigned to us, was not fulfilled. This is a true meaning of wanting. Soul wants to become something else or have something more because it keeps expansion of awareness. Every new expenditure is planned by God, which as His only child, we required to obey and follow. Also, as I mentioned above, we are here due to our past actions, which we want to clear out through our current incarnation. But what I have learned, understood, and my ego accepted after nine months being in the space of Guruji Yogananda's teachings is that our main goal is to find God and worship Him us our Father, our One parent who gives us all parents, friends, lovers, etc.

All the time I was questioning the quote *"Seek ye first the kingdom of God, and his righteousness; and all these things shell be added unto you."* Where was it? I was looking for the answers in Agape community, I was looking for the answers around, and I didn't get them. When I stopped looking for it and be in the space of trust, I received the best solution for my problems and guidance. By my active way of being, I was connected to people. I learned how to move from place to place. I saw beautiful places, and I was in service to others. It was great, but I didn't receive help where I was looking for it. It came to me through different people and different places. Sometimes I felt disappointment. To transform this feeling, I needed to be honest with myself that I wanted gain from these meetings and forgive people who made me believe that they have solution for me. To forgive those who, by goodwill, made me believe that they treated me like a friend, but it was only courtesy, curiosity, offering me their services, or purposeful short time connection. Again, I started appreciating for the things that came along with ease. Because of that, life was easier and I was able to appreciate people who really reached out to me with the job opportunities or a new place to live. Thanks to that, I was able to keep myself up and follow my intuition to buy or pay for things what made me grow and happy to share with others. Every time when I was relaxed, I received a phone call that lets me move forward. It was precious. When I started trusting more in myself and signals that I received from within, I went to the right people. Everything was flawless. When I started listening to others and do their suggestions, it didn't work at all. Only when I allowed myself to trust, then right connections were made to support me in the exact situation. I stopped doing unnecessary moves to do things to feel better about myself or to deal with everything by myself. Instead, I started being open and honest with others and observe how people react. I wanted to see their actions, not only their talking. Also, in friendships, I wanted people to share with me their achievements, not only what went wrong in their lives. They diminished their own achievements and power, and what they forgot was how wonderful and powerful they were. That's why we met in these communities—to regain our power and be supportive of each other standing up again in a more conscious way instead of being the same. I started distinguishing my circumstances from my newly met friends'. I saw my path more clearly and noticed what my friends didn't have at that time. Namely, it was lack of faith. They had families and friends, and most of them were residents or citizens. And a lot of them were citizens from birth here. I was by myself without anyone who could support me and without a "legal" status, and I had more courage and strength to keep them up and myself on the right path. Instead of appreciating myself for my commitment to myself and also others for their growth, I put myself down. It was an ongoing journey to trust myself and my abilities to stand up for myself to one day stand powerfully for others.

On my path, I met wonderful people who were successful or had money because some of them were born in rich or have successful families. They had good education, skills, or gifts that they succeeded in before. Traveling around the world was the natural way for them because they had money and families around the world. The United States wasn't strange for them because they had visited the country many times to meet family or spend time with friends or had legal status to work here as a citizen or had other possibilities to look for job legally in their professions. Some of them work and traveled and succeeded in Europe also. I made a lot of assumptions that we were all on the same stage, because when we met, they acted like they had no support here, no possibilities, and that they were without money, which was not true. Each of us had support on different levels, and my friends really were in the winning places because they had supportive communities and a supportive government here.

I saw them through my eyes and experiences I had here. When I noticed that it was only miscommunication, I started clearing out. I started asking about their lives before when we met, and I found out a lot of good things about them and their lives. I needed to distinguish that so as to give all of us possibilities to talk equally without comparison from my side and letting them feel good about themselves. I asked questions about what they liked or what they did, and because of that, they contributed to me by learning from them. That kind of communication served us all, and because of that, we became friends. They contributed to my life by sharing with themselves in powerful way instead of putting themselves in the mode of victims and telling me what didn't work out. People, when they want to have closer contact with others, share what is wrong about them or their lives. Because of that, they have a lot of friends, friends that have the same way of communication, forgetting that it doesn't serve anybody. Being here, I nearly started believing again that I was wrong on how conversations are supposed to look like, but I got other tools or people who woke me up. I also met people who deliberately came to the USA to live here. They secured themselves the legal status and had very good income because they had online businesses or made good connections here.

Sometimes I started to have negative conversations with myself, saying that I was not so predictable like others people who wanted to move to the United States. Forgetting that, I was on an awakening journey where only trust and intuitive guidance can make me free from comparison and unnecessary material safeguards because I will always be supported and surrounded by people who will serve my path and help me evolve as a soul in the human realm. When I noticed that, I started to appreciate my journey and courage, because not many people would decide to come to a new country where their immigration status can be called illegal or undocumented and don' t hide. Honestly without knowing anyone like minded and their goal wasn't to earn more money or security, only following a dream of helping others understand that life is about growing, loving, letting control go to start trusting, and liberation of the soul.

In the first lesson of eighteen sent by Self-Realization Fellowship, I find out who we really are, how the soul became trapped in the body, how we can regain our divinity back, and what Kriya Yoga is.

In Guruji Paramahansa Yogananda's lessons, we receive straight away knowledge about our divinity. Everything is put in easy-to-understand way. Guruji's goal was for every soul was to find God first so one can regain its birthright like peace, love, health, all the wisdom from within, and unlimited abundance that is acquired through intuitive guidance that is directly from God. He explains very clearly what our goal as a soul is and why *Kriya Yoga* is the way to release the bondage of body identification. All the universal principles that I cited above at the end of each chapter can become not only theory but Living Truth for all of us.

Kriya Yoga was called the *Royal One* (*Raja Yoga*). It is the ancient science technique of God realization. *Yoga* means "union." *Kriya* means "action." It refers to the physical, mental, and spiritual practices that bestow that conscious contact with the Infinite Source of all creation. From all kinds of yoga such as *Bahti Yoga, Jnana Yoga, Karma Yoga, Hatha Yoga, Mantra Yoga, the Royal One* is the fastest way to self-realization. Hence, it can release, in the fastest way, all of us from the karma cycles, which all of us are bound through our actions from previous incarnations and the present one, which I mentioned before. Because of that, soul can finish its cycle of reincarnation and stay in God's bliss for eternity. Self-realization means that the body, mind, and soul knows that we are one with the omnipresence of God. Pure child of God realizes Itself as Christ Consciousness.

When a soul descends to the physical body chakras in our bodies, our spinal cord starts turning downward, then the soul starts to identify itself with the physical body, and everything that's noticed through the five senses of the body is accepted as part of the real world. The mind becomes limited by the senses and loses connection as one with all. The divine immortal spirit identifies itself, for example, as Magdalena or another human being and, as a result, loses its real identity, which is Christ Consciousness as the beloved child or son of God. Then it starts living on planet Earth disconnected from everything that sustains its well-being—cutting itself from the Source; destroying everything around that the mind sees as danger; cutting down forests and trees; polluting rivers, oceans, and air; and building nuclear power plants in the name of protecting the boards and others "bad" people. It becomes so greedy that the mind sees only what's lacking and buys excess food and unnecessary things. Then tons of food decays and is thrown away. Minds are so fearful that they would do everything to survive, even at the expense of the health of its own body and respect as a human being. A fearful mind lacks discernment and becomes a medium for these who take advantage in the name of good will for all or individually.

Kriya Yoga helps reverse chakras upward to superconsciousness awareness, and the soul goes back to its own identity and is free from duality. The mind becomes quiet and peaceful; the heart is devoted to God. It is in tune to the intuitive guidance from the Creator, and all earthy drama stops affecting the soul. The Ascendant soul see Reality and feels God in everything and everywhere all the time and start living in this world without losing its divinity. Many self-realized masters said, *"I am here, but I hadn't come from here."* This truth is for all of us. That kind of knowledge and freedom the soul experiences when released from the body is the act of a body's death. By practicing Kriya Yoga, the soul regains its immortality before the body's death. It gives the soul life with fullest potential on the earthy realm.

Masters like Jesus, Bhagavan Krishna, gurus of Self-Realization Fellowship, and other saints knew when their bodies would make transition. They were able to inform the disciples when their time was ending on the Earth.

Every person that practices Kriya Yoga is called a yogi. Thanks to Guruji Paramahansa Yogananda, we don't have to go to India for enlightenment and give up our daily duties to become a yogi. Between us, many Americans travel for enlightenment there and pay a lot of money to be self-realized. What is the most important in the teachings is that we need to be in this life and do our chores. Renunciation is not the way for all of us. Our assignment is to bring

God consciousness in our daily lives: to feel God, to speak to Him, to know that He is in all our body parts and expresses Itself through our work in this world. That's why it is so important to start practicing see Spirit in everywhere—in our bodies, in our positive thoughts, in our good actions, and also see Him in others. Skin color doesn't matter. All internal organs and blood have the same color. Most importantly, beyond this physicality is only Divine Life, Pure Light, which sustains all Creation including our bodies by flowing through the medulla oblongata.

Only through a true guru that the soul can attain self-realization. Guru means Gu-darkness, Ru-Light. A guru is a connection between the Spirit and soul. He helps release all veils of forgetting that we are souls that came to planet Earth to learn and evolve, that we are not from here. Our true existence is as spirits. Our life experiences only help us become aware of that and learn from them, not be attached to them and create drama in our lives. We all have the same power and same origin. Thanks to the guidance of a self-realized guru, called master in the Western world, we can be free from others' opinions, and we can only rely on our intuitive guidance in every aspect of our lives. We stop being dependent on outside information and sources. We become more aware of our lives and actions. We will be able to discern who really speaks truth and who lies. We will know who is good company for us and who doesn't serve our well-being. We will be more loving and compassionate. Our life will then really start to have meaning. A real guru have no private gain. He takes care of soul evolution and helps souls regain a direct connection with God, like Jesus did with his disciples. In India they are called devotees. They are not passive people who are held in ignorance to be gained power over, only souls looking for enlightenment to know their true existence and help others to do the same. Our goal is God and unity in Spirit. As a result, there will be unity on the earthy plain. Mahatma Gandhi accepted Parahamansa Yoganada as his guru even though he was meditating for years before. He wanted to be closer to God, and he was initiated into Kriya Yoga by Parahamansa Yoganada as well. He knew that he could achieve his final goal, which was shamadhi, much faster through an enlightened guru than through many years of meditation by himself. God sends us a master or guru because He cannot teach us by Himself. We are so lost in the outside world that we are not receptive enough to feel His subtle presence or hear His thoughts. That's why a God-realized guru becomes our connection to Him at the beginning, and this connection is eternal. Love and friendship stays forever between a guru and his devotees. All this information we can find in the *Autobiography of a Yogi*.

The Self-Realization Fellowship lessons have been started translating in many languages. In 2020, volunteer groups started translating them to Spanish, German, French, Portuguese, Italian, and Polish. It was planned that later on, it will be translated in different Indian dialects and other languages so that everyone who wants to know the Truth and find God in themselves would be able to practice it in their own languages by themselves. In every lesson, we receive explanation written by Paramahansa Yogananda, step-by-step techniques that help us meditate deeper and prepare those who want to be initiated to the Kriya Yoga in practicing this sacred science.

Also, Self-Realization Fellowship has Online Meditation Center opened in 2020 so that all devotees can meditate all together in different languages around the world. It was surprising to me how fast it had been growing when I noticed one year later that meditations were led in Japanese also by SRF nuns from there. By group meditation, we receive bigger support in our adventure to our main goal. Our consciousness grows faster, and we know that we are not alone in this spiritual endeavor.

Now I understand why my soul chose this path of self-realization. As I mentioned earlier, my friend prepared my astronomy reading in Poland one year before I left for the USA: that my soul is finishing the reincarnation cycle of *love*. My soul wants to unify with its own Christ Consciousness to live in God and be One with God all the time on the earthy plain. My soul wants to love unconditionally.

Raja Yoga was given to the Earth as the science technique of God realization by Bagavanh Krishna millenniums ago. The Lost technique in the Dark Ages were revived by Mahavatar Babajiand renamed from Raja to Kriya Yoga. He passed to his disciple Lahiri Mahasaya. Guru

Lahiri Mahasaya to his disciple Swami Sri Yukteswar. A Jananavatar[1] Sri Yukteswar was beloved Guru of Sri Paramahansa Yogananda. Before Kriya Yoga was available only for monks. Thanks to Lahiri Mahasaya's request to Babaji, Kriya Yoga started being available to all people who were looking sincerely for God. Jesus Christ was practicing Kriya Yoga and he knew that True Life is Spirit not the body. He showed it to us through healing of others and His own Resurrection that body can be always revived. Our physical body is made from mass of atoms, which is kept by mind. The mind needs to be anchored in the Truth to bring healing to the ill body and kept it healthy. Jesus passed this yoga technique to his disciples like St. John and St. Paul. Gurudeva Paramahansa Yogananda left all this knowledge in his writings and the technique of Kriya Yoga in Self-Realization Fellowship series of lessons. He made transition in March 7, 1952. His body is in Forest Lawn Cemetery Mausoleum in Glandale. The Paramahansa Yogananda body was under observation of the Mortuary Director of Forest Lawn Cemetery by twenty days before the bronze cover of the casket was put into final position and entered to the crypt. The body didn't show any decay. It was unique experience for the officers of Forest Lawn. The reason was given of this phenomena was practicing Kriya Yoga by Gurudeva. Gurudeva's work guides us through basic lessons of Self-Realization Fellowship and Kriya Yoga. He is in Spirit right now. It means that he can communicate with us every time and everywhere and guides us during practicing meditation and Kriya Yoga, as well as through intuition to solution in our lives. *By practicing Self-Realization Fellowship lessons, every soul individually can take journey to God. Thanks to that, all misperception what God is through all religions can be discovered by ourselves. When we want to experience the Truth, we need to look for it within, where all the knowledge and Reality exists. Outside, we find only faulty picture of Real Life.*

What Paramahansa Yogananda said about meditation is that "first we can feel peace of our soul. Meditating deeper we can find peace of God. When our mind is peaceful then all thoughts become transformed into pure intuitive feeling." By communion with God

---

[1] Jananavatar—"Incarnation of Wisdom."

in deep meditation, we start perceiving and feel Him in everything and everyone.

It took me two years to adjust and accept these teachings. Thanks to them, I was able to understand what Jesus meant when he said, "*Seek God's Kingdom first, then you will find everything in Him,*" without the misconception that I had before. I had been seeking everywhere with this question in my head: Where is the kingdom of God, and how can I find it? I was looking around. I was changing communities and meeting new people. I had new experiences, and I didn't know what I was looking for. I was in doubt until I found my true connection. Then I started looking for guidance from within, inspiration, and peace there. My main goal was to be in tune with my own intuitive guidance to be free from the ideas of others. I wanted to rely only on it and to be reliable to others when they need me to come back to themselves. When we close our eyes, we see the Infinite Space. In this darkness, we will find peace, guidance, and communion with All Creation. We will realize after practicing Kriya Yoga that we are the infinite—having body, not being the body. Only then we will see God in physical world in the flowers, trees, animals, and even in insects. He created it all. People with whom I was looking for recognition come and go. I took classes that brought me great insights about myself, but I didn't find the answers of what I was looking for at that time. I remember like Rev. Cheryl corrected me, saying that "life is for me" in one of the Oath of Manifestation classes after I said out loud, "God is for me." God did not exist for me at all and for most people including members of my family. Some of them know God only amicably from what is said in church and how He is presented there. I wanted to know more. I wanted to see more. I wanted experience more. A right technique of meditation really gives us awareness of *who we really are*. When we enter in the field of our Higher Self, all stress and uncertainty disappears and there is only knowing. We are in the flow then. We become more trusting and feel safe, and we allow ourselves to open to the truth that help is always on the way. The ideas come, and new people enter in our lives. All is in the process of growing. Then we can discover how capable we are to love, to act, to serve ourselves, and without harm, to be a role model to others.

The Mayan called themselves Masters of Time, and they navigate us through the illusion by TZOLKIN in our incarnation process to evolve our human consciousness; thus, Kriya Yoga quickens our evolution in a very fast pace. Sages of India called the veil of cosmic delusion *maya*. Everything meshes. We are here to evolve as individual human being, to unite in one unchangeable consciousness called Christ Consciousness. Our Supreme goal is to see in everything and everyone omnipresent Spirit, God. When we realize that God is in each of us we stop hurting ourselves by small self, called ego. We start more to listen to our Higher Self who wants to bring harmony, health and love as real experience in our lives. Those who practice Kriya Yoga can accelerate their own evolution in one lifetime very fast. It will not come over one night as I understood since I started my process of evolving, but with patience and devotion, it will come for each of us individually in the right moment.

> *He sees truly who perceive the Supreme Lord present equally in all creatures, the Imperishable amidst the perishing. He who is conscious of the omnipresence of God does not injure the Self by the self. That man reaches the Supreme Goal.*
>
> —*The Bhagavad Gita XIII:27–28*

CHAPTER 8

What Is Our Function Here?

God is Love and all the Love there is mine now. I shall endeavor to see something lovable in everyone I meet, in every situation in which I find myself, and as this I shall accumulate a great degree of Love to be deposited in my bank.

—Ernest Holmes

Since I discovered Landmark Worldwide and Self-Realization Fellowship, I followed my path. Living in Culver City, after work, I would spend my time in the Landmark Center. I was in contact with Self-Realization Fellowship through e-mail. I was volunteering with the translation department, and also I read Self-Realization Fellowship lessons, learning from them how to meditate, using additional techniques that was given, and expanding my awareness of *who we are*.

Volunteering with Self-Realization Fellowship was a wonderful experience. I remember when I got e-mail from the translation department accepting that I can translate for them. I posted the test of my English language knowledge. I slept only two hours, but I was so joyful that I was so vitalized the next day, more than any other day. My body acted like I slept the minimum eight hours. When we are doing what we love or we receive a good news, we can really revitalize our body's energy without any problem. These moments of meaningfulness in our lives are really precious. We feel alive and unstoppable.

My assignment was to check the Polish translation of Paramahansa Yogananda's book *Man's Eternal Quest*. When I read the translation, I felt like I was reading a school textbook and not an alive wisdom. That's why my "check in" had a lot of correction. It was too much, and it didn't pass at that time. But I had opportunity to add on YouTube Polish translation of Brother Chidananda's speech, the president of Self-Realization Fellowship. The title was "Satsanga with Brother Chidananda—2019 SRF World Convocation." Thanks to that, I had my own contribution, and I learned a lot. I was learning about Self-Realization Fellowship, Sri Yogananda's teachings, and also technological stuff like adding subtitles in YouTube and saved them in SBV format. It was great experience. The subtitles were provided in many languages. Everyone can have this Convocation experience by pressing setting gear at the right bottom corner and the subtitles will be seen in your chosen language.

Being in the space of Landmark Worldwide, I saw a lot of transformation. I witnessed how marriages were restored. One of my new friend shared with us that she came to the Landmark Forum as her last resort, sheet anchor. She participated in the Landmark Forum because she "hated" her husband so much after five years of their marriage. As a result, her husband also participated in Landmark's program, and they lifted up their relationship on the higher level.

I witnessed how another marriage was restored in front of us. We were all in one room, about two hundred people including assisting staff. We stood and applauded them. It was so moving. I saw during the rest of the program their affection to each other, and they put themselves in the Advanced Course to create their new possibilities in life. In these two marriages, there were also children. Can you imagine how wonderful the role model these children gained in the form of their parents to lead their own adult life, where there is love, communication, and support for each other? All the transformation lasted less than three days.

Some of marriages can be revived, and some had to be let go of. I remember my marriage and relationship. We didn't fit in. We had two different views for life. We also had different kind of interests. We didn't have anything in common except our son. My ex-husband liked to go to the forest and collect mushrooms. For me, being in the forest means to relax, not walking in fast pace and looking around for mushrooms. He said that he relaxed that way and it gave him happiness. When we came back home, he went to bed for a nap because he inhaled a lot of oxygen, which made him sleepy. He also loved fishing. It is the most boring sport for me. He came home from fishing and again for a nap because he woke up early in the morning. The trips that we had together were thirty-five kilometers, mostly every weekend to his parents' home. Our son and I were forced to go there. There was nothing to do there, only watching TV, some political discussions, and what good food was to eat for lunch. That's all. On Sunday, it was a duty to go to the church not to make my ex-parents in law upset and after that, a short walk to the garden plot which my ex-parents in law owned or back home to watch TV and to eat lunch. I had nothing in common to talk about with my ex-mother-in-law because she told me all the time that I was supposed to listen to my husband. Hearing that, I felt my whole body tense, and it made me feel anxious inside. I believe that her mother-in-law was the same to her or worse. Her son was always right in her eyes, and the most important concern was food, lack of money, and nothing else. It worked for her, but it wasn't my world.

I was always a dreamer and saw good in life, while my ex-husband saw everything in shades of black. His attitude was so controlling and despotic that I started believing in that kind of life. There was no communication, no common interests, only duties. It was killing life. It was full of struggle and never enough money. I was never able to pursue my own hobbies: horse riding, playing tennis, or even dancing. There was no space for dreaming and going toward them together. It built resentment and misunderstanding all the time. Also his parents were involved in our lives. We were kind of dependent on them, so there wasn't any possibility to create something new and good for us as a family. Once, my ex-husband's father offered him to pay for his higher education, but he wasn't interested.

When I wanted to study, the offer wasn't on the table. I was a woman. In their world, only man had the right to grow.

I believe that every marriage is for a reason, to create something new together for ourselves and for others. When we start focusing together on something bigger that serves all, our trivial problems disappear. They cease to exist when helping others is at stake. Then marriage can grow.

Once when I was in Downtown Los Angeles at a homeless fair, I saw a married couple who came to the homeless organization representative to ask how they can support the initiative and give accommodation to a homeless person or two.

My dream has a purpose. I want to support others in releasing all their pain, which is unreal, and start living meaningful lives and bring truth to the world who we really are and recall each of us our own nature, which is joy, love and light.

I understood that my partner needs to live his dream to see life like I do or even have higher consciousness that I can learn from him. That life is to evolve, full of possibilities, full of surprises, joyful, good, and trustful. Then we can support each other in our dreams. I realized that creating something new is not easy by themselves. This is wonderful to create something with a partner and have mutual support. I released the need of having a person whose most important concern is what to put in his stomach and he is not aware how life works. When we dream, we are not hungry and there is always food on the plate and a good one. There are meaningful friendships and encounters with other people. Everything in life has meaning. There is a book written by Katherine Woodward Thomas, *Calling in the One: 7 Weeks to Attract the Love of Your Life*. There are techniques releasing old beliefs, relationships, and prepare for a new one—a fulfilled one. The change always starts from each of us.

Being in the space of Landmark or other communities where service to the world is important, I felt safe to share with my dreams with them. I was understood. We all were dreamers and supported each other in growing and pursuing what was important for us.

I remember after Mary Morrisey's live event, I nearly passed out when I made an appeal, fundraising for myself because I wanted become a master life coach for her institute. If I was asking for money on behalf of someone else, it wouldn't be problem for me, but I asked for myself. Even it was in a good cause, to serve others, I was terrified for a moment. It was my view of myself: judgmental and full of unworthiness. At that time I didn't get any support, but this experience let me to learn to ask for more and stand up for myself. Now I know there is no fear to ask somebody about help or support here. Those who go with courage through life had the same or similar experiences that I had. That's why we understand each other.

A lot of people, mostly women, were taught not to ask for themselves; and these syndrome is still in us. We put ourselves last.

My friend from the Self-Expression Leadership Program shared with us that thanks to that program, she told her family for the first time what she really wanted for a Christmas gift. Before, she never asked. Also, she understood that she had right to speak and express herself and what her dreams were in front of the nearest ones without hiding herself.

How many times have we hidden ourselves in conversations with others, mostly with our family because they don't want to listen? They knew better and outshout what we say or don't give us the chance to finish our sentence because again they knew better and what we speak is nonsense. How many times have we tried to prove that what we say is reasonable, that we know the topic because we follow it. Did it help? No, they still see us through their own eyes and listen what they want to hear. If they don't like, they cut off the discussion. What I have learned is to stop proving my point of view. I don't have to have their agreement to follow my dream and be fully expressed even if others don't respect it.

People like talking about politics, make opinions, make boring discussions that don't lead anywhere. They love to complain about the government and politicians or laugh at those who have the courage to put themselves out. It is easy to laugh or judge sitting on the chair and make comments what others say on TV. People has opinions what this or that politician is supposed to do or not do or how he acts, etc. But none from these passive commentators has tried to stand in public and speak their own truth in front of millions and put themselves at risk to being judged. It needs courage and strength to do that. It doesn't matter if that person is right or not, but for sure, this person has the courage to express his or her own point of view. People close themselves at homes and sit in front of TV and they think they are a good citizen because they vote. They listen to what others have to say instead of having the courage to ask themselves what they are up to and stand in front of many and share it to give others possibility to join and make difference in the communities for better, not only with those who agree with them but also those with opposite opinions, and respect them. It is called enrollment to life instead of passive watching others' lives. None of us came to the Earth to make opinion of others and hide themselves. Everyone came here with a divine purpose. A lot of people forgot this. We all forgot. But now we have opportunity to start recalling our true roots.

Those people who try, who are really fulfilled, they don't need applause from outside. They don't care what others think. They enjoy their lives. They neither overdose alcohol or other addictive substances, nor do they overeat. They minds are focused on something else to be alive: to be in service to others. They treat everyone as their nearest family. They stopped favoring some people and tease or humiliate others. They have the same love for everyone. That kind of being is very graceful, and everyone can be that kind of person.

The simplest task, and also the most difficult, is to stand in front of the mirror and look at your reflection. Be with yourself. Look in your eyes. What do you see there? Can you feel or express love to this person? Not many can do that and from this person starts true love and acceptance for others. Most people run away from themselves. I used to do that very often also. We see a strange person in the mirror and cannot stand our own reflection. When we don't see ourselves, we cannot see others. When we are separated from ourselves, we are separated from others. And here starts the ego war: arguing with each other, judging each other, blaming each other, disrespecting each other, etc.

That's why we need to do work with the person in the mirror. You could hear this in inspirational words of Mahatma Gandhi as well as Michael Jackson's song "Man in the Mirror." This is the key to the peace and love in the world.

The person in the mirror is always with us, never leaves us. No matter how much we want to escape from ourselves, we will not be able to do that. Thoughts in our heads are always present and mostly comparative. They judge others, what they do or did not do; what others think, what others should do or did not do. All these is seen through a limited prism, the prism of our limited minds, a very narrow point of view. When we have courage to share our perception of the world to others and most importantly to those whose worldview disagrees with us, then our mind become more open and we become more tolerant for ourselves and others. We start noticing that the other person has right to express his or her own worldview. When we start sharing this diversity together, then we learn one from each other. Our communication is on a higher level, and our consciousness rises. We lift up ourselves and help others to do the same, instead of holding tight to our old convictions. Then life becomes more interesting and more colorful.

When we wake up in the morning, we can ask the question, *"What can I do for myself and others to feel good to be in alignment with my True Being?"* or *"What do I want to create for myself today to feel really good?"* Thanks to these questions, every day can be different and meaningful for each of us.

Love and happiness were given by God to us. When we are loving and happy, we evolve automatically.

The last five months in Culver City passed for me very fast after I had found my purpose being there, and at the beginning of January 2020, I still didn't know where I would move out. Once when I doubted I asked the lady if I can prolong my stay, and she said that a few days before, she made the arrangements with a new person. It was blessing for me because I knew that I would find a new place to live. I let go these problem to God. At the end of December, I received the one-month notice to release my room, as we both agreed at the beginning. It was surprising for me because we never signed any agreement at the beginning when I moved in, and as we knew each other more, I didn't realize that people who knew me didn't trust my word. The lady asked me twice before if I wanted to prolong my stay at hers. So I knew that she really wanted me there, but I kept telling that I was moving out. I wanted to give Life a chance to support me in it. I really wanted to move on. Later I found out how many Americans and people who lived here were looking for covering documents to everything because they don't trust one another and would do everything to protect themselves from one another, not realizing that they're acting against themselves.

One day I was in Landmark to assist. It was about the middle of January. My new friend Louetta asked me if I wanted to stay with her at her place. Louetta worked as a staff in the Landmark Center at that time. She took me to her apartment, and I said *yes*. The room was available from March. So I needed to find a place for a month. I contacted my friend Heliberto, who I met in Agape International Spiritual Center on the Oath of Manifestation class. He lived in Glendale. I was once at his house when he hosted me and other friends from the group to prepare our final project for Agape's self-awareness class. At that time, I started speaking out loud about wanting to write a book, and I didn't know how. From my friend Julie Ann came out, "Just start writing," but I wasn't ready for the message then. It was too easy, but later it turned out to be the truth. To be a writer, we don't have to go to college or university and learn how to write. We can attend if we want to improve our knowledge about writing and literature, but this is not the only path to become a writer. Not everyone can afford this. We have a lot of support from other sources as an artist. For example, Santa Ana College has non-credit classes to learn how to draw and paint. I believe that there are many resources we can use to evolve our creativity without paying thousands of dollars. The only thing we need to do is allow Life to take a course to express through us and manifest our reason for being here.

When I contacted Heliberto, he agreed to let me stay in his house for the whole February. At that time, he was in Paris, so I had his beautiful house to myself. I paid for the room, and I felt like I was in heaven. I was able to rest at last, out of Culver City and the rushed life there. I stopped assisting in Landmark too because I knew that

I would be in their program for over seven months from the end of February. I wanted regain my strength before that and my coming back to Los Angeles. I was in bliss. There were beautiful mountain views, fresh air, and peace. Some birds sang from midnight there. It was a time to reconnect with myself and nature. When I let go of my weekend work in January, the one with the elder person, to be able to attend the Introduction Leaders Program later in February, I had only one job in Beverly Hills—to take care of Victoria. The rest of the week was for myself to continue my spiritual growth and writing.

Thanks to having free time, I started practicing meditation regularly, using the techniques given in Self-Realization Fellowship lessons. I applied to volunteer in Lake Shrine, and I came back to writing my book for which I didn't have time in Culver City.

Once I went for a meeting with Maryam who was responsible for volunteering in Lake Shrine, it took me two and half hours to get there from the place where I was staying. I was enjoying that journey, and I knew if I was going to volunteer there, I would have to live closer. I was coming back to Los Angeles next month. At that time nobody knew that induced pandemic would stop our social meetings for a long period of time.

When I met Maryam, she asked me who brought me here. I believe it was a very important question regarding what Jesus explained, saying, "No man can come to me, except the Father which hath sent me draw him." It meant that Jesus accepted only these disciples who were ready to receive the message, follow the Truth and initiated by God. Spirit was giving him intuitive guidance. In my case and in the case of the other devotees of Sir Paramahansa Yogananda, he accepted us because God sent us to him and his teachings. It was the souls' contract. So when Maryam asked me the question, I said right away, "Divine Mother." Paramahansa Yogananda very often called God as Divine Mother, and in my case, I identified this name with the nature as Mother Earth. I recalled right away the monarch butterfly that sat on my lap and was washing its antenna. As I mentioned before, every time when I was there, this butterfly was there, greeting me. Even in this exact day, I received a sign from the monarch butterfly. The gates were close, and I thought that I was not able to get into Lake Shrine property to be at the meeting on time. To get to other entrance, it would take me another half an hour by feet. Suddenly, the butterfly appeared and I knew that a way would be found. In a few seconds, a car approached the gate. The gate started opening. I walked in, and the person said that I wasn't supposed to be there. I told him that I have an appointment with Maryam. Suddenly, all the doors were opened for me. I walked through the Temple doors, and another person opened the back door of the Temple for me, where I was able to use the stairs and walked down to the lake area. He pressed a code to open the gate to the lake, and I was heading to meet Maryam. She was waiting for me at the Visitors Center. We greeted each other and sat in the alcove. She explained to me about volunteering in Lake Shrine. Above her head was a Guruji's picture. She asked me which one of the volunteer program I wanted to choose. My attention went right away to the Sunday school. My heart expanded every time I looked at the inscription "Sunday school" on Maryam's piece of paper. I stayed with that. She connected me later through e-mail with the Brother Sarvanada who was responsible for Sunday school.

Every time I was in Lake Shrine, I felt like my soul was at home. Being in the Temple, there is a very strong feeling of the presence of Gurudeva Paramahansa Yogananda and embracing peace.

After meeting with Maryam, I went back home by bus. I was so happy. I got off near my place where I stayed to do some shopping in one of my favorite grocery stores, then I walked back home. What I noticed in this chain of stores is that it depends on what kind of society lives there and what kind of awareness they have then the store changes its own energy. The food was put differently on the shelves, and it changes the energy field. In one store there was more harmony; in others, it felt like disorder even if it had the same good quality products. It really matters what kind of people come and how products are arranged on the shelves to enjoy shopping. There was a lot of nervousness there. A few months before, I started noticing that I was sensing different kind of energy in different places and stores. It depended on what kind of people that were living the area and who did the errands. I thought at that time that everybody can sense it, but later on, I discovered it was another gift that I was born with.

Taking care of one-year-old Victoria in Beverly Hills gave me a wonderful opportunity to get rid of an old subconscious belief about favoring boys and men over girls. She was so full of light and courage. The more bigger and stronger her body was, the more she tried to do. She was so free and enjoyed being by herself and exploring what her body can do. She loved to run and climb. More higher was the best.

She resembled myself. I remember how I explored my body's strength. I climbed trees and wooden towers in the forest at my family's town. I loved walking and swimming. I loved to make flips in the water and on the ground and jumping. I caught beetles with my hands and then put them in the jar for a while. We played in the playground different games. I walked barefoot in puddles. I played badminton, and I was good at all my adventures on the physical level. I participated in all our playground games, and I was one of the best. Jumping in a rubber game with my peers, I taught myself to stand on my hands and reach the rubber on their neck level to score and pass. In my PE classes, I was able to do the handstands and bend my body in an angle. We called this position bridge. I jumped over obstacles. The more higher, the better. I loved diving into water. I loved do flip in the air and jump into the water. I was unstoppable. Others were tired, but not my body. I had never enough. I was skating and learned by myself some figures. It was fun. I never was afraid of animals like dogs or horses. I was very attracted to them.

When I was six years old, I taught myself how to get on a horse without saddle or reins. Nobody taught me. I just knew how to treat horses. My grandparents had an apple tree. I picked apples up and gave them to my grandparents' neighbor's horse. Then I found a tree trunk and climbed on her. It was a horse for working in the field. I was so happy every time she made a move while she was grazing. Once, she was scared by her owner. She kicked him and run away. I didn't know about that accident, and when she was found, I climbed on her and felt safe with her. When I was bigger, I had some more adventures with horses, at that time with saddles and reins. I loved it.

The same Victoria's body was very agile too. She was so spontaneous and alive in her way of being. When her parents would let her evolve in this, she will be unstoppable and really happy. She will be enjoying her life.

When I was taking care of her, I let her looked into my backpack, because I knew that she was curious. Once she took out the wallet, and I noticed that I was missing my TAP card that I used in the buses and trains. I wasn't able to find it. Later, I asked her father to look for it, but he wasn't able to find it either. What I understood was that I lost the TAP card probably in the bus in the morning, and thanks to this small girl, I was able refill another spare one on my way home. If it wasn't for her, I wouldn't be able to use the buses the next day because I didn't have any change to pay on bus or time to go and refill the spare one. The universe gives us guidance through other people, circumstances, and situations to take care of ourselves. It is not important how big or small these people are.

Another miracle happened, thanks to her. When I would go walking with her, I loved to buy latte coffee for myself in coffee shops. Sometimes we went to grocery store. Mostly, when Victoria was sleeping in the stroller that I would do some errands. So I had my debit card with me all the time. One day, when we came back from the walk, I was unpacking the stroller and noticed that the debit card was not in my pocket or the place where I used to keep it. I knew that this card was around. I asked in my mind, *Guruji*, for the card to be found, and suddenly, Victoria appeared from the hall and held in her small hand my debit card. I knew that she was guiding intuitively, because it was a few seconds after I have sent the thought. She always had a habit keeping new found things for her to explore, but not this time. As soon as she found it on the hall, she approached me and gave it back right away. She knew that it belonged to me.

As I mentioned before, children know because they sense everything and their guidance is only through intuition. When people don't know that, then they say, "What a smart child" or "How did she [or he] knew?" or "So wise," etc. It is only the soul and the unseen realm. We all are geniuses and we all used this guidance until we went to school and started gaining intellectual knowledge and others told us that something was wrong with us when we acted differently or thought differently. To fit into the society, we became like them. We dream away our life, unaware that there is other realm that guide us through feelings and other senses that are beyond our bodies. We put ourselves in the space that there is something wrong with us and jamming these feelings, not trusting ourselves that maybe we are right in what we feel and not what other people are saying to us.

The time in Glendale was passing fast. Meanwhile, Heliberto came back from Paris after a week and half. Thanks to that, we reconnected with some people from Agape International Spiritual Center and threw a party. Also, he introduced me to his Hispanic friends from the Unity Church in Burbank. He was the reason that services in Spanish were able to continue there. I heard for the first time the original Mariaches. It was a lot of new encounters and fun. I started using Spanish there also. It was in very basic way, but I was able to practice.

When Heliberto left for Colombia, I stayed behind to enjoy the rest of the time by myself.

Once, I went to Paramhansa Yogananda's tomb. I met there a person who was on a business trip from India, and he shared with me his story and how he found way to guruji's teachings in India. We both meditated together there.

Meanwhile, my son went back from China to Poland for his holidays. After one week of staying in Poland he found out that the coronavirus pandemic had erupted in China, and at the end, he stayed in Poland and move to Wroclaw to settle down there.

When it was time for me to move back to Los Angeles, Louetta offered me to pick me up from the place where I was staying to her apartment condominium called Madrid. I felt like I went back to the beginning. My first trip away from Poland was Madrid, Spain, where my son was born. As I mentioned before, I was dreaming about modeling at that time. This time I received a job offer promise from a new met friend from Introduction Leaders Program who was the owner of a fashion company. Thanks to that, I learned how to apply for EAD card or job permit. The waiting time was sixty to ninety days. After two months, I received the whole documentation back from the immigration office with the request to insert eligibility to apply. At that time, it turned out that I needed wait until January 2021 to get any eligibility to stay or work in the USA. In February 2020, I received a Notice to Appear that I would have a master hearing at the Immigration Court in Los Angeles. Life gave me the whole year to prepare me for this hearing.

Being at the Madrid condominium, most of the time I spent writing a book and practicing Self-Realization lessons. The job that I had in Beverly Hills was finished. Victoria's parents started working remotely. I was so grateful for the generosity of the girl's father for paying me for two weeks even if I wasn't working for the family anymore. It helped me cover the rest of the rent in April. It was a blessing.

In March, I registered at Evans Adult Community School to improve my English. I passed the test to the highest level there. It was the right time because a week or two later, the governor of the state of California announced a stay-at-home order, and schools were closed. My classes started at the beginning of April. I joined the class by Zoom. I met new people. I have learned a lot about Los Angeles and new inventions. We had guests on our Zoom classes, for example, the husband of our English teacher who worked for the company that owns *League of Legends*. I found out about the *League of Legends* World Championship. The tournament is hosted by Riot Games and is held every year to online game fans to spend time together and play. The *League of Legends* World Championships has gained tremendous success making among the world's most prestigious and watched tournaments.

The other guest was a person from NASA Jet Propulsion Laboratory (JPL) in Pasadena. It was an exciting encounter. I had so many questions for him. The person was working with the team on a current rover called Perseverance. The name was chosen by kids from American's schools. The vehicle was prepared for voyage to Mars, which was launched in July 2020. The journey from the Earth to Mars lasted about ten months. The rover was prepared to find some life on Mars. We found out that its maximum speed is two miles per hour. The communication between Mars and Earth is delayed for about fourteen to fifteen minutes. The journey is only one way.

At the moment there is no possibility to bring the rover back to Earth. NASA doesn't have possibility to refuel a rocket and relaunch it back. The scientists equipped the rover with batteries to prevent from losing connection during orbit when it changes position. In previous models, NASA lost connection with the equipment on Mars during orbit rotation. The scientist said that the NASA laboratory is more sterile than in American hospitals. Everyone wears masks and sterile overalls when working at that project. The scientists want to prevent bringing life from the Earth to Mars. Their research wouldn't have sense then. They are looking for life there and find the way to bring tests to the laboratory in Pasadena to have more possibilities for research. The rover was equipped with a small laboratory, but not as advanced like they have in JPL. Also we found out that the launch window for Perseverance had only two weeks, because in July 2020, Mars and Earth were the closest to each other. If they missed that time, the next launch would be two years later. Coronavirus didn't prevent scientists to work on their project. I asked them why they are so interested in Mars. He said that scientists do that for curiosity. They love to learn and explore new things. It was so wonderful to speak with this person because we all felt his passion for his work and we all were excited about everything he said.

I also asked about SpaceX. While NASA does small steps on Mars, the private space business has bigger vision. Few weeks before, our topic for our English Zoom class was about entrepreneur Elon Mask and his adventures to Mars. That was the first time I heard about Elon Musk and SpaceX. The person told us that NASA and the space private business support each other in launching rockets. The idea of Elon Mask is to build a city on Mars for people to live there. At this moment as we were informed by our guest, it would be only a one-way journey. There was no way back to the Earth. Also, we found out that the Jet Propulsion Laboratory is open to the public twice a year for free. Everybody can see these new technologies and met people working there, like scientists with different scientific backgrounds and the astronauts. Because of the pandemic, everything was suspended, but it was good to know for a future plan to visit this place. I was appreciative that we got all the knowledge about it firsthand. He was a person who truly enjoyed his work and was involved with the newest scientific project to Mars. At the end of our space adventure, our teachers invited us to watching all together by Zoom the movie *The Martian*. It was great ending up our classes about space.

Life all the time was giving me surprises and knowledge from the best.

Living at the Madrid condominium, I was suddenly attracted to gemstones. Louetta had a wonderful library with everything that I love. I bought some crystals who spoke to me, and I still had my gemstones from Poland like pyrite or chrysocolla. I bought a book, *Crystals for Beginners* by Karen Frazier, which was my first step to know more about the crystals and gemstones. What I have learned by myself was that we are attracted to the certain gemstones or crystals in different moments of our lives. They raise our vibrations to help us overcome some issues that don't serve us anymore, for example lapis lazuli resonate with the fifth chakra. This metamorphic rock helps to find our own voice and express ourselves fully. Many times we shut down and not share our wisdom with others because we have convinced ourselves that we have nothing to say or are not allowed, which is lie that we say to ourselves on a daily basis. Chrysocolla resonates with fourth chakra, the heart one. When we want our hearts to be more open, it is good to have this crystal to help us to be more loving. There are gemstones and crystals that resonate with lower and higher chakras, such as orange or red jasper, which is responsible for the root chakra. It balances anger and sexuality and heals women's anger at men. On the other hand, it calms men's sexual aggressiveness toward women. It also helps balance physical sexuality with emotions in gay and heterosexual relationships. There are kyanites that resonate with sixth chakra, our third eye and help among others with creating pathways from one thing to another, getting us out of the rut, memory recall, grounding. There are agates, quartz, and other crystals that resonate with different chakras depending on their colors. There are crystals or gemstones that protects us from absorbing negative energies such as obsidian. There are many books about crystals and gemstones. The topic never ends. Crystals have healing properties, can helps us gain some balance, and become as an introduction to the spiritual world.

During the coronavirus pandemic, my youngest brother, Pawel, created a family group on Messenger so that we all could be connected with each other and our mother on a daily basis. As I mentioned before, this time was a blessing, allowing reunions for families around the globe. We had time for each other and became closer. Once, Bartosz sent to our group a sneaker's image for fun, and that image helps to determine which cerebral hemisphere is dominant in our brain. It turned out that mine was right-hemisphere dominant, which is responsible for creativity. I believe that thanks to writing and being intuitively connected, my dominant hemisphere became the right side. Before, I used only logic and didn't see that I can create something new by myself. Martin, my son, had a balance of the right and left hemispheres. So he equally uses logical mind and creative one. The rest of my family and friends to whom I sent the image had left-hemisphere-dominant brains, which means they are very logical. So with how many people there are in the world, there are so many possibile ways of seeing things differently because every brain creates its own illusion of perceiving things.

Meanwhile, I received guidance to connect with my new friend Kirin, who was looking for a place to live with her partner, and we were considering living together. At the end, I moved in with them to a new place in May. I stayed at Lauetta's apartment for only two months. It turned out that I made the right decision because she and her partner were moving to a one-bedroom apartment in a beautiful town in Palos Verdes one month later, which is about twenty-two miles away from Los Angeles. When I made the decision based on my intuitive guidance to move in with Kirin, I didn't know how it would end up, but it turned out to be the best outcome for all of us.

During the induced lockdowns, there was a huge reset. A lot of people were laid off. The government and cities were of very much help to a lot of households in the USA. A lot of people had more money than when they were working before. So it allowed a lot of them to rethink what was most important to them. People had more time for themselves and families. They had become much closer to one another and united. They had possibilities to evaluate their own lives and took new steps for their future, steps they hadn't considered before. A lot of people evolved, and they started looking for new solutions and raised their awareness to feel safe and thrive. I saw the artists who united themselves to lift up people around the world. I saw other people who, through social media, were helping others look for the good things in the current situation. I was a part of that. There was more love, understanding, and compassion. I also felt a lot of fear around. It was because of a misunderstanding of Life and the lack of knowledge that our minds create every experience in our lives individually and globally as a collective consciousness. The point of power is always in the present moment. It means that *now* we have the power to choose which thoughts could nourish us such as love, health, happiness, and courage beyond present circumstances. People who knew that were calm. For instance, in one interview, Neale Donald Walsch said that he asks himself four questions on a daily basis and encourages everyone to do the same to receive clarity for themselves: (1) Who am I? (2) Where am I? (3) Why am I here? (Why am I on this planet?) and (4) What am I going to do about it? If you live this way, fear and confusion will disappear. We find peace and wisdom from within about the purpose we have in every situation.

My time in the Madrid condominium was about to be finished when one day, I woke up with fear about money. I wasn't able to keep my mind calm. I felt an emotional disturbance. My savings were running out. I knew that the people I was going to live with would be counting on my rent payments, and I only had savings enough for one month's payment. Suddenly I received a very strong feeling, a thought from my heart: *Never doubt in Me!* Thanks to that, I relaxed. My mind calmed down, and I started being trustful again that everything would work out. At that time, my Introduction Leaders Program was suspended, so I had more time to practice Self-Realization Fellowship techniques from the lessons. And I asked for prayers concerning health issues for my family and friends. I knew that I was safe, but with their scattered minds, I wasn't so sure about them. The prayers were kept up for three months by the nuns and monks of Self-Realization Fellowship, and it really worked. I felt at peace that they were taken care of. Once, I was guided to learn more about prevention to be safe because the air was very heavy with thoughts about coronavirus at that time. I didn't watch TV to save myself from all the subconscious programming and news about how dangerous coronavirus was, so I called my mother. I knew that she was watching TV and that she was fearful, but when I called her, she was panicking. All the fear and information she heard, she put on me. I asked her to stop because it would not help anyone. I tried to calm her down and asked her to tell me only what kinds of precautions I needed to take. She relaxed and gave me all the useful information that I needed. During our call, I was on the bus with a lot of people, and this conversation left me with a feeling of nervousness. I needed to do something with it to calm down my mind. I opened Instagram and spotted right away a perfect affirmation posted by @thedivineabundance:

> *Wherever I go there is a*
> HEALING ATMOSPHERE.
> *It blesses me and*
> *brings peace to me and*
> *all those around me.*

I read it many times, and I started feeling peaceful. After that I suddenly sensed that the pandemic was in the past. I felt relief and looked around at the people I was with on the bus. I discerned nothing but peace radiating from everywhere. At the same time, I received a thought with the words I heard from one of the spiritual teachers: "What the human being experiences as a current situation, for the Universe, it is the past." I started treating this global experience as part of the past, and I tried not to be involved in any discussion about the whole situation. I started looking for good things in this experience including the mandate to wear masks, which prevented people from breathing properly by making them inhale carbon dioxide from their own lungs to weaken them. As a result, it could be the body hypoxia that causes the mind to be more anxious than usual and to start seeing more danger everywhere and in everyone including life-giving oxygen and the fellow human being. I had a lot of resistance toward this mandate, but I found one good thing in it: we all at last could look at each other's eyes instead of our mouths while speaking. This allowed a true soul-to-soul connection. During this time, I was guided to contact my stepsister, Anna Pawlak, through Messenger. She lives in Poland, and we haven't met in person yet. It turned out that her husband was in the hospital diagnosed with coronavirus, and his state was very serious. He was in pharmacological coma. I asked Gurudeva Paramahansa Yogananda to heal him, and I received the image showing that Guruji was with him. I knew that her husband would be all right. I sent her this message. She was grateful. We were in contact often at that time. After two or three weeks, she texted me good news that her husband woke up from the coma. He recovered step by step, and about one week and half later, he was released home. She shared with me later that the doctor said that her husband's state was so bad that only love could heal him, and it did. Later on I spoke with Teresa, Anna's mother, and she told me that her son-in-law was really stressed about and fearful of this situation. It was the cause of his infection, which turned out to be very dangerous for his life because doctors didn't know how to treat it at the beginning.

At that time, I was reading the book *The Holy Science* by Swami Sri Yukteswar, a guru of Sri Paramahansa Yogananda, who translated this book into English. Self-Realization Fellowship has all its copyrights reserved.

Swami Sri Yukteswar describes in his book all the period cycles on the planet earth called *Yugas*. The whole period lasts 24,000 years, which causes a celestial phenomenon of the backward movement of the equinoctial points around the zodiac. The sun also has another motion by which it revolves round a grand center called *Vishnunabhi*, which is the seat of the creative power, *Brahma*, the universal magnetism. *Brahma* regulates *dharma*, the mental virtue of the internal world. When the sun in its revolution round, its dual comes to the place nearest to this grand center, the seat of *Brahma*, which takes place when the autumnal equinox comes to the first point of Aries. *Dharma*, the mental virtue, becomes so much developed that man can easily comprehend all, even the mysteries of the Spirit. The autumnal equinox started falling at the beginning of the twentieth century, among the fixed stars of the Virgo constellation and in the early part of the Ascending Dwapara Yuga, in which we are in currently. Swami Sri Yukteswar continues to share that: after 12,000 years, when the sun goes to the places in its orbit, which is farthest from Brahma, the grand center, the mental virtue, *dharma*, comes to such reduced state that man cannot grasp anything beyond the gross material creation. The other hand, when the sun in its course of revolution begins advance toward the place nearest to the grand center, *Brahma*, the mental virtue begins to develop. This growth is gradually completed in another 12,000 years.

Each of these periods of 12,000 years brings a complete change, both externally in the material world and, internally in the intellectual or electric world and is called one of the Daiva Yuga or Electric Couple. Thus, in a period of 24,000 years, the sun completes the revolution around its dual and finishes one electric cycle consisting of 12,000 years in an ascending arc and 12,000 years in the descending arc.

Development of dharma, the mental virtue, is divided into four different stages in a period of 12,000 years.

The first stage is called Kali Yuga, which lasts for 1,200 years with its before and after 100 years *sandhis*, the mutation periods. The mental virtue, *dharma*, has its first stage. The human intellect is so diminished that it cannot comprehend anything beyond the gross matter of the external world.

The period around AD 500 was the darkest part of Kali Yuga and of the whole cycle of 24,000 years. At that period widespread ignorance and suffering in all nations. In AD 1599 the human intellect was so dense that it could not comprehend the electricities, the fine matters of creation. In the political world, generally there was no peace in any kingdom. When Kali Yuga was in the 100-year transitional, the mutation period in the effect was a union with the following Dwapara Yuga, man began to notice the existence of fine matters, the attributes of electricities, and political peace began to be established. In the political world, people began to have respect for themselves. The civilization advanced in many ways, even if their nature was not clearly understood.

Dwapara Yuga lasts 2,400 years with its 200 years before and after *sandhis*. In 1899, on completion of the period of 200 years of Dwapara Sandhi, the time of mutation, the true Dwapara Yuga of 2000 years has commenced. It brings a rapid development in man's knowledge. The human intellect can comprehend the fine matters or electricities and their attributes, which are the creating principles of the external world, what we experience right now. Also in this period of the cycle, Time has the great influence as it governs the universe. No man will be able to overcome this influence except those who being baptized in the holy Aum vibration, blessed with pure love, the heavenly gift of nature and become divine. These comprehend the Kingdom of God. That's why Swami Yukteswar wrote *The Holy Science* to let us understand that it is our time to reach out for spiritual knowledge and that men require loving help one from the other. That book was requested by his paramaguru (guru of his guru LahiriMahasya) maharaj Babaji.

The Aum vibration we can hear after closing our eyes and ears. The sound resembling the sound of the ocean it is the Aum vibration, the sound of all creation. It is the Holy Spirit that Jesus said about. In the Aum vibration, the Christ Consciousness exists as One, the unity, the True being of each of us.

Swami Sri Yukteswar continues: Subsequent Yuga, what the humanity will be heading, is called Treta Yuga. The period lasts 3,600 years with 300 years before and after its *sandhis*, the periods of mutation. *Dharma*, the mental virtue of a human being, will be in third stage. The human intellect will be able to comprehend the divine magnetism, the source of all electrical forces on which the creation depends for its existence.

The fourth stage of the mental virtue is called Satya Yuga. The period lasts 4,800 years with its before and after 400 years of the mutation time, *sandhis*. *Dharma* will complete its full development.

The human intellect can comprehend all, even God the Spirit beyond this visible world.

The scientist proved that our planet Earth has millions of millions years. We can only discover for ourselves that the cycles of 24,000 years of Daiva Yuga held place many times.

Reading the book of Sri Yukteswar and exploring the Mayan sacred calendar gave me the confirmation that we were here many times to evolve in our planetary and solar consciousness. We are really creation of God, the Spirit who divided and manifested Himself as a human being or other creature and nature in this and other solar system.

Also, it gives understanding that during induced by mainstream media pandemic, people who passed away or in other situations they went back to their own divine nature. The physical body would never be an issue for them anymore, and it has stopped limiting them. It only let them find eternal bliss on the vast sphere of Spirit Who is everywhere. It means also that we can communicate with them all the time. They will guide us to relief from our pain of their loss if we listen. They want us to know that they are safe and happy. They want us to experience their bliss here on the earthy realm by love, joy, and happiness. We are connected with our parents, loved ones through Spirit. They contact us through dreams, by the suddenly calling of the phone and with the background music, with beautiful loving words, or an inscription appeared on the display, "I love you" or "I am okay." They guide us to people who experienced the death and have come back to share the truth with us like Anita Moorjani or others who know that life is Spirit and they communicate with the unseen realm all the time. They guide us to the books that contains the Truth. They guide us to videos that resonate with us to receive the answer. They guide us to right teachers and masters. They love us beyond all conditions. They want us to be happy. They are with God and in God. Being on the physical realm, we feel disconnected from our Creator. I remember when Heliberto came from Europe and during our conversation, he said, *"You never was disconnected from the Source."* It was like an awakening for me. I thought that I knew, but that day was like an a-ha moment. I was on the beginning path with Self-Realization Fellowship teachings and I felt a lot of disconnection at that time. It is a never-ending process of recalling ourselves what is our true Source of origin and appreciating our own way of growing and being.

That's why loving ourselves and others is so important. When our thoughts and love become directed toward our Creator, the Spirit who manifests Himself in each of us shows us how to love each other and we start losing our identity as individual and our whole being starts to be filled with unconditional love. Then we can see how we are precious and important for our God. He never loses sight of us.

> *He who watcheth Me always, him do I watch; he never loses sight of Me, nor do I lose sight of him.*
>
> —*Bhagavad Gita VI:30*[1]

---

[1] *He who perceives Me everywhere and beholds everything in Me never loses sight of Me, nor do I ever lose sight of him,"* a literal translation by Paramahansa Yogananda.

CHAPTER 9

How Would You Like Your Life to Look Like?

In the beginning was the Word, and the Word was with God, and the Word was God... All things were made by him; and without him was not anything made that was made... And the Word was made flesh and dwelt among us.

—*John 1:1, 3, 14*

When I moved to a new place, I continued writing my book, recalling and practicing the Mayan sacred calendar by tracking days with different energies and being in the space of preparing myself for initiation for Kriya Yoga. I applied for it in March 2020. It is good to have around so powerful energies like Jesus Christ, Baghavan Krishna, Mahavatar Babaji, Lahiri Mahasaya, Swami Sri Yukteswar, and my direct guru Paramahansa Yogananda who help us in our daily lives and, most importantly, their protection for our soul to be on its own path to God and to make right choices in the material world. They are like mediators between what we think we need or want and what Spirit chooses for us to evolve on the higher realm.

Once, when I reread the book *The Incarnation Code* by Hanna Kotwicka the description of my archetype with the mirror energy, my attention was attracted to the word "sensitivities." I read the interpretation many times, but it was first time when my attention went to this word. The same day I attracted the article about empaths by a French psychiatrist. When I read it, I started see myself, my way of analyzing, and other similarities of what I was doing was mentioned there. Out of all, I learned that there are only 20–25 percent people in the world who are born as an empath. I started knowing my body's abilities more and more. I discovered new knowledge for myself, but I didn't know the meaning as of this realization, how would others benefit from me knowing that I have empath's body. I heard this word from time to time mostly from new male friends who discovered for themselves that they were empaths. This gave them ability to become a healer.

I remembered about the CDs my friend Paula sent me for my birthday two years before. On the CDs, there was a recorded the book by Dr. Judith Orloff—*The Empath's Survival Guide*. There was the exercise to help identify what type of empath the person is. Also there were the tools and strategies how to stop absorbing stress and how to protect yourself from narcissists and other energy vampires. When I was listing to these CDs, I learned more and more about my body's abilities. I was a mild physical empath and 100 percent emotional empath at that time. Later, my body abilities were evolved more. Dr. Judith Orloff explained in the book the difference between having empathy and being empath. Having empathy means our heart goes out to another person in joy or pain. Being an empath means that "we feel other's emotions, energy and physical symptoms in our bodies without the usual defense that most people have." Dr. Judiff Orloff is a psychiatrist and empath, both physical and emotional.

So she speaks from her own experiences. For example, a physical empath passing by a person who has pain suddenly feels this pain in his or her own body. Emotional empath feels all the energy of the environment and also takes others feelings as its own. For empaths is very important to be in a loving and joyous atmosphere, then they can function very well. When they are in an environment with negative energy and people who are dismissive or depressed, those people drain from them a lot of energy. Empaths are very loving and openhearted human beings. They give away their own energy to people to make them feel better. As a result, they tend to forget about themselves and not having adequate energetic protection, and then they'll feel like they have lost their own energy. I remember this feeling when I was in the Agape Community. As I mentioned before that being with the people there, I felt many times like I had lost my own energy. But not because I invested my energy wrongly as Rodolfo said, but I didn't protect myself as an empath. I didn't know that I was one of them and didn't have guidance how to protect my own energy at that time. My heart was so open and wanted to be for everyone that my energy was sucked out from me by others. It was too much for me, and one day, I decided not to go back. Leaving Agape Community, I felt at the beginning that I betrayed myself. First of all, claiming that I wanted to be an Agape license practitioner. It gave me the courage to take a Greyhound bus from New York City to Los Angeles to be around the community. Second, I got a lot through this community. I really loved being there, and I stayed in communication with people who I met there. I learned how to be more aware of myself and beliefs with which I grew up through the workshops. It was a huge step forward. But when DeAnna sang a song during the Sunday services, my tears started falling down. This song spoke to my heart. I realized that I was sabotaging myself by stopping to write my book and I left. It was last time when I was on the service.

At that time when I decided to leave Agape International Spiritual Center, I thought that I was imagining things. But now I know that my decision was right. My Inner Being was protecting me from things that didn't serve me and didn't understand. I really wanted to evolve and know the true God. I wanted to have an actual personal experience. My soul was yearning for this divine communion. Later I understood that Agape International Spiritual Center was the first step of my spiritual growth. The true understanding and guidance as a soul and person, I received from Self-Realization Fellowship teachings. When I started practicing lessons, I understood more. Also, participating in Self-Realization Fellowship services and watching recordings during lockdown helped me to obtain more and more awareness of self-realization and real communion with God as a Consciousness within me.

Dr. Judith Orloff described how empaths sense the energy of the environment. When they approach a room, they know what is going on. They sense everything. They see the bigger picture. Regular person have perceptions based on their experiences, on what they see or hear. The empaths feel harmony or disharmony in the environment without looking in it. Also the empaths don't like to be around a lot of people because their way of being can overwhelmed them. As I mentioned before, when the environment is positive and harmonious, they can really feel good. But when it is too much mixed energy and loud, it can be too overwhelming. And many times I was feeling that way. The empaths are like a sponge, and they are vulnerable in their way of being.

As I listened to the CDs, everything started becoming clear to me. I remembered one of the supportive persons on ayahuasca ceremony telling me that I was very sensitive to the higher energies. At that time I thought, *So what, what was special about that?* Another thing was recognizing energies in the grocery stores and other places, also reluctance being in places where there were a lot of people governed in one space, feeling nervousness and division at the JFK airport right away when I landed.

Later on, this feeling was confirmed by my observance and listening to what the people were talking about. The Americans deal with the division all the time, and they cannot find solution. For sure, letting people by law keep guns in their homes will not prevent homicides at schools and on the streets. Violence and fear attracts more violence and fear. We need to learn how to trust Life again. Affirmation is the best thing to start right away for feeling safe when we are walking, doing errands, or working. For example, "I am always safe," "Wherever I go, I am safe," "I can trust life, life is good," "I am protected," "I am divinely guided to the places where I am safe," and so on. Positive affirmation is the best conversation with ourselves, then we can attract only safe conditions in our lives and people who we can trust. Affirmation, repeated over and over, gives peace to our mind when we are not able to sit and find peace in meditation because we are at work or other places. Gratitude and appreciation, allowing Life gives us better experiences and leads us to the truth who we are and what gifts we brought to the world this time.

From Dr. Judith Orloff, I found out that empaths don't need big doses of medicine like the others receive. That's why a small dose of one pill kept my body intact even when my doctors in Poland told me that it was impossible. Also, she mentioned that empaths are people who take on themselves clearing all family generation karma. That's why I went to all the workshops and I was looking for solutions that are not conventional. I took a lot for myself so posterity of my family can live fulfilled and happy lives without violence and addictions in their homes. It is good to start healing your life because you can heal patterns that are repeated for ages in your family. It is not only about you when you take these steps for yourself. Everyone wants to be loved, respected, and fulfilled. Good to know that our healing brings healing to the planet Earth in the next generations and also that the karma patterns in our families will be healed. Our deceased ancestors count on us. Souls who chose to be children or young person who died in accidents or passed away because of illness were very brave souls. They chose this way to heal family patterns that have been going on for several incarnations. We cannot see this way from our human perspective because we were taught about unfairness, lack of love, sin, guilt, and grief. We were warned to protect ourselves from each other to survive in this life, be detached from our feelings, and close our hearts. Nobody taught as that every sudden death has a bigger meaning: one on the family plane and the other on the global community. We saw how people gathered on the streets when an African American man was killed by a policeman in the US. People saw it as unfair and a family loss. That accident brought the family to the higher level of forgiveness, and also human consciousness was evolving on the global manner. That means more responsibility for individual choices, forgiveness to ourselves (we do mistakes all the time, and we judge ourselves badly for everything instead of being forgiving our own slips), more love, more tolerance and equality in our lives.

Forget what you were taught about death by your families and by religious dogmas. The journey on the planet Earth is a soul evolution always to love. It is love to yourself, another member of your family, or community. You can call people as an enemy and point out their behaviors, but this people are the best blessing for you. We need to remember that who we treat as an enemy was hurt also in the past and their behavior is to protect themselves, not to be hurt again. There are many reasons people act in the certain way, and we cannot understand them. It is only a calling for love from you, and these people are not even aware of that. They are really lost in their pain and separation from themselves. When a child dies, don't waste their death by holding grief in your hearts. You chose this experience before you appeared on the Earth: to heal yourself, by forgiving and loving. The parents who chose healing this way, they are the faster in evolving their souls. It was a way for their souls to bring evolution to themselves and their nearest families. From an earthy realm, we can see it as a painful experience, and IT IS. But when we realize that every incarnation is for the soul to evolve to their highest potential of unconditional love, we can find this love and compassion for ourselves then. It is not an easy path to open your heart to yourself instead of holding on to the wound and dying every time when the death anniversary comes. Many times parents keep guilt when the child dies because, in their minds, they didn't do enough so that their kid wouldn't die. There are no coincidences in being revived or not. This soul, who was your child, still lives, and you can communicate with them every day. From being in Agape classes, I met a person who was communicating via mediumship with her deceased son, who explained to her about life after life, and she shared that with audience. We need to realize that we are here only for a while to evolve as a soul, so enjoy your lives and release the past.

I had in my hand the booklet from the book by Robert Schwartz, *Your Soul's Plan*. For those who suffer from loss of their loved ones, you will find the answers there. Only be receptive to the message that is given to you. Remember, when your mind starts denying it and talking to yourself that it is impossible, it means that you forgot your Divine nature and origin. For those who are reading with open mind, life becomes more meaningful and makes more sense.

When I was in Tamascal Park with girls for Queen Up Your Act, one of the girls who stayed with me in the same cabin told us that when she was reading this book, she was crying because she started remembering everything. There is another book written by Neale Donald Walsch, *Little Soul and the Sun: A Children's Parable*, that children remember who they are and parents will be able to remembered too.

What more did I learn listening to Dr. Judith Orloff's book? That an empath can be a great healer. She said, "We don't need more entrepreneurs we need more healers right now." Nowadays, the empaths are the blessing to the world. The new communities of healers start being created to heal people individually and collectively so energy would be lifted up in the world. Those who are on their path to become a healer need to learn how to embrace sensitivity and activate their gift to heal the planet Earth faster.

Another thing that I discovered listening to Dr. Orloff's book that the empaths choose people to keep their distance so as to keep their energetic filed clean. I noticed that I really enjoyed when I was in a new place by myself to explore and sense the environment. Also I realized that being here at the beginning, I spoke very clearly and fluently when it was about important things which I was interested in. The things I said could change another person's day or even life by looking differently in their situation. Life is really good. When people were not interested in and were looking for connection in small things like cooking and how delicious it was or what was a beautiful weather, I started forgetting words and I shut myself down. The weather for me was to sense and enjoy. It didn't matter if it was raining or shinning. While cooking for me was to give healthy fuel to my body, nothing else. I taught myself how to choose food intuitively, or my body taught me how to be connected to it when I am choosing food. That something is stated organic doesn't mean that my body would love to have it as a fuel. A lot of things are exaggerated here. Sometimes the word "organic" on the label doesn't mean that is edible for the body. Every time I choose food intuitively, it turns out that it is the purest it could be. I avoid reading ingredients on the labels because it stops shopping from being enjoyable. I put out the intention that I would choose the best food for my body, and I say thank you after it is done. Thanks to that, I know that I would be attracted to the food my body would need to receive for good-quality fuel. Thanks to that, shopping lasts shorter as well. Most people who want to eat healthy food choose it by reading labels. Their minds are tools that logically choose nourishment based on that they are told what they're supposed to eat or drink from outside sources such as magazines, TV nutrition programs, or nutritionists. All are good, but our bodies know what is the best for them at the exact moment without being overloaded with information about what products people buy (such as supplements) or counting calories. Their choices are what is written on the sticker and not always what the body needs at that time. We all can learn from our bodies how to choose the best food for ourselves. The healthy food industry has become a new machine to earn money. Mostly people in the United States are unaware that they overpay for food that's called organic. In many countries, good-quality food is a norm, and the prices for it are regular; they don't make customers to overpay for it. We need to remember that our intuition also guides us to the right food for our bodies at every moment. It is possible that each time, we choose differently. We are attracted to certain shelves or certain colors on the packages without making a mistake; we are doing the right thing. Everyone has a different body, and every body can communicate differently likewise by intuitive feeling, like when we touch a grocery product we want to buy. Becoming aware and tuned to our bodies is all that we need. So instead of reading labels, I choose to enjoy shopping and be aware of my body's signals to every product that I am attracted to or touch when I want to purchase. I love this exploration.

    Likewise, I received another explanation as to why my attention was subconsciously directed to the men who I wouldn't have intimacy with. They were attracted to me, but they were in their own relationships. Intimate contact is not easy for the empath. They are like a sponge and absorb other people's energies. When I was listening to Dr. Judy Orloff, I understood my behavior more and more. My awareness was attracting men whose ways of being weren't for me. They would not respect my boundaries as I wanted them to. Subconsciously I was protecting myself from emotional pain as an empath who was vulnerable. My mind and body soak everything more deeply than others. Having emotional pain after my marriage and being like a sponge for other's emotions, I was choosing subconsciously to avoid men who would be interested in a relationship with me. On the other hand, growing in a society where being in a relationship was the most important thing, I decided not to be involved in any. Really, I was thankful for my common sense, but I didn't know why at that time. I felt like a victim, but the truth is that I created these encounters only to trust and listen to my intuition to receive all the answers when I would be ready to accept, adopt them, and be ready for a meaningful relationship without unnecessary pain. At the end of Dr Judy Orloff's book, I stopped judging myself, only appreciating being open to knowing myself and digging deeper and deeper. It is precious to know thyself.

Many people use sex to release their own stress, instead of clearing themselves from the day before going to their bedrooms. Some of them drink, smoke, and treat their partners as another toy to play with. Their bodies are soaked with nicotine and alcohol. They disrespect themselves and their partners in the alcove. Every person can be overwhelmed by this kind of treatment, but the empaths sense even more and mix their sensitivities with their partner's moods and absorb all as their own. When the partner is loving and joyful, it serves intimacy and a healthy psyche, but when the partner wants to release all the stress and anger into your body, it can cause a lot of emotional disorder in your whole being. It can be a feeling of being dirty, angry, or emotionally unsatisfied. After a while, your body can start ailing because you soaked in all your partner's stress and emotional pain. An empath's body is infinitely absorbent sponge. We need to start treating sex us connection between two divine beings, to treat each other with love and affection, not as a way of performance or releasing our daily problems. Our bodies are very sensitive to the way we nurse them and how we let it be treated by others.

Once my friend asked about a sentence that is repeated during wedding ceremonies probably in every religion: "Until death do us apart." The words that came out from me was that *people translate this vow very literally. They think that death means only when the body dies. The truth is that death appears also when the marriage doesn't function well. Life is to evolve, and when there is no opportunity that partners can expand, the relationship comes to death.* People, instead of feeling alive in their marriages, feel like a dead person. There are only obligations toward one another. They don't have any excitement growing in their marriages. In some relationships, people, to get some excitement, start to quarrel. This kind of excitement doesn't serve to anyone and our bodies. We need to realize that God doesn't look at us and beholds the wedding ceremony. He is us. The guests and family are the witnesses, and we want to please them and convince ourselves that it is time for us to get married even though we are not ready yet. The parties that we throw after the wedding are for guests, not for God or even us. He responses to pure love in our hearts. He doesn't need alcohol and other addictive substances to have fun and celebrate the event. When we drink, smoke, or dance, we think that there is no God with us. Unless we are aware of that, we work hard to please our society to become a good husband or wife. In most cases, it doesn't work, and we don't know why. We only have it in our minds to satisfy others like our family, who believe in us and want us to be happy. But they don't know that marriage is not the only way to happiness. This is only a societal belief. God knows that, and He warns us by sending a thought: *Don't do it, You will not be happy, You are not ready yet, "You don't know everything, or Let it go and don't marry this person because you are not for each other.* But we don't listen to the Spirit. We listen to our parents or aunts who made the same mistakes. When we are at the altar and speak the words of the vow, we put a cross on our shoulders. God is with us even then. His will for our happiness was rejected, and He has to wait patiently until we understand our mistake and allow Him to help us rise up. At the moment we decide by ourselves to listen to others instead of our inner voice, He starts agreeing with us. Our will becomes God's will. And through the law of attraction, He gives us what our thoughts and beliefs are about marriage and life in general, absorbed from our society. He tries to be in communion with us and protects us even in the worst-case scenarios in our lives, but mostly we still do not respond to it. Due to misunderstanding the word "death," there are so many unhappy relationships kept till partners end their lives. On the other hand, people who are divorced mostly feel guilt and put on themselves a name tag that says, "I am a failure," not knowing that it was made up by society. They don't let themselves to be open and happy in a new and more fulfilling relationship. They are afraid that they would fail or that their partners would hurt them again. They promised in front of everyone that their first marriage would last forever, and the relationship didn't survive. They blame themselves by thinking or using statements such as "*I should have done it or said it,*" "*I could be better,*" "*If I only knew, I would've made myself more available,*" "*If I do more,*" "*If I could be more polite,*" and "*If I only did this or that, for sure my marriage would've worked out.*" Those people live in the past, unaware that they do the same mistakes over and over without knowing that none of those relationships would work out from very beginning. We cannot to make up for things or words we have done or said in the past and make people happy again without realizing that we married a younger version of our mother or father in a body that looks different and that we behave as our parents did in their relationships. So it is impossible that our marriages would be happy unless we break the chain by stopping ourselves from duplicating their way of being toward ourselves and our partners. First, we need to stop treating ourselves like someone who is unworthy of being loved or enjoying their own life. We need to know that behind the words "*I am a failure*" is huge guilt and "*I am not good enough to be happy.*" All these things are made up by our societies—a human mind—and not by our Creator. He always wants happiness for us.

The truth is that the only damage we can commit is when we betray ourselves, when we sacrifice ourselves to make something work knowing that it would never do. We lose ourselves by trying to make up to our partners. We act against Life. We often fake love to our partners to survive in relationships that don't work. We blame partners. We compromise with them, and very often we cannot look at our eyes because we know that this is a huge lie. We afraid to be honest with ourselves because it would push us to tell the truth and make changes in our lives. God is with us during the wedding ceremony and in the divorce. In both cases, we have blessings from Him. Sometimes more often He blesses us when we stop proving how good we are and let go of what doesn't serve anymore. He will take care of us. Divorcing or splitting the relationship is the best thing that can happen to people who don't fall for each other. They have possibility to grow in the different environment and meet the right person for themselves. Spirit is in each of us, and He didn't choose stagnation on planet Earth, only evolving for us. We have right to be happy with other people who really care about us and respect us and our choices, people who celebrate our mutual individuality. It is really precious when we start feeling love again. This feeling fills our whole being. It is natural way of Life: to be in love. When we ask, our Creator will release us from any guilt and shame that we keep consciously or subconsciously. Thanks to that, we will be free from them, and we will stop caring about what our environment thinks about us. This gives us unlimited freedom to make our own choices in harmony with our souls and inner voice. We never meet the expectations of others, so it doesn't matter how much we try to please them. Everyone has only one responsibility: to be happy in their own lives, which means to stop listening to others and make communion with themselves. This will bring true happiness and peace into their and our world. One day, I found Louise Hay's "Meditation for Building Self-Esteem" on her website www.louisehay.com, which resonated with me to let me move forward when I started to build my small business as a Heal Your Life leader and Reiki healer:

> *No person, place, or thing has any power over me unless I give it, for I am the only thinker in my mind. I have immense freedom in that I can choose what to think. I can choose to see life in positive ways instead of complaining or being mad at myself or other people. Complaining about what I do not have is one way to handle a situation, but it does*

not change anything. When I love myself and find myself in the midst of a negative situation, I can say something such as, "I am willing to release the pattern in my consciousness that contributed to this condition." I have made negative choices in the past, but this does not mean that I am a bad person, nor am I stuck with these negative choices. I release old judgments and love myself unconditionally.

How to start? First and foremost, we need to be honest with ourselves. Ask the following questions:

- ♥ What was the reason that I have become so judgmental, angry, and gossiping person?
  Sample answer: *In my environment, everyone behave that way.*
- ♥ When did I start believing that fear prevailed over life?
  Sample answer: *I was warned by my family. They taught me that life is difficult and dangerous. They say: 'You are not good enough to win with your life. You are not capable to do it'.*
- ♥ What happened that made me feel nothing inside, that I feel more like a dead person?
  Sample answer: *I needed to compromise my life with others, and this put me into the space of emptiness and not being fulfilled.*
- ♥ Who told me that life is grieving instead of loving? What did I see or experience that made me believe in it?
  Sample answer: *I saw how people react around me to the death, and I accepted that grief is only what we can experience or in my culture, understanding of the death is the end of life and we are losing our beloved ones. Death is unfairness. Good people die, and the bad are still among us.*
- ♥ When did I start believing that life cannot be filled with happiness?
  Sample answer: *I was hurt so many times that I gave up. I don't feel happiness any more.*

- ♥ What is the reason that I feel only regret and bitterness?
  Sample answer: Nothing good is happening in my life. I feel like I am invisible for others.
- ♥ When did I lose faith in life and said that this is the way it is and I cannot do anything with it?
  Sample answer: Every time when I tried something new, I failed in it. I am not skilled enough.
- ♥ When did I start believing that my life has no meaning?
  Sample answer: Whatever I did for others wasn't appreciated. They took me for granted.
- ♥ When did I give my power to others that I feel powerless now?
  Sample answer: I always ask for advice from others because I don't know everything. I am afraid of making my own choices.
- ♥ When did I start telling myself that I am not good enough and I am hopeless?
  Sample answer: I heard this many times from my mother, and she is always right.
- ♥ What happened or what I am telling myself that I feel stuck and feel less and less?
  Sample answer: I am afraid of failing and taking responsibility for my life.
- ♥ Who did I listen to that I don't believe that life can be changed for better, and because of that, I don't even try?
  Sample answer: Everybody make jokes of me and told me that this is impossible.
- ♥ How long have I been waiting for change and nothing happened?
  Sample answer: I hope that life would change for me. I do not know how, but I still believe. I cannot do anything with that it is right now. I need to wait for better times. I hope that it will come one day.
- ♥ What am I telling to myself that I am afraid moving forward?
  Sample answer: I am waiting for the right moment. I cannot do anything right now. This is not a good time for change.

- ♥ What is the reason that I am afraid of life and see enemies in everybody, even in my own family?
  Sample answer: I am afraid of life because people are unfriendly. Everybody pushes me and tells me what I am supposed to do or not do. They drive me crazy. I cannot talk openly to certain members of my family because they don't like me. They judge me all the time.
- ♥ What does determine my behavior toward other people? What is my gain?
  Sample answer: It depends on the other person's behavior toward me. I give back that I receive. When people treat me well, I treat them with respect. When they attack me, I behave the same. I don't like when people take advantage on me. I fight.
- ♥ What beliefs I keep about myself?
  Sample answer: I am not good enough, I don't know how to do many things, I am a failure, nobody wants me, and I am a phony person. Love and success are not for me. It is too late.
- ♥ When did I start believing that I do not matter?
  Sample answer: When I noticed that nobody paid attention to what I said. They didn't listen and believe me. I was omitted many times.

When you answer the above questions for yourself, will you be able to consider that your beliefs about life and yourself are not true? Will you give yourself one more chance, knowing that it was only your thoughts and feedback from your closest family members who acted in disrespectful ways toward you that made you believe that you deserve being treated that way and cannot do anything about it? Your view of yourself and life is through the prism of what your family told you. If they said that you cannot change your life, you start believing that you cannot. When they told you that you don't do enough and compare you with others, you believe that there is something wrong with you. You took their negative feedback and words and take it as something that's true about yourself. What would your life look like if you transform these negative beliefs into positive ones? How would it be for you to find yourself again and rediscover life anew? What new possibilities would this to bring to your life? Can you imagine that life would look totally different from what you see and experience right now? Do you know that you have power over your destiny right now by changing thought patterns to experience yourself in a different way?

When we look at our lives in the objective way, we can see that our past accomplishments and behaviors were nothing but expression of love in the way we knew how to love, act, and react. Every time we remember people who weren't happy because of our way of being and they didn't appreciate us and the things we did right, remember that they were focused only on what we did wrong or didn't do at all. They started blaming us for things we didn't understand or not doing their way. Their lack of self-control made us to believe that everything that was wrong was our fault. We tried to please them to hear something good about us and stop being punished for things that weren't even relevant to merit that kind of reaction from them, which was exaggerated. Those parents or close ones acted that way only to make us believe that they were right and had a justification for their own bad behavior. Sometimes they used the power over us as an adult person to feel an unhealthy satisfaction from blaming us for their unsuccessful lives. As a result, we started doubting in ourselves, giving up on ourselves, blaming ourselves, and having negative thoughts patterns. Through the law of attraction, Life brings to our experiences only things and situations we expect to receive as negative beliefs. The more we experience similar situations, the more we believe that life is really bad and unfair to us. We blame ourselves for not being good enough and wise in our life choices, and we start punishing ourselves for making another wrong decision, which cuts us off from our good outcome in life endeavors. We made decisions based on what other people would have done in our situation, and therefore, we disconnected ourselves from our Source of Life.

What if, instead of the above negative answers, you start using more positive ones as affirmations and start using your imagination to create your life in a harmonious way to evolve and expand?

Will you try speaking to yourself in a kinder, more loving, and less judgmental way? For example, instead of repeating to yourself, "*Nothing good is happening in my life. I feel like I am invisible for others,*" you can learn to affirm constantly, "*I am capable of finding good things in my life. My life becomes more colorful day by day. People only reflect to me what I believe about myself. I am a loving, joyous, and wonderful person.*" Or you can try this one:

> *I know that I am a pure Spirit that I always have been and I always will be. There is inside in me a place of confidence and quietness and security, where all things are known and understood. This is the Universal Mind, God which I am a part… Through the Great Law of Attraction everything in my life what I need for my work and fulfillment will come to me. It is not necessary that I strain about this. Only believe, for I am strengthen in my belief, my faith it would make it so… I enjoy life for each day forth brings a constant demonstration of the power and wonder of the Universe and myself. I am confident. I am serene and sure.* (from *Three Magic Words* by Uell Stanley Andersen)

Here are a few questions in which we can use our imagination:

- ♥ *What would be like if I feel alive again?*

   Let yourself feel it now. Don't be afraid. Let this feeling in. Feel it with all your being. Doesn't matter if doubts come up. Soak in that aliveness. Indulge yourself with this loving feeling. Bathe in it with the whole you. This feeling is True you—free, loving, and happy without boundaries. Enjoy this moment.

- ♥ *What would I do that time?*

   Feeling this aliveness and love, describe to yourself what really matters to you. What kind of work would you like to have, where you feel fully expressed? Maybe you will remember your dream from your childhood or later years and you were afraid to move toward your dream for some reasons at that time. Don't be afraid to describe in detail what kind of life you would like to live. What kind of person you would like to become and what kind of people you would love to be surrounded. You know that you deserve the best. It is True You who feels this joy when you are dreaming. When you need to speak aloud to yourself about things that matter to you, do this! It is good to hear your own voice. You will see yourself different: as a very valuable wise person. Love this person unconditionally. This is You. Write it down to remind yourself every single day. You do matter and all that you do!

♥ *How would I feel being that alive, loving person every single day?*

Say to yourself and write it down. It is so precious when we wake up in the morning and we feel good about ourselves and life. Doesn't matter what others do or think. They have the same issues with self-worth and negative thinking that we have had. When you doubt in your truth, reread again and again what you have written and keep faith that it was answered. These things matter to you. God is with you always. He responded to the asked questions through you. He wants you to wake up and regain your own power. He is the cause behind you reading this book. He has been guiding you to this title so that you can find the truth about yourself and how you can change your life. Life speaks to you right now. This is your life, no one else's. You can bound relationship with God and His desires for you, or you can listen to people from your environment who very often told you, "No, you cannot do this or that." Due to that, you repeat to yourself, "No, I can't do that. This is improper. How can I manage by myself? What others would say if they find out?" Our thoughts and words have the power to determine our choices.

- *What am I willing to let go?*

  Answer honestly what you willing to let go of. Maybe it is the word "no" to yourself and replace with "yes." Then you see how life can be enjoyable. Because of that, you can become more tolerant person and you let others to experience their lives in their own precious way. Maybe you need to let go of judging yourself. You would notice that instead of judging, you will feel more love for yourself and others. Maybe you need to let go of meddling in others' lives and take care of your own. It is so liberating when we let other people live their own lives. Then you can realize that you are not responsible for them except for yourself. You are free to make your own choices. Maybe you need to let go of complaining about everything, such as yourself, family, job, and the world around you and replacing it with looking for good things. When you don't know, what is it that you need to let go of right now, ask about guidance and life will show you. How? Probably you will know right away to what you are the most attached and you don' t want to let it out from your hands. Might you will receive a thought, what it is. It can be an unpredictable situation, and you will see your reaction to it. It can be inner feeling or a voice from nowhere. The guidance can be in the words of the song. You can notice a huge poster with the exact words that you need to see. Our resistance to new things or situations speaks to us mostly. The words that we say or the way we behave determine if we are in space of love or fear.

The dreaming starts from the awareness that our lives can be changed. Then we ask these questions: What do we like? What do we love to do in our lives as occupation? What is the reason for our presence here on the planet Earth? And thanks to that, the journey to your greatness has started right away. We all are the same. Be honest with yourself. This lets you get back your True Power that you lost on the way and love to Life. Follow your inner guidance to things that are important to you, and every day will become filled with love and joy. You will meet people who are like yourself. You will combine your heart with them. They will be your new community who support each other in their dreams and adventures.

Every time we need to remind ourselves that we have the right to be the way we are from very beginning of our journey. Our minds were taught since we were kids to compare ourselves to others all the time. There is nothing wrong with us. The deep acceptance of this fact only can bring us to unconditional love of ourselves and overflow to others.

Once, I received an email from the Los Angeles City Council regarding the Angeleno card. I was informed that the mayor of Los Angeles gained more funds because of the pandemic, and I received the card, which allowed me to pay my rent. It was a one-time support from the city. I was grateful for how Life supplied me with the money without borrowing after losing the job. I had everything that I needed to write my book, evolve in English, and continue my spiritual endeavour with Kriya Yoga and my connection with the Spirit. It was precious. I felt at peace and trusted that everything would work out for my highest good.

At that time, I took a break from the Introduction Leaders Program because Landmark Worldwide, LLC, suspended all their courses in late March 2020. Four months later, the programs were relaunched one after another on Zoom. My Zoom Introduction Leaders Program started on July 30, 2020 and finished on April 9, 2021. The course contained weekly evening classes, assisting agreements in which we had a lot of breakthroughs for ourselves by calling our friends and families. Also in the program, we had four weekends in which we were on Zoom all day long. It was a lot of fun and there was a lot of connection between participants. We learned from one another and enjoyed being all together.

I remember when we watched a video on our first Friday class of the program at the end of February 2020. It was mentioned that every Introduction Leaders Program was led in a certain way, so the one that would start in 2020 would be totally different and new. The leaders who led the weekends told us that they would lead this program like it would be their first time even though they had led for over decades. When we were introduced to new content, nobody could predict that the massage would be given in a different way—by internet without personal touch. Everything was virtual. I believe it was really convenient for every participant of the program. We saved a lot of time without getting to the Landmark Center and having to go back home late. We really were all blessed because of that, and the whole program cost me only $100. Relaunching the Introduction Leaders Program made me really think about why I wanted to participate in the course. I reattended the program without any expectations and promised myself to participate more actively than in other Landmark courses. It was a huge breakthrough for me during this program.

I danced with nearly two hundred American women to their favorite hits and felt a connection with them on Queen Up Your Act in 2018, and two years later, I wanted feel a connection with the participants of the Introduction Leaders Program by sharing about myself, being supportive to them, and being open to receive support. It allowed us to have breakthroughs in our lives and by sharing about ourselves individually to others who deal with their own issues and don't know that they have choice to live differently and become a compass for others to change their lives. The transformation can occur only this way—as a ripple in the pond, one after another.

One day I realized that I had started being interested in people's lives here. Being on the Introduction Leaders Program, I regained enough courage and confidence to ask questions about them or their lives. I started loving learning more and more. I began to admire the cultural diversity in the United States. I have faced adversity here and praised them because it gave me back my own power to deal with my own circumstances. Thanks to that, I started reaching out to more and more people. As a result, I was evolving and becoming more confidant in settling down here without giving up on myself and my heart desire's to grow and be connected, knowing that I can make difference in other people's lives in the place where I was right now. The most important thing was I started regaining my self-esteem, which I lost after I came to the United States by putting into my head the idea that something was wrong with me because I didn't speak

English fluently and because I was not able to meet my needs the way my family wanted me to. I was on my journey to transformation, and my courage was awarded every time in the form of better income, respect toward myself, and the ability to learn, grow, and experience life more in me.

Several times I was at the Beverly Hills library. When I walked in there the first time, I was astonished at the space and the ambiance it had. Once, I met a young woman there, and I started asking her questions about her work and how she was doing. When we were chatting, I noticed on the woman's face resignation and boredom. I asked her for her name. She told me in her language. Since I have learned that every name has a meaning, including mine, I asked about the translation of her name into English. She translated her name. The name was *Dream*. I was stunned. She had such vivid name, telling both of us how we were supposed to live our lives.

We can see a lot of people sick in the hospitals. They don't see any link between their thoughts, the way they treat themselves, and their diseases. People put themselves into those beds by giving away the power to others and through their own thoughts, which created illnesses in their bodies. They are reaching out to the doctors for miracles. Most of them listen to the doctors and give up on themselves after hearing a negative diagnosis by a doctor. They are fearful and powerless, forgetting that all the healing power is in them. There is only one condition to be healed. We need to stop doing what brought us to this experience, which is lack of awaremess, unhealthy thought patterns and beliefs about disease, among others, and that this is the outside cause. We are one with our Creator. We have His power, which can give us the best life ever in a healthy body or kill us one after another. What will you choose for yourself? Are you still afraid of letting go of things and thoughts that don't serve you anymore to be healthy and happy? Or you will start trusting the process of life and release everything that's out-of-date and all the authorities to become the only authority for yourself by communion with the Creator within you?

We all were children full of expression, joy, and curiosity. Every day was a new adventure. Life was safe for us. When we started adult life, we had so many ideas and hope that everything would work out and everything would be possible. We trusted and had huge faith. Suddenly, one day we stopped believing in good and in ourselves. We started listening to others and comparing one to each other. Maybe we failed in something and we said to ourselves that we don't deserve better life unknowing that it was only experience for us to learn. We determined ourselves as the failures and decided to play small to feel safe and unhappy. We started turning from a happy, full-of-life person to a bitter old one, full of duties and never fulfilled. Our attention went to things that didn't work, and then we started having more and more experiences that wouldn't work. Some people say that life sucks. But life is the same like it was before: full of air, full of good surprises. Nature is still lavish. Life still gives as possibility to invent and grow, meet new people, see new places. All is for us. Only our minds have narrowed and don't see the possibilities. What is the worst thing that could happen to an immortal soul that had started identify with the physical body and believed in things like aging? Don't you think that it is ironic? By erroneous thinking, we believe that life is ending when our body reaches some kind of age. We forgot that our body is a vehicle or a cloak through which Spirit expresses Itself, creating illusion of being recognized through five senses. Body is not source of all. Source of All gives life to the body and maintain it. And when time comes, the body is released by the soul, to let it come back to eternity to Real Life. Identifying with the body, we live in illusion not knowing anything about True Reality. Many people say to us, "I live in reality and I am realistic." What do they mean by that? Do they know who they are? Do they see True Life? Mostly, what they mean by telling this is that life is the way it is. I need to go to work, to pay bills; I have children, I need to focus on them; I don't have time, my husband or wife won't let me; etc. They sound like they don't have a choice. They believe that they have to live that kind of life. They got used to it. They use that term with resignation and sometimes with desperation, which has nothing common with Real Life. We are the *Word*: *"In the beginning was the Word, and the Word was with God, and the Word was God."*

Why don't we start looking in Life with childish enthusiasm and trust that all is possible, give another chance to ourselves, and start believing in ourselves? Start cocreating again the best version of ourselves. Sit behind the wheels of adventure, take a risk, and see where it leads us. Let's taste how much we can trust life and surrender to it and be the role model for our children and people who we love and lead them to their own greatness. New aliveness is waking up in us, and the Light in us again starts to shine.

> *I am beyond everything finite…I am the stars, I am the waves, I am the Life of all; I am the laughter within all hearts, I am the smile on the faces of flowers and in each soul. I am the Wisdom and Power that sustain all creation.*
>
> *—Paramahansa Yogananda*

CHAPTER 10

What Is Your Calling?

I open my heart to receive the Love of the Holy Presence. It descends upon me, and enfolds me now. I feel it's warmth and sweet abiding love. I let compassion well up in me for myself and for others. I turn to this Divine Holy Presence to honor my true nature and the true nature of others.

—*Agape International Spiritual Center*

When we start being aware of ourselves, we begin to realize that a lot of the beliefs we carry come from people we trusted the most. Also, we repeat automatically out-of-date proverbs, which only create in our experience unfairness and diminish our greatness to justify our unwillingness to change. At the beginning, when I started awakening through the self-awareness classes, I realized that my judgment about men was based on only one person: my ex-husband. I had an "Aha!" moment when I was sitting on the bus. I received an unexpected thought that people think men who respect their mothers are mollycoddles. When I noticed this, I asked myself for very first time, "Okay, Magdalena, and what do you think about men?" After a while, I realized that these were my thoughts. Knowing that I am the only person who is responsible for these thoughts, I acknowledged them as my beliefs. At that time, I didn't know from who and when they came into my awareness. Even though I was often treated disrespectfully by my stepfather, I really love my male peers. We really enjoyed time with one another, and we respected ourselves the best we could. After four years on the path of self-awareness, I remembered the moment when my ex-husband said this. It was in Spain when I was nineteen years old, and we had just met. He said this toward another man, my cousin's friend who loved to spend time with his mother and sister. He could afford for fully exclusive trips abroad and that he traveled with his two favorite women. I realized that my partner was jealous of him. At that period of time, I started believing in my partner's nonsense unknowingly even though I had very good experiences with other men and people in general. The only person who I was not able to communicate with was him. I was so naive and believed in everything that he said about me and other people without realizing that he had a lot of behavioral issues toward men and his mother. It reflected in his relationships with other women. Looking back, I can see now how jealous he was. Another one of his beliefs was that rich men are bad and disrespectful, not recognizing his own behavior toward me and his son. His jealousy, lack of self-esteem, and disrespect toward women impacted his friendships with the men who helped him a lot in his work and led to unnecessary pain in his own small family including himself. It is very important to recognize the core beliefs and who or what implanted them into our subconscious mind. We need to ask, "Are these beliefs ours, and do they unite or divide?" My ex-husband's behavior was dictated by his small-town environment, in which was accepted credence that by fighting and being disrespectful, they would be winners. We have a lot of men who were harmed by this type of upbringing and by outdated proverbs such as "Men do not cry; only women do it" or "You cry like a woman; be a man." These were expressions used on the little boys, who were innocent children. This kind of saying still continues to be said in many environments nowadays, making men emotionally immature. They weren't allowed to openly express their emotions by crying or even screaming their pain, fear, or loss as a child and later as an adult person. It can cause aggression and a detachment from emotions. Add dissatisfaction, a lack of control, and alcohol in the mixture, and we have ready-made domestic violence and mental abuse. Do we still want this?

Most women agree to this kind of treatment by their husbands because they don't know that they have a choice. That's why it is very important to rebuild self-worth. We are missing nothing. A lack of self-love and respect causes disharmony in our homes, bodies, and the world. We need to distinguish life and people who we are surrounded with or married to. Life gives us good experiences all the time and moves us toward new things. We receive support, help, kindness, love, and a smile from a passerby all the time. We obtain jobs to pay our bills, we get a raise at work, and we have new cars, homes, and children. Also, we are fired to be able to move to the better work opportunity or open our own business, changing our current occupation for a completely new one to thrive. So why do we take as a granted belief that life is against us and bad? The people who we are surrounded with give us a feeling of being overwhelmed and less. That's why, without discrimination, we call life bad instead of being willing to change and letting go of the environment with people who don't serve our growth and only put us down. When looking at life in this way, we can discern that we have had moments of triumph in our experiences. We felt powerful and appreciated. Now it is time to regain this power. There is so much love and wisdom in us. We keep them away from ourselves and others by denying our excellence.

Once I had a conversation with my friend Kirin about the expression "I am sorry." I said from nowhere that *the word "sorry" is used too much*. In my own opinion, it has no meaning for many people. We use it automatically because it is accepted by society. We know that every time saying "Sorry," we would be known as a good brought-up person. However, when we use this word too much in every situation, we start feeling less and less. Many people feels sorry that exist, as a result of bringing-up or past experiences which determined about their self-esteem. Every time I said "sorry" because the door was slammed or in other small situation to be kind, I felt guilty without reason. Noticing that, I decided to use more often the words "thank you" in this kind of situation rather than "sorry." For example, "I am thankful or happy that nothing happened. Next time I will be more focused." When we say it that way, we feel good without negative emotions, and our subconscious mind catches and gives us possibility to be more focused and aware.

When we do shopping in grocery or department stores, how many times have we used "I am sorry" or, casually, "Sorry" only because we went in other people's space. The store is a public space, and the shoppers don't own it. When we cut in front of a person, we usually say sorry and go back with the feeling of shame that we were rushing. As a result, we don't notice the person in the first place, or we can say, "Thank you for being patient and understanding. I am learning how to do things without rush" or whatever reason it was. The words "*thank you*" give us and another person to feel appreciation. We are gifts for each other. Both parties start feeling good about themselves, and really good conversation can be brought it up because of that. The word "sorry" makes us wrong and think that we owe somebody something. People take it with kind smile but nothing changes in their awareness. Every time I wanted to use "I am sorry" because of what my background was, where people taught me to use more often "I am sorry" to them, many times for nothing than "thank you" to me for good things what I did to feel encouragement and support while nothing changed in their behavior, I stopped and started thinking what kind of gift I am for that person or the person for me. Then I say, "Thank you for being you and for giving me the opportunity to be myself in this or that way," or I use different words for both of us to feel good. It takes a few seconds, and they are worthy. Why I am bringing this topic up? The reason is that after overusing the words "*I am sorry*" here and there, lessening myself and feeling of guilt for something, I noticed a day or two later that what I had said or did helped the person when the subject or situation arose. I realized that my clairvoyant ability and right consciousness were gifts for every person I touched, helping them with what they were dealing with. It didn't matter if they noticed this or not. It was information for me from the Spirit to stay on the path, be myself, and stop feeling bad all the time.

Now it is your time to think about a situation when you said, "I am sorry," feeling guilt that you maybe shouldn't have spoken up or reacted, and later on, it turned out that for the person, your courage to speak up brought a blessing to their experience. Maybe they were saved from something that didn't serve them. Or their consciousness arose, they were able to move forward, and an unpredictable good thing happened to them. We don't know why we speak, act, or react in certain ways to people we care about. At that moment, we are unknowingly aligned with our Higher consciousness, and we learn the reason later. Sometimes we have saved people's lives unknowingly by making them late or making them change direction, and we weren't aware of that. Now let's look from your perspective. Think back to when you were angry at someone who cut in front of you, blocking your way inadvertently, and you needed to change direction and go to a different spot, which was more flawless, or when you found what you were looking for. Maybe you were late somewhere because of traffic due to a driver who was too slow or too fast, and you judged the person, wishing them all bad things consciously without realizing that this person helped you safely get to your destination. How many times have you thought that someone owed you the words "I am sorry" without knowing that he or she was a blessing in disguise? However, when we did something and knew that we messed up with the person, let's say, "Forgive me for my behavior or 'for being late.' I did my best at the time. In the future, I will do things differently, or 'I will be on time when you need me.'" Say these words with meaning. Forgive yourself for unwanted behavior and affirm how you want to act next time. You will see how you both feel. It gives an opportunity for a deeper connection and keeping the promise next time. We will never be perfect as human beings, but we don't have to put our traits and unwanted behavior on others, later blaming ourselves, saying sorry, and repeating the cycle all the time. We need to be conscious that every thought and word has vibrations behind it. We want to use thoughts and words, which change our undesirable behaviors and build up our self-esteem and which we lost in the past because of our nearest environment, and reach the point of self-love, appreciation, and acceptance for ourselves and others to move on with our dreams. Overusing "sorry" or "I am sorry" doesn't help in this process.

We all were born with a minimum of at least one dream, which we usually don't follow. Mostly our dreams are in disharmony with what our parents and families choose as an acceptable thing we should do as our occupation. We pick our adult path and profession that, in the eyes of our closest ones, makes us look independent and makes them proud of us. That means we earn more money than they did or do. We do that as our duty as a kid with a good upbringing. We try the best we can. We started liking following the dreams of our parents, causing unnecessary disharmony with our hearts. We had hobbies that we gave up as an adult person. The reason was that we treated them as youthful interests that are not safe to do as an occupation. It is commonly accepted as unknown, and according general beliefs, it would not bring us good money. We stopped focusing on them because they did not fit our worldview as an adult who is busy earning money in a serious job to provide for ourselves and our families. As a result, we put our lost dreams onto our children. We encourage them in the things that we used to do or wanted to do and had no courage to follow. I was in this second group. Most of us selected occupations that support our beliefs on how we were supposed to earn money. We wanted to be teachers, businesspersons, economists, lawyers, doctors, nurse assistants, sales persons, or some other occupation that is recognized as well-paid or a good position. When we want to travel, we try to get ourselves hired in traveling agencies as tourist pilots or become stewardesses. We get ourselves hired as a cruiser crew member. We have a lot of ideas about how we can see the world and have decent money. I believe those kinds of occupations are ones we choose when we come from poor families and want to change our fate for the better, one better than our parents'. Mostly it becomes a short-term adventure. The reason is that we were pushed to have families because of our age or because our partner blackmailed us. Then we want to find an occupation that suited to an ideal family picture, being together, bringing up children, and being the best parent we know how to be. When we settle down with expectations smaller than what we once thought our life would look like, we stop living our soul path, only our family's or partner's expectations. This way of living is accepted by societies as the order of things. We were taught that we're supposed to forget about ourselves and live for our children and teach them the same. We sacrifice ourselves for the common good, which is our family. Our children grow up and many times have their own issues and grievances toward us. They stop communicating or contact us only on a very casual level, mostly when they are in need. We give them our attention all the time, and there is no end to it. Meanwhile, we blame ourselves for making mistakes as the parent and think this is our fault. Once, I was wondering why my son really didn't trust me and came to me only when he needed something. He was able to cut me off and got along with it, stating that I was toxic because I knew more than he understood. He didn't need any contact with me. He told me many times that he loves me, but our conversations were rare and general. Many times, when I shared about myself authentically and about what I was doing or planning to do as being with higher consciousness people who encouraged me to do it because they were my new teachers, how to obtain my own power, and making my own choices which were true to me to transform my life and support others, he judged me and defended others. To him, I was the one who was wrong. He contacted more often my mother, and I felt like I did something wrong and that I owed him. He really introduced this to me that way, and for many years, I believed that he was right not because he said that but because it was society's belief of how the mother is supposed to act. I believed him as I believed his father before until I started clearing all of society's beliefs and expectations of me from my closest ones. Sometimes I had feeling that I needed to compete with my mother for my son's love and trust. And I found the answer. During our sharing in the Introduction Leaders Program, my friend Venessa recognized her syndrome of abandonment and, as a result, her way of being. She always needed to be a perfectionist and really dealt with life by herself even though she had husband and family who really loved her, but she felt alone. I saw a lot of myself in her, isolated, but the most important insight she had, which I was able to connect to my son's behavior toward me, came when she remembered the event, the result of which being she lost trust in people and the most important person in her life: her mother. Venessa was five years old when the situation occurred. Venessa's mother took her to the family in Mexico. She met for the first time her grandmother. These people were strangers to her even if they were the closest family members of her mother. Venessa was taking a shower while her mother left the grandmother's home without saying anything about where she was going and when she was coming back for her. It was a huge shock for her finding herself without mother and in the new environment.

In Martin's case, when he was five years old, he needed my love the most. We started living without his father at my mother's place at that time. Meanwhile, I received the opportunity of going to London for six months to earn more money for both of us. I didn't say anything to him to prevent him from feeling sad or bad before I would leave. He "lost" one parent a few weeks before when I decided take him and move to my mother's. Martin's father was preparing himself to work abroad at that time. He didn't have time for Martin anymore. So when it was my turn to leave for London, without saying anything to my son, I left him sleeping at my mother's home. For a young child, it was traumatic event. Even he wasn't aware and didn't know how to call it. He felt abandoned. Many of us have this syndrome and live with it, unaware of it all our life. We don't trust our parents and people with whom we deal. We stop being emotionally involved with them because we are afraid of being abandoned again. And truly, we trust only those who've never left us. In my son's case, this was my mother. When I realized it, I felt a huge relief because I understood his behavior. And now, when I am far away again, following my heart, he doesn't need me to deal with his own busy life. None of his friends' moms did what I have done, and for Martin, it was unaccepted and incomprehensible. He made his own assumptions why I left for the US, and he kept himself to this story because it was convenient for him. Society can be very cruel when we want to get out of the matrix in which we have lived most of our lives. Once, I was in conversation with my other friend Alison about my realization about communication with my son. Through this, she was able to recognize when the disconnection occurred between her and her younger son. We both felt relief and laughed. We affirmed the truth that we are the best mothers for our sons. They chose us as their mothers to work on their own evolution. Unless we realize that the issue of our children is their subconscious behavior toward events they are not conscious of, we take it on ourselves and think it was our fault instead of forgiving ourselves and understanding that we acted the best we knew at that time. A lot of women were unprepared as the parents, and we didn't know that. Our behavior was directed according our society's beliefs. We had no free choice. Our illusive decisions were made automatically, and we thought that it was our free will. Meanwhile, our souls are dying and yearning for more, but we don't listen because we want to be a good husband, mother, father, or wife and have a duty to our families even when we are not ready for it. Can you see this pattern in your family? It is time for a courage and being honest with yourself, recognize your own choices as delusional happiness, and introspect on what you can do right now for your soul. Then live accordingly to its choices instead of your small ego to be happy and fulfilled. Our souls imprinted their dreams in our hearts. This is how they wanted us to express ourselves in this lifetime—to grow and unfold the beauty from within, and that would enable our soul to level up own consciousness in the spiritual world.

When the Introduction Leaders Program was suspended, I had a few calls with my assigned coach, Carlos. He asked me once, "Magdalena, why don't you want to succeed?" We both went through our school days in this call. He told me about his own experiences in school and what he promised himself at that time. It determined his behavior and how he was showing up in life. When he shared his experiences, I started recalling mine. In class, I knew the answers to the questions or mathematical solutions many times but I never raised my hand. I would wait until my other classmates would raise their hands. I never was sure that my answers were right. I kept the knowledge to myself. I never was the person who wanted to shine in class. I was afraid of being laughed at if I was wrong. The students who raised hands were called "toady" by peers very often. I believe it was one of the reasons that I decided not to be active in school. For most of my life, I was the one who supported others, helping them shine or gain success or do work from behind the scenes with the thought that my time would come one day. Also, I remembered the situation from the Heal Your Life training when I made a space for a friend so that she could pick up the stone with the inscription "success." Because of that, I received my crystal in the shape of a heart. But this event left the image in my head that love and success cannot go in a pair, that I have to choose again, this time between God and success. So I had another breakthrough after realizing that I didn't know God at all. My new friend Omkari said something once when I shared with her my understanding about spirituality and success based on the image in my head after the Heal Your Life training. She said, "Magdalena, I don't agree with you. We put a lot of times in our heads that being spiritual means we cannot be successful or have money." In another conversation with me about the same subject, she gave the example of Paramahansa Yogananda, who came from India to teach us about the true God and gave us Kriya Yoga as a direct path to the Spirit. He had many ashrams, and Self-Realization Fellowship has a lot of beautiful temples. He left a lot of books and writings so that we could know the Truth of our Source and understand Bagavan Gitta, or the Holy Bible. Also, he spoke publicly. All this work brought a lot of money for him and enabled him to share as humanitarian work. Paramahansa Yogananda was the only spiritual teacher and master who was invited to the White House by a president of the USA at that time. Simply put, the *gurudeva* knew the true God, who gave him all that he needed to complete the task for the Spirit on the planet Earth. Now I understand that the Spirit doesn't want us to choose between Him and our earthly happiness, to sacrifice one thing over the other that we both love. He wants us to have the whole Him without exceptions, which is love, health, fulfillment, and money. All of these are His creation.

Guruji Paramahansa Yogananda wrote a prayer:

> *O Father, I want prosperity, health, and wisdom without measures, not from earthly sources but from Thine all-possessing, all-powerful, all-bountiful hands.*

But to have all of God's richness and fulfillment, we must find Him first. Why? First of all, we all have ideas about what we're supposed to do in our lives, but most of them are based on what we have seen, what we were told, or what kind of occupations are fashionable to gain good money or be in service. All is based on what the outside world determined for us as successful or the best way of earning income. Most people focusing so much on the money that they forgot that all the goods can be taken in the next second through different events in the world or in the nature. They close themselves off in their mansions and become their own mind's prisoners. In the United States, children from very beginning have been taught not to trust neighbors and to not disturb them because they can call the police. Because of that, a lot of citizens closed their lives, open only to the small groups of family and friends. They only use others to achieve their own goals without being connected. A lot of people here are afraid of one another. The media helps them believe in it. So society gives us ideas of being successful, fashionable, and healthy; of how to earn decent money; and of what is good for us. An example would be most technology companies giving us a new product every few months, and all they say is that we need to have it because it is the best. Look around your home and notice how many things and devices you bought as necessary and how many have not been used at all or used for a short period of time. It was "good stuff" for a while, and now you have storage of "useful" and "necessary good things" at home. Regarding food, look at how much you buy just because they are on discount and later on throw it away. These are the reasons for many to find God within—to know what it really is that you need to live a good and healthy life. We want to learn how to discern what is good for us and what society says we have to have or be.

There is a prayer written by Paramahansa Yogananda about discrimination:

Heavenly Father, I am charged with the light of Thy divine discrimination.

I am awake with the light of Thy divine discrimination. I shall sleep no more!

Bless my understanding, bless my thoughts, bless my activity, that I may use in all things that divine discrimination which quickly leads to Thee.

Sit with yourself, and you will find God within you and turn to the wisdom that you have always had without getting up from the bed. Try to meditate to meet Him. He will give you a peaceful mind, creative thoughts, clarity, more joy, discernment, and a vision for your life. It will give you more courage, and you will stop doing things that have stopped serving you years ago. You will not be afraid of change in your life because you will notice that you grew up from your environment, and without pain or regret, you will start finding people who will lead you along the way to a new life. Each person is a blessing in the ladder of your growing consciousness. Secondly, we can start looking for the Spirit in the small things that we do on daily basis. Unknowingly we use His power to work, dance, eat, walk, make plans for trips, meet with friends, plan a new home or family, etc. All the power we have is borrowed from Him. When we start our journey to self-love, which, for me, means a journey to love the Spirit within me, we can start with small things to appreciate that which we do for ourselves and others, like being thankful for our health. If we don't have a healthy body, we can be thankful for the years when our bodies were healthy. It can bring true joy to our hearts, and as a result, it will heal the disharmony in our bodies. When we appreciate the small things that we do, we grow, and it gives us a sense of self-worth. We start seeing that we are really important. We start realizing that not everything and everyone is for us. We show love to ourselves when we start looking for a new job and new people who encourage and respect instead of put us down or use us. We really start noticing how much we have disrespected ourselves by letting our environment treat us as a "useful thing" to please their egos. When we find God in ourselves, He will pull us to do things that our fear stopped us from doing before. We are not the same. We can only move forward with courage and a passion for life. It gives us freedom to experience new things that we have never dreamed would be possible. That's why God is first to give you courage and faith that you are here for a purpose.

So the question now for each of us separately is, *Will I still live in a fear because I lost my identity as a child of God, or I will do my best with the knowledge what I have right now to regain my birthright and fulfill my purpose being here?*

My purpose is to awaken love in each people's heart and bring understanding of who we really are. My intention is for this message to reach everyone. Why? The reason is peace in the world and there will be no boundaries any more. The planet Earth will be ruled by Spirit, awakening Christ Consciousness in every soul. This is the divine plan for all of us on this beautiful orb. We all have power and wisdom that sustains all creation.

The fruits of our individual healing from limiting beliefs labors are for the benefits of all. And from this space of oneness, we see that harmony is a true experience in our lives. We become a true conduit for God's expression in, through, and as our lives.

All the experiences that I had in the USA was for a reason. I saw my whole childhood during my first four-and-a-half years living here. I was brought by God (my soul calling). I experienced abandonment, not being treated equal, being unwanted, omitted. Money wasn't for me, and I received messages from people saying I am not so important as I thought. The reason was that there were other people who, in their eyes, were better than me, and they were familiar with them. I was moving from place to place over thirteen times in such short period only to noticed how I was pushed and moved many times by my parents like an unnecessary thing. I never had peace to truly be myself and find time to learn more on deeper level and rethink what was really important to me and who I would like to become in the future. To recognize this, I needed to go deep in the presence process to heal my childhood to reestablish my knowing who I Really Am, regain my own divinity, and determine what was important for me as a human being.

So God knew better. Being here, first of all, I had to leave for three weeks the West Coast for the East Coast to understand that my home is Los Angeles and its area and recognize that multilevel marketing, which is very financially liberating, is not for me. Why? It would keep my consciousness still on diseases and focus on gaining material goals. There is nothing wrong with that when people desire it for themselves. They grow as a human being and as a leader because of that. They accumulate money by sharing good quality products and help others achieve their financial freedom and health. A good leader brings the best in their people. Because of that, the leader's income grows and those who cooperate with him/her. Most importantly, these people can rely on themselves. Joy and excitement accompany them all the time. Through MLM, your awareness can grow regarding the quality of products and money. You start choosing more deliberately what you eat, and your priorities changes. You start seeing what is important for you as an individual human being. Thanks to that, the soul develops itself. But there is a lot of ego also. The monthly sales plans (which can be exciting when we reach our financial goals, making us feel good about ourselves and what we are capable of), sometimes don't have integrity. Many times, we put our goals ahead of connecting with people. This is what is still missing in the world of sales the most—connecting without gaining, and when a deal finishes, a sales representative or agent stop communicating with us. Life can give us more when we do things selflessly, when our purpose is to grow and be in service to others. Then cooperations are on long-term. So I chose my path of trust and released all the layers of doubt that separated me from my soul's fulfillment as a Heal Your Life leader, Reiki healer, and using other modalities to expand awareness and learn how to be in service of others later on. I love knowing that I have the power to heal my body by myself consciously. As soon as my mind was healed from disbelief, I released thought pattern which was a cause of creating the chronic illness in my body. Everyone is created from light. Light manifests itself as an atom, cell, and tissue; and it sustains all organs. I love to call God and ask Him to talk to me, and I affirm His presence in my body. It gives me security that He is always with me and wherever I am and that I am safe and protected, and honestly, I have no control over my life. Many times I needed to let go of control over my finances and other things that Creator was able to manage it much better than my mind could imagine. I love remembering that if it wasn't for Spirit, my body and identity as a human being wouldn't exist. It gave me sense of self-worth many times when I was doubting or comparing myself with other people here. This is the ego's play. So I focused on writing affirmative prayers, continued writing my book, and continued being open to the next step that I needed to take to become who I was affirming as I am and learn how to appreciate myself for what I have done and do to obtain the trust in myself and my skills. As I learned it, I stopped putting myself down and let life provide me what I needed at that time. I started regaining my self-worth and asking for more from my source of being, God. Healing my inner child, I started feeling worthy of my divinity.

Writing affirmative prayers it was like opening new world for me because I wasn't praying person at all. I have started loving to write them and shared with others who needed them on Instagram and Facebook. The prayers written by me depended on what kind of challenge the person has had at the moment.

The ones that are in churches are dogmatic and are meaningless when we repeat them without understanding. Repeating formulas that are general and are misunderstood for most of people don't serve anybody. We are all unique, and each of us need to find themselves which way is the best for us to be in communion with Spirit and find a prayer for yourself. It can be "thank you for my life" or "good things in my life." The one what keeps us feel in communion with ourselves, true God, and it will start to fulfill the reason why we appeared on this planet in this particular day, month, and year. This incarnation process started in the spiritual realm and ceases there. Knowing your incarnation purpose by learning to use the Mayan sacred calendar on a daily basis, your life will stop being a puzzle for you. You can foresee what it would happen in thirteen days of the wave.

You can see what theme can be continued in the wave started with the same archetype that current wave finishes. It would be forty days forward. Also you can find the reason of current situation by checking what was happening in the wave that was finishing with the archetype of the present wave have started. This means forty days back. Through looking over every year, each of us can recognize what we did, why we did it, and the reason behind what we do right now. It was written before we were born in the Mayan sacred calendar. That's why we can foresee our future and what's left for us to do on the energetic level. This is your TZOLKIN, a circle of your life. As I mentioned, your life stops being enigmatic for you, and you start to understand your choices. Because of that, you feel more free and loving for yourself and others. You stop comparing yourself to others. It is you—your feelings, your emotions, your decisions, your individual growth, no matter what others do or not do. Remembering your dreams and starting making steps toward it by using Tzolkin gives you the freedom to make your own choices and expect the best outcome because you are unique in the realization of your dreams, and fear stops being the issue. When the Spirit calls you by sending a God-realized master, follow his teachings. They will support you to find God within you. I received my initiation to Kriya Yoga in June 2020 by having a small ceremony in the bedroom, binding my soul with the masters of Self-Realization Fellowship as a path to God and ascension. It is good to have awareness that I will not be here for eternity. When the time of incarnation ends, I will go back home to the Spirit. I am an unlimited soul with a full potential, and so are you. Every prayer is answered by Him. You will tune through meditation into your inner guidance. It will help you release all concerns, and you will become a free soul. Your awareness will grow more and more. For everything that you will do or achieve, you will stop being attached to the outcome. You will be happy and know that everything that is great is done by Spirit through you. We all are His tools on planet Earth to support ourselves in growing and bringing peace to our homes.

God wants us all to evolve and be united. He wants to express Himself through all His souls, not only few. You can see some of them on TV or read about them. We need to understand that fulfillment is waiting for all of us, but we need to find time to be with ourselves, to reach for our Creator's guidance to find our true calling. God's laws are love, forgiveness, compassion, unity, joy, abundance, health. Awareness of that and using the law of attraction correctly, which means using to expand (eternally young and healthy) instead of being constrained (getting old and full of diseases): where your focus goes and belief is, you will receive. The law of attraction can bring you to the space of who you really are by vibrating willingness to find out. We all have our Source power to create our lives by choice and by connecting with the Source to make right decisions.

Asking empowering questions (e.g., Who Am I? How can I evolve and expand in love?) It will bring you the truth. Using daily intention on how you want the day to look like (e.g., full of joy, love, unexpected good), affirm it, and be love and joy on that day, and unexpected surprises will come. Using imagination and appreciation, being trustful that all you need to find the truth and grow will be revealed and given to you. Our birthright is to know and experience God and His good in our lives.

We have laws made by man, and they are changeable all the time. Every government makes changes one after another, and it will never end. We see divisions through nationalities and color of skin. We have boundaries where one country considers to be better one from another. Because of that, we have visas to nearly each country. People, instead of feeling free to do what they love to do, need to prove first that their will is not to stay long enough to settle down and earn money in the country without permission. We all know that this law is useless. People want to go to countries which economy is on a higher level and their purpose is to earn money. They will stay and have earn income, which will be sent to their families. The truth is that these people are in the service to others. They mostly do the heaviest work to support their families in their own countries, whose governments have a very low awareness of abundance covering with "a good care" and diminishing their own citizens' birthright to have good income for their professional work in their native countries. We all are taken care of by the country of our birth. We receive everything that people in governments with different levels of awareness determined what would be our birthright. As a citizen of a "richer" country, people have more opportunities to grow, learn, and apply for jobs they want without being pushed to choose between their skills and lesser work only to provide food for themselves and their families or growing. Undocumented immigrants have to do that all the time. As a result, very often they are treated worse by the close minded citizens of the country if they don't know with whom they interact. Every undocumented immigrant is treated equally as a second-class, not-necessary-or-wanted citizen. So what do better situated citizens to adjust themselves to this situation? Mostly they take advantage on those unaware of their rights immigrant people, giving very dangerous work. I remember in Spain how my ex-partner had to clean outside windows on the twelfth floor without protection because it was a private apartment. He had nightmares that he was falling down from the building. Other immigrants work with asbestos, which kills their bodies. The undocumented caregivers are treated as someone who only needs to provide care by many people who didn't experience what it is like to find themselves in a new country without choice of better work in which they were skilled in their homeland. And now we have another instance of hypocrisy when becoming a resident or citizen of a new country. Only people who have families in their countries can receive residency right away. It's like they are saying, "You are welcome. You are our person, and we will take care of you." Another way to receive residency is to be delegated or receive a good job, but these kind of jobs can have only people who graduated from the universities and have useful professions for the country. By "useful," I mean the ones that can bring more gratification to the country. But the jobs that are given to undocumented immigrants—like cleaning sewages, housekeeping, or other low-pay "insignificant" jobs—cannot bring glory to the country, so the people are treated differently. If you don't have a plan to stay in the new country with support from family or friends of your family or find a good employer who respects you and your work, you are treated as an unwanted person. It's like they are saying, "You are here, so we'll take advantage of you and pay you less or give you a worse job. And you're supposed to appreciate us how we are so generous to you." Also, there is a fear of deportation from these who are undocumented because it is said that they take a lot of jobs from the citizens of the country. Immigrants who are on their own without documents are called undocumented, and as an undocumented person, you are really unwanted here. It's like they're saying, "We can only protect our own. You are unwanted." You first need to talk to a lawyer if you want to stay. As an example through my experience, most lawyers take cases in the United States when you have a sponsor or family here with legal status because they know that they win the case. So they financially take advantage of the person who has all they need to be legally here and only doesn't know the law or cannot fill out documents by themselves because they are afraid. People make mistakes by getting married for the documents, and later, they suffer in their relationships and cannot divorce for many years as Homeland Security will decide that it is enough long time, that the person can or cannot stay in the country by herself or himself as a resident. I had a friend from Europe, and she came to the United States. And after a while, she got married to the person who she loved. She received residency in the United States. But after two years of their marriage, they broke up and got divorced. She received documents from Homeland Security that said she needed to leave the USA since she is no longer married to their citizen and she was not married long enough for Homeland Security to accept that her marriage wasn't a scam. We all think that we are free. Are we? We can be free only to a certain level—the one we are allowed. When we ask for something more, which is granted to others as something natural because they were born in the country, even though we are good people and want to give to the communities we live in, we receive a feedback saying, "You do not belong here." So do we still want to live in the world where is division and hypocrisy is accepted by law? Most of the people who are rejected are these who are fearless; they want to experience their lives as a child of God and try exploring themselves more than they thought they could. For some people who don't speak, for example, native English, they couldn't learn in schools as children, so as an adult person, it is an adventure. And learning English or other languages as an adult is a first step to another evolution of our soul wherever you are.

Joining the European Union was a salvation for all Europeans. It became a way of development for all union citizens. Less developed countries have become more prosperous. Migration has become a natural thing under documents of the country of birth. The European Union became a true role model. Different nationalities with unlike cultures and languages are treated equally. The European countries with lesser economic standards were lifted up so that all citizens of the European Union have the same rights. They have equal access to work in which they can use the skills they learned and studied in their birth country. They can have the same good income for their work, receive the same retirement equivalent, and have the freedom of traveling without visas, only their country's birth ID. Also, no one pushes them to speak only one general language. Brussels has very well-built translation departments. There are translators who speak many different languages. There is one person who speaks thirty-five languages including Polish and Mandarin. Can you imagine that these people who speak so many languages learned by travelling and meeting other diverse cultures? It helped them understand everyone they communicate with. You can say that the United States is the same from very beginning. I would disagree. I see them with my own eyes, and as I mentioned before, there is a lot of division, fear, and also money disagreements here. In fifty states and major territories of the USA, everyone uses English. Cultures are varied but are assimilated to one—the American one. There is a lot of controversy in this country, and a lot of people from older generations here believe that the United States is the best country ever. Also, children in schools are taught that too. They repeat unknowingly the mistake of their parents. There was a very well-known culture movement here in the '60s when people came to the United States to improve their lives and feel equal. They stopped teaching children in their native languages, and a lot lost their culture because everyone wanted be a good American. Everything in the United States is prevented by law, and you are allowed to do as much as you want as long as you agree with rules given automatically by law. For example, a lot of clerks who work in the lower level governmental or state jobs lack resilience. Even though they have contact with a person in front of their desk, the post office windows, or other places, some of them act like Automats. The rule is the rule, and there is no other way. Because of that, they are very detached from themselves. They are afraid a lot, mostly of losing their jobs. By losing touch with humanity, they lose the opportunity of moving forward to a better work or new opportunities. These people don't travel much and have no opportunity to see different cultures, only believing in the power of their country and not living accordingly to the power within them, which is more impressive. That's why a lot of people including Americans have had enough of living this way. They attend the transformational programs, and communities to find a meaning in their lives and they find real purpose of life, and at last, God who is behind all this. Not the one that is given by ages on the cross and puts people down. They have had enough of living in the old paradigm and listening to out-of-date authorities. Nationality and religion always leave us with division, asking us who has as better or worse roots. There is no such thing in the eyes of God. He put us in the certain families, nationalities, and religious to overcome everything what is not Him within us. When we stop identifying ourselves with our nationalities and start looking at ourselves as a soul under God's law, we begin feeling better about ourselves. We'll understand that we have a right to be in the place where we are. We'll stop disrespecting ourselves and other people. We will feel more connection with each other not only on the formal level but as friends of one another's. We will start feeling love, joy, and more courage to move forward with our heart's desires. Our mutual awareness will grow. One will pull up the other. This is called soul brotherhood.

We need to understand that we were born in one country but we are citizens of the whole world. Everyone would have a choice where they want to live. This choice would be available to everyone, not only to those who have money or have businesses. Even these people having businesses for example in the United States need to return to their own countries after a few months to get another permission.

When we all start using spiritual laws and we all start thinking about peace, love, unity, as a result, we will regain our own common sense, the boundaries will disappear. The government will not be needed to dictate how we'll supposed to live because we will feel connection to the Spirit and Mother Earth. We are the bridge between heaven and earth. The real equal exchange will be given to us through spirit not according to human beings who are not you.

We can start creating this world right now in harmony with the omnipresent, omniscience, and omnipotent Spirit using universal principles and the tools that evolve our whole being.

In the current circumstances, we need to stop believing in the institutions and see that there is a human being working there. The person is eligible and capable to make their own decisions when they allow themselves in your case. The law is one for all people in the country, but there are some hidden information that can support your individual case and help you receive, in accordance with the law, an outcome different from other people, also there are lawyers who really take care about your case and not taking advantage of you because you have family here. The lawyers who reject the other cases, which are not so easy, or want to twist the facts to a good meaning to win the case are not good lawyers. They have the paralegal assistant who fills out everything on the computer for them or prepare the case, but they are not ready to commit themselves to learn more and change their attitude to the lawyer profession. The good lawyers are looking for other avenues which support your case according to its status and accordance to the current law. There is always way out. Where our focus is, believe and we receive it. We need to appreciate these people who know the governmental states or city laws to use their own common sense and their true soul nature instead of doing everything mechanically or taking advantage of your unawareness that there is another way.

I have Divine Power within me. This Power gives me life and everything that I need. There is only one Truth in my life that I Am the Divine Being created by God. I Am one with His omniscient Mind. Therefore, my financial freedom and happiness is my birthright. God doesn't make mistakes in His own plan. His Mind is lavishly abundant and so do I. I am in harmony with His Mind. There is no lack, no limitation, and nothing to fear. I Am one with God. I Am thankful because God thinks and expresses through me. I receive rich divine ideas to bless my and others lives. God always gives truly to me. Abundance is everywhere just look around. Opportunities come to me from everywhere and from everyone. I evolve in everything: in my work, in my mind and being in my own heart. Love and Joy is in harmony with abundant life. I am healthy and prosperous. I do what I love to do. I spread love and kindness to everyone. I am so joyous, happy and thankful. I Am blessing to the world. Whatever I touch it turns into precious gold. I Am successful. Thank you, thank you, thank you, God. I am truly grateful for my Life! Amen.

—*A Statement of Truth by Magdalena Julita Byra*

You realize that all along there was something tremendous within you, and you did not know it.

—*Paramahansa Yogananda*

CHAPTER 11

What Is Abundance, and Can We Experience It without Pain?

I have a great life. I stand on my own two feet. I accept and use my own power. I explore the many avenues of my being. I am willing to learn new ways of living. I feel totally complete and whole. I accept and use my own power. I am deeply fulfilled by my life. I give myself what I need. It is safe for me to grow.

—Louise Hay

We came to this world with gifts and talents, yet most people settle for the lowest-paid job that helps them to get by. We suppress our creative sides, only allowing those closest to us to truly see and experience our genius but mostly they are not recipients of our gifts. We need to exit from our comfort zone and allow Life to provide for us people who would really appreciate our talents and gifts, those who want to pay for our art, service, or product that we have to offer. The only difference is that whatever we have to offer needs to be in harmony with God. It means that our services or products will not destroy planet Earth, only help Her to recover. Animals will not suffer anymore due to greediness of the human mind. Our action supposed to be focused for the good of all, not only our own goal such as gaining mountains of money. We came here to serve, and because of our honest service, money comes to us. Money is good and only then does it comes easier and more abundant when our focus is on God's features such as love, peace, joy, forgiveness, health, unity, creativity. Most new entrepreneurs know the secret of life, and their wealth is the wealth of others. They are really successful people in every area of their lives. They grew up from an old understanding of becoming rich, where money is the only focus and where you take advantage of other people to get richer without taking care of employees or the environment. They remembered that God is within them and having the right mindset and meditation is a tool to be in communion with His guidance. After that, the right actions follow without hurting anyone.

Charles Fillmore, in his book *Prosperity*, gave a great recipe to release all our debts and receive God's prosperity:

> *Your thoughts should at all times be worthy of your Highest Self, your fellow man, and God. The thoughts that most frequently work ill to you and your associates are thoughts of criticism and condemnation. Free your mind of them by holding the thought "There is now no condemnation in Christ Jesus." Fill your mind with thoughts of divine love, justice, peace and forgiveness. This will pay your debts of love, which are the only debts you really owe. Then see how quickly and easily and naturally all your outer debts will be paid and all inharmonies of mind, body, and affairs smoothed out at the same time. Nothing will so quickly enrich your mind and free it from every thought of lack as the realization of divine love. Divine love will quickly and perfectly free you from the burden of debt and heal you of your physical infirmities, often caused by depression, worry and financial fear. Love will bring your own to you, adjust all misunderstandings, and make your life and affairs healthy, happy, harmonious, and free, as they should be. Love indeed is "fulfill-*

> ment of the law." Surrender your debts to God along with your doubts and fears. Follow the light that is flooding into your mind. God's power, love, and wisdom are here, for His kingdom is within you. Give Him full dominion in your life and affairs. Give Him your business, your family affairs, your finances, and let Him pay your debts. He is even now doing it, for it is His righteous desire to free you from every burden, and He is leading you out of the burden of debt, whether of owning or being owed.

If it wasn't for Spirit, we wouldn't be able to breathe. All the power we have is borrowed from Him.

Life always gives me the tools and signs to move forward when my mind sees no way out. Knowing that I came to the US for a reason, my soul calling and not my ego's wanting, kept me in the process of growing and moving forward to prevent me from focusing on gaining a little material security and let my heart dream to die. The above thought always reminded me that the journey is of my Inner Being, my Greatness, who chooses the exact way of fulfillment, expressing Itself creatively; and financial security will come from that. The soul has gifts and talents to bring in a unique way to this world that are required right now that we can move forward in our consciousness as a collective on the planet Earth.

From being here, I saw a lot of people who came to the United States to earn some money and go back home. Sometimes it takes them many years. They are afraid of losing higher income to go back to their countries where their families are, and they are missing the place where they were born. Those who have legal status here believe that when they gain a little material security, they will be able to go back to their native countries with retirement benefits and savings to live better in their countries. A lot of them don't think about learning to change their circumstances here for the better. They focus only on the money. They suffer inside by being in the place that keeps them going financially, but their hearts are in their own home countries. They sometimes have adult children here, and they don't want to let them go to live their own life. Their focus is divided. They lose their health because they want to control situations in two distant places, which are the United States and their homeland. They don't feel that they can change their circumstances for the better. They miss their countries after having lived abroad for over twenty or thirty years. They never feel like they're home here. If only those people realized that money is not only the purpose behind them coming to the United States, nor is it bringing their families for a "better" life. There is no better life if we miss our homeland and have worn-out bodies because of hard work and misunderstanding our life's purpose. We must know the truth that we are souls, and as souls, we can designate any place as home. Our origin is the Spirit, who created the whole planet and the universe, not only our homeland. The soul reaches all dimensions, not only the location where our body is placed on the planet Earth. As body identification, our ego cannot see that. It sees a disconnection between the places we were born and where we are now. The younger generation is more open to changes and is not attached to their country of origin. They can find home wherever they go.

Mostly, these people are not looking for staying with one kind of nationality. They enjoy variations of culture and learning from each other. As we know, we are all Spirit and our body is only a vehicle for Spirit, which is divine and eternal. Thus, body age has nothing with mentality. It only depends on the environment that we grew up and with whom we choose to stick with. Thanks to open-minded people, we can grow and shine beyond age. When we are with limited-minded people and stick to our outdated beliefs, we are not able to grow and move beyond the 3D reality, which is illusion.

The Soul wants to be in process of evolvement, likes changes, loves to explore Itself, like a small child does all the time. It loves everyone and everything. The Soul is courageous and has confidence of Itself. It sees Itself in everyone and everything and can affirm what He wants to boldly follow the heart's desire because it is granted as a manifestation. The abundance comes from that. We call ourselves successful then. To bring success in our lives, we need to see it in the small things that we do daily. We need to acknowledge ourselves. Why? Because when we don't appreciate that which we do, we neglect our achievements in our lives. When we start noticing that we really did a good thing for ourselves, it brings us joy, and we want to do another one to challenge ourselves. We've had many situations in our lives that were scary and made us feel overwhelmed, but we did it because we had a goal in our minds—that our life will become much easier, that we will have more adventures, that we can learn something more, or that we will be able to act differently in a better way than we used to. It is us growing. We start seeing ourselves as being able to move in our lives only by doing it step by step, one thing after another. This is the way to succeed in our lives and feel abundant. Whatever we do, things that we call big or small ones, we must do with love and appreciation for ourselves. We will then gain more self-esteem, which builds up more momentum for us to have breakthroughs in our lives. By being more organized or cleaner, we make space for new growth, and it really matters that we do. The Spirit supports us in it. For example, when we stop messing up our houses and put things away, the place can be kept clean for a longer time. Then we will have more time to do something else. I taught my mind to be focused and put things away. It was my own training. I wanted my mind to be in the present moment. I often express gratitude and appreciation for myself when I do things I once resisted or postponed. I feel my love expands and love for myself. This has become second nature to me. With the other things like being in communication with others regarding to money commitments, we don't have to be on time with the payment if we don't have money, but we need to be in communication with the people who give us service or lent us money. It builds mutual trust and confirms that we are on our way to pay or give them the money back. Being on time at appointments, events, or meetings with friends—this is another way to show your love for yourself and for people you interact with. Every time we worry about being late, we can affirm, "I am always on time." And even when we do not arrive at the exact time, it can turn out that nothing was happening and that the event will start in a few minutes because there were delays. By repeating the affirmation that we are on time, we relax, and it becomes our new habit to appear timely. It really works in my life, and it will work in yours.

Speaking the truth beyond any circumstances is my way of being. Very often people are afraid of telling the truth or admitting that they messed up. They are afraid of being judged or even being fired from work. When I started trusting life, I recognized that no one has power over me. The people who I have met are only the Spirit's tools to teach me about myself, to provide for myself, and to provide something for them such us good work, friendship, information, service, or a good product. And when the time comes, I will release my codependency or providing service to move forward to the real better life and appreciate the lessons that I have learned. Some people stay in our lives because they are authentic and loving, and some of them, we need to let go because we are on different levels of awareness. I stopped being afraid of expressing myself authentically. I know that God is always with me, and He knows that whatever I do, it is right thing with the awareness that I have right now. Having this kind of attitude, we don't have to be afraid of other people's feedback. The other thing that puts us in the way of growing is keeping our word; it builds mutual trust. This indicates we are reliable people. My issue was to learn how to keep the promises I've made to myself. Many times I've broken them for the sake of others; I provided my time and service for free to help others, forgetting about myself and what I wanted to create. I procrastinated many times. One example is when I was writing my book or preparing myself for workshops, I did homework from English classes and many other things that I said yes to something, which took me away from what I planned to do that day, and I justified myself with my current circumstances, lack of "legal" status, and many other things. Regarding my undocumented status, I received an awakening thought" *I have nothing to lose. It's now or never!* Thanks to that, I started feeling powerful again and repeating the affirmation "*I am ready and suitable to work on my divine life purpose now*" to regain my confidence and my focus.

I have started receiving thoughts and signs regarding the Heal Your Life workshops. Every time I was looking for any confirmation, I received a picture of myself speaking publicly on the Mer-Ka-Ba workshop in Poland in 2017. This was the confirmation that I would be a Heal Your Life teacher. I remember a little uncertainty then in my voice. The reason was that I had this thought in my mind: "*How would it be possible in a foreign country, without being known by anyone there and with my English not being at the native level?*" The picture reminded me that I said the word and that there was a time to pursuit it, as I decided at the beginning that it would be my life's work to learn and teach women how to love themselves and how to live a fulfilled life. It was a huge learning process to become who I am right now. To really stand for myself and put my growth first, we need to find balance in our lives by choosing our priorities and following them. We all trained ourselves in something, even in bad behaviors or actions toward others. For example, we want to take revenge on other people because we think they have acted unfairly according to us. Creating new habits or a new way of being is nothing else but transforming old, unwanted behaviors into new ones by practicing them and being aware of them. Thanks to that, we can see our progress and find joy in being capable of living the best.

Once, I saw Oprah Winfrey spoke about her success, and she mentioned that she spoke on behalf of all her ancestors, mostly women, who weren't able to speak up for themselves to stand and show their greatness. As I mentioned at the beginning of my book, whatever we do to clear our old family patterns to bring light to the world, we clear past karma. It helps new generations live in a different and a much better world. And our families' bad patterns of behavior will be erased. Our ego doesn't see that, but our soul knows that. That's why we need to recognize that this journey on the planet Earth is for a reason, not only to earn money later to get ill and old but to bring harmony in our families and experience love and evolution in the universal consciousness. It starts with one dormant dream in your heart. Be willing to change, and life will take care of the rest.

Living in Los Angeles, I was learning a lot and saw my old beliefs or judgments about other people who were successful or have money here. When I was ready to have a breakthrough, I received videos or links that showed me that these people here are awakened. People who are really successful, they work in harmony with God and with their higher self, their soul. I received a link from my friend that showed a very inspirational speech by Jim Caviezel's as a tribute to Maria, the mother of Jesus, who guided him in his life and career. He played Jesus in *The Passion of the Christ.* Listening on YouTube to *The School of Greatness* by Lewis Howes, we can learn about these awakened souls. You can find the interview of John Paul DeJoria, who was homeless person that became a billionaire, and discover what values he had that helped him succeed financially and also as a person. Neale Donald Walsch was a homeless person who found his calling to become an author, screenwriter, and speaker. Oprah Winfrey invites guests who can inspire you to help you stop being afraid of moving forward. They live with values, which helped them find themselves and serve as an inspiration to us to bring the best to our lives, including abundance, and help other people understand that none of our circumstances can put us down unless we allow it to. You can stop living with their lives and start creating your inspirational story, then you can be fulfilled as a person and a soul. You have the same potential to become the best version of yourself in this life time. It is never too late. Dr Wayne Dyer said, "Don't die with your music still in you." We all showed up here with a purpose.

Once when I listened to a Self-Realization Fellowship service, one of the brothers, a SRF monk, talked about the *Horn of Plenty Bank.* He showed the small paper box on which was prayer affirmation of Paramahansa Yogananda's: *"Teach me to feel that Thou art the power behind all wealth, and value within all things. Finding Thee first, I will find everything else in Thee."* The purpose of the box was to put money in every day for forty-two days, using the prayer affirmation to the consciousness of God's wealth would possible to grow. When the Horn of Plenty Bank is full, we give away this money to someone else as a gesture of kindness or to a cause that matters to us, and we stop being attached to this money. We start to understand that the Spirit is the one who supplies all of us. It opens up our awareness to real wealth, which follows our calling. You can start asking God through prayer to show your individual path to real abundance. He will answer and lead you in every situation, small and big, to be able to express Himself through you in the form of abundance and eternal satisfaction of knowing God within you.

Later it turned out that for over two years, my hearing in immigration court was postponed through current circumstances in the world. Life gave me time and chances to focus on what I want and follow it safely.

I contacted Heart Inspired Presentations LLC, through which I was certificated. I was informed that it was a requirement to buy license and insurance. I asked if I could change my last name on the certificate to Byra, and I received a yes. I was happy that I could start leading these workshops under my mother's maiden name. The new possibilities started opening up to me as soon as I decided to reach out for them. I started reviewing the Heal Your Life manual that we received on the training and prepared myself for the workshops.

At that time I was living near the Polish retirement home, Szarotka. It neighbors with Our Lady of the Bright Mount, the Polish Church. These were the places where I took my first steps when I came back to Los Angeles from New York by a Greyhound bus.

I thought that I could give workshops there. I called Szarotka, but I found out that the facility is closed for people from the outside because of the virus. I went to the nearby parish to speak with the Polish pastor. I called the church office. The person who answered the phone was a woman who I thought that she worked for the pastor in the church. I was at the parking lot. Meanwhile, I noticed the Polish pastor driving out the rectory. I thanked my interlocutor, saying that I saw the Polish pastor. And I wanted to hang up, but she was confused because she didn't see me and claimed that she was with a pastor. I was looking around and didn't see any woman except myself. Despite this, we hung up. I asked the pastor if I could start workshops there, and he said that they are closed. Only the church building was open for services on Sundays, and there were a few devotees who came. The next day, I called the woman back. It turned out that she worked for the Polish church, but it was the different one, a National one, and she was the pastor's wife. They both were Polish. The difference between those two Catholic churches is that the National one isn't under the Vatican. They split over 150 years ago. The reason behind this was the language. In those years, the Catholic church didn't hold services in international languages, only Italian or Latin. That's why some clerics who wanted to hold services in the communities with the national language decided to split, and Vatican renounced them. Thanks to that, the priests can have wives and are able to lead their sermons in the languages they wanted, and their sermons differ a little from the Roman ones. I found out about it later on from the pastor of the Polish Catholic National Church. I was invited to see the hall, and I fell in love in it. Also, I was informed that there were two studios for rent. Before, they were rented out as Airbnb, and many people from Europe, the United States, and other places rented them. So I was delighted at the opportunity that came up; I would be able to live next door to the hall in which I wanted use for my Heal Your Life workshops. The community that attended there was mostly Hispanic. Additionally, there were Filipinos and a Polish couple.

I started planning my first Heal Your Life workshop there. I prepared flyers and gave information around.

Meanwhile, the governor ordered to close churches and other places where people liked to gather in California. As a result, citizens were scared, and streets were depopulated. People suffocated in their houses. If only they knew that there is knowledge and tools for their problems with fear; they would have chosen to decide about their lives. During this so-called pandemic times, many people have admitted that they made wrong choices by relying on third parties to look for solutions to their problem instead of listening to themselves and their own feelings of what was right for them. Being secluded and intimidated was practice of many bad leaders in history, and people still haven't learned from history that it is another attempt at taking their free will and imposing power. Before, it was on national level, and this time, it's on a global one. I was allowed to come and prepare workshops outside of the church hall in the beautiful place near the nonfunctional angel fountain. I was naive in thinking that people may come, but it gave me an opportunity to learn and practice using the Heal Your Life manual. It was a very relaxing day with sun and green bushes around.

One day I sent an e-mail to my introduction leaders group about exchanging money for work. One person replied and introduced me to WorkMarket platform. The platform was established in 2010 in New York and gives possibilities to foreign vendors or employees who were looking for employment, partnership, or wanted to hire people and got connections. This platform was mostly for technological companies or people who work in this field. Because of that, I called on July or August to IRS to find out if I have my tax number, which I had applied in January this year. It was 2020. I found out that the IRS was opened after few months break from lockdown not so long ago, and I received my ITIN. I was delighted. It gave me an opportunity to fill out the W-9 form instead of the W-8 on the platform. There is a difference in deducted tax. Those with the W-8 form can fill out with their country ID and look for employment connections here.

Having ITIN, the person can be self-employed. It can be one of the steps to become a permanent resident of the USA. Mostly people started with this tax number to help them to pay their taxes and be self-employed. Also ITIN gives opportunity to apply for EIN (entrepreneur number) right away.

One day when I asked about guidance I received the thought, *Self-Realization Institute*, which I would love to connect with many healers and coaches for this and have on-site crystal bowls, healing baths, yoga classes, meditation classes, visualization classes, sacred Mayan calendar, Heal Your Life workshops, and many other holistic avenues that clients can utilize to be healed spontaneously with the realization that they are immortal souls to become their own authority and start living in harmony with their own life purpose. This is so wonderful feeling when you are awaking and start realizing that you are not your body or mind, and you came here with a purpose. The soul has power over the body, the mind, and the soul lives in the present moment, and only the mind keeps holding people to the past or future. So by having a connection with our soul, we can start healing our disharmonies now so that in the future, we can be happy and healthy and know the truth as self-realized souls. A positive mindset can only keep maintain results after visiting any healer, coach, nutritionist, doctor, or teacher. We need to realize that power lies in each of us. That's why we are responsible for our awakening well-being and happiness permanently.

From living with people, I was able to understand at last that I gave a lot of my time without experiencing reciprocity. There was a lot of miscommunication. Many times I felt that I was used. It was my learning process. I had a lot of insights while reading Louise Hay's book *You Can Heal Your Life,* not only patterns that I had subconsciously, but about judging others' behaviors; which I liked or didn't like. Once, I opened to page on relationships. It was said that when you are upset or annoyed about somebody's behavior, ask yourself when do you behave that way.

I learned about myself a lot after asking that question. Thanks to that I felt free from judgmental attitude toward others every time. I felt lighter. It made me possible to laugh out my behaviors, and I left others to do what they wanted to do. It stopped being my business, and it created space for me to be loving and patient without pretending. One time, I was wondering why my friend with whom I used to live didn't take care of her body when she needed to instead of giving a lot to her partner.

I understood that she was in love with him and wanted to show her love and appreciation to him. She also acted that way to me, which I really appreciated, but also, I told her that it was too much. In my case, I was overwhelmed because I didn't do as much as she did regarding our mutual household chores. Mostly it was about cooking. She was happy that she was able to cook for her partner and serve him, but I saw how many times she neglected herself because of proving her love to him, forgetting that she was a blessing to both of us. I believe she had overcome this, but before, I noticed that even I wasn't interested in cooking or treated specially, I started acting like she did too. Instead of taking care of my writing or learning to workshops, I was spending more time in the kitchen than usual. When I realized it, I understood why I was doing that. I wanted to relieve her even she was the creator of this situation. She felt somehow guilty and dependent on her partner for a while, and that's why she was overcompensating. I felt pity for her, and I started taking her duties on myself. I was giving my time voluntarily and sucked in a lot of emotions from living with them. At that time, I didn't know that some other dormant gifts started awakening in me like Claircognizance. We know that we know. In my case, I knew that at the backstage was not like my friends showed outside; but not knowing that my body has this kind of ability, I thought all the emotions in my body I was dealing with then were mine. Many times we disregard our wisdom because we don't trust ourselves, only we believe in an apparent image made to show to the public by others not always true. I understand now why I was guided to move out to the Guardian Angel Church faster than I planned before. My soul wanted me to take care of myself again, but I didn't learn the lesson then. I put myself into a chaos bigger than I thought. I had a pattern in myself that made me to take on myself the obligations of others even though I wasn't the cause of their own chaos. I was only needed to take care about their created turmoil, and at the end, I didn't have possibility of making my own decisions or even saying something on my behalf. When I recognized this pattern in my mind, I was thinking, *Why do I behave this way?* I was always the one who needed to pay the bills without exceptions, no favors for myself but doing huge favors for others, which later became obligations. Every time when I chose my duties to which I said "yes" over others, it created chaos, and I was blamed for that. The cost I paid, it was big. I was left without any right to stand up for myself and a place to live, but it was worthy. Life had started releasing me from my karmic circles, at last. Before I moved to a new place (the Gaurdian Angel church), my friend took care more about herself, and she and her partner shared their responsibilities more often. When a woman wants to show her love through cooking, that is great, but when this cooking becomes obligation, then very soon she becomes a servant and prisoner of her own understanding of love, which gives her some kind of control over her man and family. When we wake up and understand this, then it is not too easy to let go of control. Thoughts of guilt come up, unworthiness, and other low-energy emotions. True Love is for nothing. We don't have to prove our worthiness through some kind of behavior. This way, people trade their own love: I will do for you to show my love, and you show me your love. Both partners are looking for approval from each other and don't believe that they deserve love from the partner for nothing. This kind of relationship doesn't work for a long time unless it becomes transformed. All uncertainty that partners have at the very beginning start coming up to the surface. People, to cover this, try more and more, yearning for approval and creates a vicious cycle of not working relationship at all or partially. When partners know their own values, then the relationship is whole and complete. No one needs to prove their worthiness to be loved when they feel love, compassion, and respect for themselves; and this love reflects in their relationships.

    I asked another question about being attracted to men who were in relationships, because I started having feelings back to one of my friends who I felt for many years before. The answer to the question came out from within right away. I dug deeper and found that this pattern started in my past lives. My soul communicated with me through pen and a piece of paper. Because of that, I understood my behavior with other women who had small self-esteem. I wanted to help them and be a friend, but they treated me more like a competitor and not the person who they can trust. To heal their wounds, I put myself down and started feeling powerless. Again, I understood that I could never help them this way. I would only lose confidence in myself and purpose of being here. I decided that I can only help the women who have low self-esteem by supporting them through my work as a leader, but first, I needed to regain my self-worth back through Louise Hay's work because I lost a lot of confidence here and then by giving them tools how to love themselves and get back their own power and self-esteem to follow their dreams. It would bring harmony to their own relationships and life. We are all the same. We are equal; nobody needs to compare themselves to each other and envy each other. We all are unique and powerful beings; and it doesn't matter if we are in a woman's or a man's body.

    When I understood that, I was hurting myself by giving away my energy here and there, voluntarily letting others' obligations overtake mine and not appreciating myself, I started using the affirmation *"I am willing to change. And also I am willing to change my life for the better*" followed by other affirmations, and I really started feeling more joy and confidence. I started to remember myself when I was flying out of Poland, full of joy and trust and seeing purpose again. I love being happy. Thanks to that, I stopped worrying about money and the circumstances I was in. I started feeling my power coming back.

I let myself visualize accordingly to Shakti Gawain's book *Creative Visualization*. I had the Polish healer, author, and trainer Ewa Foley's CD, which guided the visualization. In the visualization led by Ewa, similar to Louise Hay's, it was finished by putting our desire into the pink babble and releasing it to the ether. It meant that the dream was from the heart. It's another way than Mer-Ka-Ba to live accordingly to the heart's desires instead of ego's. And angels will take care of our dreams by letting them manifest in the easiest and most harmonious ways. Ewa Foley's spiritual story started in Australia and led her back to Warsaw, Poland, to open her personal development institute, Conscious Living Institute, with her friend to train personal development trainers nationally in two year program near the '90s. (Her website is www.foley.com.pl.) She bought a license from Hay House to use Louise's tools in Polish. Also, she connected her work with those of other inspirational spiritual teachers to help transform not only the Polish community. Ewa Foley is an author of a few books, among others is *Fall in Love with Life*. She is a seminar leader and speaker but also a mother who lost her son in the accident. He was at the age of twenty-seven years old. Ewa shared with us when I was in her workshop that instead of being supported in her grief, she was the one who cheered up others after the loss of her son. It gave me the opportunity to think, remembering how my uncle cheered all of us up when we came to the funeral of his oldest son. Ewa Foley, after the loss of her child, started creating meetings for mothers who lost their children so that those women could grieve and at the same time heal themselves, won't hold the grief all their lives, and only remember their children and live with passion.

My cousin Tomek Byra died in the accident. He was taking photos with friends in an abandoned factory in Żoliborz, Warsaw. Photography was his hobby. Tomek was twenty-four years old when he was electrocuted after entering an unprotected transformer station. He wasn't the first one who died there, but after his passing, for the first time, the public noticed and pointed out how many abandoned factories were not protected correctly by the cities. This accident left grief in our family. My uncle and aunt and his younger brother are still dying with Tomek every year for over nineteen years on his death anniversary. But now I understand that his death had a deeper meaning for our family and that the members didn't understand. I saw this disparity as a teenager, and I was wondering why it was that way. As a small kid, I knew that the church is only an institution where people worked with a different awareness, and as a teenager, I noticed differences in my family. Tomek was the oldest son of the oldest son of my grandparents, who is also my godfather. This accident was supposed to bring us closer and connect as a whole family from both sides of Tomek's parents all together and also learn about forgiveness toward the members of the family. Our family meetings are on events such as weddings or funerals or a few days on holidays at our grandparents' house, but afterward, we are living separately and have no access to support each other in difficult times or enjoy moments together, mostly with cousins. There are fifteen grandchildren in our lineage with their families, and each of cousin individually deals in their own way with their lives. All the discord in any family leads to disconnection on a global level. Instead of connection and abundance, it creates disharmony, fear, and judgment toward one another. Many times we keep quiet and don't share what is going on in our lives with the nearest ones because we are afraid of being judged by our own aunts, uncles, and cousins. Tomek died for a reason—to bring closer each member of our family from his father's and mother's sides. There is no doubt. In the majority, we can create harmony for each of us not only by chosen members from our lineage or community. We need to transform grief into love because only love can bring healing to everyone all together. This is the truth behind why we are here. After my cousin's accidental passing, his parents, to preserve his creative work, asked two friends to make a book as a photo album. The title is *The Photographs, Tomek Byra 2000–2002*, compiled by Tomasz Ferenc and Henryk Waniek.

I encourage you to look up to his work, especially those who like old factories and tenement houses. His work is important to these who have memories of him and want to everyone to remember his life as valuable. By having time and loving what we do, we can create new things in our lives to leave for posterity. It doesn't matter how long we live. The most important thing is to live with passion all the time. Thanks to that our lives will be fulfilled. Even if we end up living for a small amount of years, we can create something valuable for ourselves and others. Never give up. We all are here for purpose and be in communion with our Creator. This helps guide us on the path of our earthly lives to enjoy them as much as we can.

Through Louise Hay's work, I knew that miracles are happening fast. Her work brought me to the USA to continue her legacy here and spread wisdom around the whole world. When I understood the core of her work, I felt privileged that I received the techniques that really make miracles in our lives as long as we practice them. Connecting with the inner child is nothing like connecting with our real nature, our inner being, with whom we disconnected by accepting others' feedback that something's wrong with us at different age of our childhood and puberty. There are emotional wounds which has not been healed to feel as a whole and complete person. Now I understand that forgiveness is nothing like releasing energetically ourselves from experiences where we were involved with people who we trusted and their behaviors made us feel less and unworthy of our existence. The reason was that we didn't meet their expectations. Forgiving and loving ourselves only bring people to us, people who know our worth and will encourage us to shine our own light. And the mirror work can only speed up our transformation.

I received guidance from my Gurudeva Paramahansa Yogananda when my mind had some contradictory thoughts about my occupation as a teacher of Heal Your Life philosophy and practicing Kriya Yoga.

He said, "Be patient and focus on your main goal as a spiritual teacher and healer. Louise did a great job. You can follow her. Her teachings give us possibility to reach more women and help them understand that love is who you are and nothing else. You don't have to work hard, give away yourself to others because they are needy. Everyone has power within themselves to create joy and love in their lives. You need to understand that part of your growing is to learn that your job is not who you are. The job gives you income and fame, but you belong to God and nobody else. That's why you put boundaries to others and tell them what you need or want.

"Kriya Yoga is remembering that you are a child of God. You are not a human, only Spirit. Spirit is strong and powerful, loving and connection with me gives you to bring peace and love to the world."

I share with my intimate conversation with Guruji to emphasize that these two messages apply to all of us: Spirit in the women's or men's bodies. We all are Spirit without gender; but incarnating on Earth into physical bodies, which are divided for men and women, our societies gave us the roles. For example, men can put boundaries because they were taught this way. However, women lose themselves on issues of others. Their bodies were many times used to their limits. That's why it is important to remember being on this planet that God is Spirit. We are Spirit. Women and men are equal. We all belong to God, and we are immortal. Kriya—action, Yoga—unity. It means that those who practice Kriya Yoga can unite with Spirit one day, and the veil of illusion will drop down forever. As a result, we will not feel separation from one another, from nature, or from the whole creation, which include universes and galaxies. Jesus Christ and Bhagavan Krishna are our main goal to achieve in our communion with God as His own Beloved Son.

Being in Introduction Leaders Program at that time and noticing mine and other participants' breakthroughs, I found great affirmations from the book *Cosmic Telepathy and You* by Hanna Kotwicka. (It was collection of publications by Tuella and others.)

> *I AM a Child of the Light.*
> *I serve with the Brotherhood of Light*
> *to bring Light upon this Planet.*

And this one:

> *I AM a Child of God*
> *embodied upon this planet*
> *to serve the will of my*
> *Heavenly Father;*
> *So be it!*

I bought the license and insurance to legally become Heal Your Life teacher. It gave me the possibility to feel that way, and I started preparing myself for another workshop, which I was planned to start when I move to my new place at Commonwealth Avenue at that time, I thought that it was a reason for me to be close to my work. I know that women are waiting for me with the message that they are about to hear and practice what they will learn from me and my experiences. I was focusing on Hispanic community women to stand for themselves beyond what they were taught and believed.

Omkari for a while was the one who helped me with preparation by guiding me step by step and giving me space to grow and understand how my message, through Louise Hay's work, supposed to look like. It was really inner work. I really appreciate Omkari's support in it.

Through my inner work, I found it very easy to communicate with my masters and my soul by writing. I asked a question, and the exact answer was poured on the paper. I was learning to communicate with my higher self and the spiritual realm that way. I received information and insights many times coming out of my heart, feeling powerful energy, hearing inner voice, or receiving an idea or a picture. But also I wanted evolve in communication during my meditation, and sometimes I felt that I was alone, but it wasn't true. I received guidance through Kriya Yoga lessons by Gurudeva, how I can be attuned to his guidance and have communion with God. Every lesson received from Self-Realization Fellowship helped me to understand more and become more penitent. God's voice is really audible.

The most important for me was to start asking the right questions in which I was evolving through pen and a piece of paper. I communicated with my Guides. They are here to help us in our earthly journey. We need to remember that they protect our soul to achieve its goals being on this earthly plane.

I registered myself to Santa Monica College's fall and later spring semester to non-credit classes to practice English on the advanced level. I enjoyed these classes very much.

After losing the job because of an induced pandemic, I was wondering each month how I would pay my rent. A lot of people had the same issue at that time before the government started helping them. One day I received a call from Louetta. Thanks to her I was able to relax for one month. It is magical when we believe that we are supported and loved wherever we are.

I remember the affirmation that I used a few weeks before when I noticed my thoughts about loneliness and not being supported in a foreign country. I affirmed loudly:

Life brought me to the United States. I am wanted and supported here.

Also this one:

I am financially thriving. I can support myself and others with ease.

After Louetta's call, these affirmations became real for a short time. Month before, I had problem paying my rent on time. I asked my family to support me. They agreed, but I knew that this help was temporary. When I was a little upset that I had to borrow money, I thought, *It would be great when I can find support through others to focus only on my dreams, not to worry about rent and other basic issue and I can support others through that.* My friend's call was the answer to this thought. God answered my prayers for support at that time. It was magic. I started seeing more possibilities to help others through this adventure. I reconnected with people who I met on my journey here. Some of them joined me. They saw opportunities for themselves and families.

The time of coronavirus gave us possibility to awaken the power of love in giving and receiving in the very generous way on every continent. There were established communities from friends and their families to support each other in these difficult times.

I remember my conversation with my soul regarding my flower in this community. She said, "My concern is about you. You cannot believe in something that cannot be you. You are this flower, this beauty and lovingness. Who you invite to this flower, they are like you. I connected you with people who love you. Be patient, they will come. You will see how good it is when you support and trust others. I am with you and believe in me. Stop manipulating others. This is not your purpose. Your purpose is joy, being in the community with these souls who will join you. Be present and peaceful."

> I trust process of life.
> All my needs are met.
> I can create fulfilling life.

People who joined me were very committed and understood what it was about. When I received money, I was able to pay my rent and support my friend so that she could pay her utility bill, which was my intention from the very beginning to support others.

At the beginning, it looked great, and we really trusted these people who worked as admins in our community. But suddenly, it stopped looking as a community project as only three people who stood as authority were allowed to make decisions. They didn't answer the questions that the people wanted to know. They didn't want to admit that what was at the beginning looked colorful didn't work out. As a community, we wanted to know how we can support all these processes. Some of them had great ideas how we all can be connected with each other, but all were rejected. We were supposed to do what we were told and be patient.

It came the end of September, and on October 1, I moved to a new address, where my new obligations were waiting for me.

In Louise Hay's book *You Can Heal Your Life*, she stated that all the experiences that we attract to our lives over and over we have need for it or that kind of relationship or addiction.

One day I asked myself why was I attracted to people who put themselves as authority, speaking about love and control me with money? When I asked the questions and stood up for the people who joined my flower, the admin people didn't listen, and at the end of our cooperation, made assumptions about me, what kind of person I was. They spoke that it was a community, but they were only words.

What have I discovered?

I saw myself as a kid and my mother with my stepfather wanted me to be obedient. They controlled me through money, saying that if I listened to them, I would get this or that, the thing that I wanted. If I won't listen to them, I would not get it. I realized at that same moment that I attracted to myself those people to see my subconscious pattern from my childhood to release it.

It was revelation for me. I felt I needed to be controlled by money because I understood that I was loved. As children, our parents say to as "I love you, but you need to do this or that" or "I love you but you can receive what I want, not what you want. You need to deserve for more and better. You are not good enough for it." With these kinds of feedback that we received from our parents, relatives, or other people such as our teachers, schoolmates, religious institutions and nowadays social media, our limited belief system about love and ourselves were shaped. As adults, it affect to us varies. We put limits with what we can do or cannot do. It is so painful how we reject ourselves and all the good that life has offer to us by putting ourselves in the shoes of mortal creatures who has to follow the rules that society imposed on us by limited beliefs.

When I understood this, I practiced an affirmation: *"I am willing to release the need for being controlling with money by people in the name of love."*

After two or three days, I received an e-mail from the person who created this community. On behalf of the collective admin I was removed indefinitely from the community. As a courtesy, I received my money back, which was part of joining the community. I was so pleased with this e-mail because I wanted quit by myself as soon as possible. My decision arose after our last Zoom meeting when instead of creating space for our full expression, the admin people offered money lottery. This lottery was sham to cover up things which didn't work out and admin people didn't want to admit this. I was thankful for that experience because I reconnected with my friend Joanna. I met new people, and I learned a lot about myself how I understood love.

Being aware of how life works, we see more and understand more. When something bothers us in the other people, they are reflection of us. Looking at this people as a mirror, I was able to find my lack of authenticity also. Many times we want to hide things from others, and we put our mask that everything is all right. Then very often we change the subject instead of acknowledging what is happening in our lives and sharing. Only then we can receive help, support, and don't have to deal with the problem by ourselves. There are bunch of people who love you, understand, and want you to help in every aspect in your life.

We judge ourselves very cruelly, and we think that our lives have to look perfect to become someone else. But this is not true. We have a lot of "mud" in us, and to be free of that, we need to acknowledge it and have willingness to change. Ask God to change you instead of the situation you are in, and you will see miracles. We attract every situation to learn, and some of them, we repeat many times until we understand that we need to notice it and let them go so that the circumstances can be changed. Then the problem or challenge will disappear from our lives because the pattern that we had in our consciousness will be transformed on the energetic level. Thanks to that, we start acting differently and solve our problems in the way we didn't see possibilities before. Our consciousness would elevate, thanks to that. Only in this way we can become a different person and our life change itself for the better. We all have lessons to learn here. Unless we learn them, we will repeat them all the time by attracting the same situations that causes us to grow.

Here in the United States, I had experiences such us attracting situation wherein people made fraudulent transactions on my bank account. Thanks to my friend Joanna, I needed to stop pretending that everything was all right because the bank would solve that problem. The thing was, not everyone brought those circumstances to their lives. It required me to look deeper. What was the reason that my money was withdrawn from my bank account? And I attracted people who wanted to use my account to pay for their things. Their awareness for sure was in lack, the opposite of abundance if they believed that only by stealing they could pay for the things that they wanted, but this was not about them. I attracted these situations to look deeper what my beliefs are about money. Why did I attract this? What thoughts and beliefs did I have that money disappeared from my life, my own bank account? How did I treat money? Did I appreciate it? Did I praise it? Was I thankful for having it to be able pay my obligations and support myself? Or did I give it away, and I did my best to rid of money because I had subconscious belief that I didn't deserve enjoying it by myself? Or was there another reason that I couldn't see the connection of my behavior and connection to others? Did I steal their time, or did I support myself through false belief that I couldn't make myself responsible for making money to enjoy life? Life is a mirror, nothing else. Instead of cursing life and people, we can only look inside and ask the questions, what kinds of beliefs do I carry about exact subject?

When I released the need for bringing up these experiences to my life, it stopped happening. I affirmed that "*I am willing to release the pattern what is in my consciousness to create this condition.*"

A lot of people curse social media, others appreciate them. I was the one who was cursing them. I was afraid of social media, I was afraid of losing myself, and I kept being resistant to learn more on how I can take advantage of the platforms to improve my life and connect with people who are real and heartfelt. I repeated mantra "I am teachable" and "This is so easy to learn." Also, I attracted guys who saw my face on social media and wanted to chat with me. These men had so low self-esteem that they steal identity of well-known people or they put on themselves the mask of a successful and generous person. People would blame social media that this is their thought. I remember the thoughts that I got from somebody who said that this was social media's fault. But the truth is, not everyone experiences this. Every time I attract a person who covers himself by putting on well-known person's identity, I thought, *Aw, the social media are bad thing. I cannot trust them. There are many bad people there.* And I knew that I gathered this thought from other people who I agreed with.

Now looking through my reflection instead of judging others how they act on social media, I have a choice to look for my inauthentic way of being where I pretended or have a kind of dialogue with myself that I hide and cannot accept myself the way I am and decided to pretend to be someone else that others can notice me or started treating as an equal? We all are one and the same, and all are worthy of being seen and loved. We have choice to fool ourselves by pretending to be someone else or become authentic, and only then life can move us forward. People think that not having achievements in their lives they are a nobody, but this is not true. They don't appreciate themselves for who they are and where they are now in their lives. God is in each of us and put us in the places where we are supposed to be at this moment. When our minds become open and ready to grow, we will see that life is not what we have thought; it is evolutionary phenomena to evolve as a human being, and thanks to that, as a soul. We are able to bring more love and good to this world, to another generation would be able to raise planet Earth's consciousness even higher to bring harmony in all coexisting galaxies and universes. It requires courage from each of us to start looking within and nowhere else.

I was talking with a new met person, Antonio, who, for seventeen years, was in the movie industry. He reached a six-figure income and said goodbye to this industry. His life was transformed along with his mum's recovery from cancer. His healing journey led him to many modalities and coaches including Tony Robbins. He opened his own network company to bring more health to the lives of his clients, but his purpose pulled him to SanityDesk Inc., where he can serve broader audience to make changes in their lives and help new entrepreneurs to put their message out through social media. I am one of these entrepreneurs. I met many others on the workshop about funneling to attract the right customers who can benefit from us. We can only support those who have similar life experiences and want to change their circumstances for the better ones. We can teach about what we confronted and how we overcame our conditions to move forward with our lives. Our testimonials that life is good and supportive for each of us if only we are willing to reach for the stars are true. When we only look at our "backyard," we struggle by ourselves with problems, and most of the time, we do not let other people help us. But we cannot do a lot by ourselves. This is a very limiting point of view, and our bodies have limits too. We came to do big things, and we cannot undertake them by ourselves. Behind every leader is a lot of people who create unique things. Without them and their support, it wouldn't have been possible for Mahatma Gandhi, Mother Teresa, Martin Luther King, or other leaders to make such an impactful difference on people. We all are creators of our experiences and in what we believe, they become the truth for us. Only believe and take this first step to your dream, and you will not be the same.

Many times we are limiting ourselves by the thoughts that we have to have money to make difference in our or others' lives. The truth is that money has nothing with who we can become for other people during our transformation and make difference in their lives. When we judge ourselves by the current circumstances and let others judge us by their limiting minds, those who have no idea what we are up to, we give our power away instead of focusing on our goals and dreams. Being here, I heard many stories of people who have nothing but still made a difference in other people's lives. No money, no material possessions, a lot of debts. They overcome their current situation by trusting that Life would give them at that time opportunities to succeed by leaving their own comfort zone and be of service to others. When we rise up beyond what is happening in our lives and stand for ourselves, we start believing that nothing can stop us in what we want to achieve; doors will start opening for us—doors to better and healthier lives. Start investing in yourself. Thanks to that, you will support others. Many companies who are helping others transform on the planetary level donate money to countries where people have no opportunities to stand up for themselves and grow unless they meet those who support them and release all cultural beliefs to move forward with their dreams. Your growth and money help those who are on the lower end of the ladder of society, and your higher consciousness helps the whole cosmos. Can you imagine how your evolution is important to our cosmic planetary family? Listen to your inner voice. Stop reasoning your decisions, and you will see yourself acting differently. Don't wait until you get sick and will not be able to take care of yourself. When we don't live purposefully, our bodies are getting sick due to lack of care and lack of awareness of our thoughts. The true life is love, joy, mutual respect, health, fulfillment, and an abundance of money.

Thank you, thank you, thank you, Mother, Father God, that everything is always, always, always working out for me. Now I have a wonderful job, great possibilities come to me. I have people around me that I love, and they love me. I accept here and now that all my affairs are directed by God. The Divine Spirit is within me, expresses Himself through me, and acts as me. I am in the presence of the only God who is the Highest Good and Love. I know that my dreams are God's dreams, because He sowed them in my heart. I know that abundance and prosperity are given to me, and I accept it with joy now. I know that when I am in presence of the Divine Spirit, no one can prevent me from achieving my dreams and goals, which lead me to financial freedom and fulfillment. I am completely free to do what I love to do. Everyone is supportive to me and my dreams. My inner freedom allows me to express myself fully, to give the best to the world. I interact with people who value the same. Thanks to my pure intention, I am generously rewarded and abundance is expressed in every aspect of my life. And so it is! Amen.

—Prayer of Abundance and Support by Magdalena Julita Byra

CHAPTER 12

Healing Is Always Certain

*I recognize my illness to be the result of my
transgression against health laws.
I will undo the evil by right eating, exercise and right thinking.*

—Paramahansa Yogananda

For most people, their spiritual journey begins when they decide that the life they are currently living no longer serves them. They begin to look for greater ways to be healthy, to be fully self-expressed, to be financially free, and at the end become one with their inner self. They begin to see that there's more life than just the material; it's about the quality of our relationships and our lives. As we look for remedies, we start to dig deep into the core of our existence and discover there is more for us than our past experiences. We are not just our names and thoughts about ourselves. It is this journey that brings us to greater healing. Discovering the truth of who we really are gives us internal peace. When the mind is healed, the body is healed. When our mind is healed, the wounds from childhood start healing, and our perception of Life is different. My journey has started that way, and during these years, my consciousness has been transformed from a victim to one with God.

I am still in the process of transforming subconscious beliefs that has stopped serving me and creating disharmony in my life and body. The work what I have done to trust Life is the most important, and it is saved in the Universal Bank for me. Coming to the US and taking many classes and workshops were precious, and at the end, it helped me find God within through Gurudeva's teachings. The biggest and fastest transformation as a person I received was through Landmark. Through Landmark's methodology, we can achieve our goals and dreams much faster than we have thought that it would be possible. And everything starts with a registration to the Landmark Forum. One year after I did the Landmark Forum, I have noticed my life has become more whole. Every step I took here was the right one, but thanks my participation in the Landmark's programs and assisting there, I have obtained new friendships and I stopped feeling alone and being by my own. Thanks to it, my confidence also grew. Thanks to it, I started considering as my job as a leader of Louise Hay's philosophy at last. What my mind thought as impossible at the beginning of my journey when I came to the USA has become real for me. It took a while, but we all have the right moment of unfoldment. We cannot rush it or postpone it. Everything is in the Divine order, and only our small yes puts us on the path to healing the world. The most important piece of knowledge that I gained was that healing is not only about our bodies. Healing has a deep connection with our roots—the conditioning from the people we grew up with like our families and friends and others who had a huge impact on our experiences even though they were not present physically in our lives. I have experienced my own healing on many levels for which I am grateful. The biggest healing of my past was the reconnection with my father on a deeper level than I thought would be possible. When my brother Piotr informed me that our father was diagnosed with cancer, it gave me the courage to connect with him, and this was the cause of our reconnection. He and his wife were my first guests on the introduction to the Landmark Forum, which was led from the London Center. The biggest breakthrough I had was saying to my father for the very first time "I love you." It healed the whole past. At that time, I understood the words that I heard many times from spiritual teachers, that love can heal past in the one moment. In my experience, it was in a second. I was on an assisting agreement in my program that day, and the coach, Cindy, asked me, "What do you want to create for today during this assisting agreement?" I said that I would like my father to be registered to the Landmark Forum because I knew that it would help him release his own resentment, which caused disharmonies in his body. She asked me, "Who is your father to you?" For a moment, I didn't know what to say. When I let myself talk, I burst out with tears and said that he was the most important person in my life and that I loved him. She responded to me, "Magdalena, I feel so much love from you to him. Call him and tell the truth." I tried connected with him three times during this assisting agreement. After the third call, he answered. I shared with him the whole conversation with Cindy and told him from my heart for the very first time that I loved him. My father unexpectedly responded to me right away that he loved me too. At that moment, everything that was causing our disconnection disappeared. The past stopped existing. It was healed. We received from Life the gift of a new relationship as father and daughter, and only this matters. This program let me connect to leaders from the Polish Introduction Leaders Program from London who committed themselves to bringing Landmark to the Polish community in Poland so that they could receive transformation. Their names were Katarzyna, Aleksandra, and Tomek. What does Landmark Forum give to everyone? It helps people leave their conditioning by making them look into their past, having them become aware of the blind spots and helping them move with dreams to the future. A lot of participants made changes in their careers to live accordingly with their values and desires beyond the age. Also, some of them saved their lives. Once, Aleksandra shared with me how a friend thanked her for standing up for him so that he registered at the Landmark Forum. He was about to commit suicide at that time. Aleksandra didn't know about it until he told her after his Forum. The mind received healing, and thanks to that, the person was able to see differently his circumstances and life in general. It was some kind of awakening to help him continue on his path to healing. Mostly it starts with creating possibilities for yourself and becoming loving, happy, boldly speak up or act. Open communication with our closest ones to release resentments and regrets toward them or toward ourselves help release walls and builds up true connection. Thanks to that, our bodies start getting more light because all negative energies were transformed into joy and love. We all are love and nothing else. We connect with our true nature, and it matters the most because then we can courageously move forward without burdens in our lives. There is a song by Naughty Boy ft. Beyoncé and Arrow Benjamin called "Runnin' (Lose It All)." There are very profound words in it: "I ain't runnin' from myself no more. I am ready to face it all. When I lose myself, I lose it all." There are all disharmonious when we stop trusting ourselves and put blame on others instead of looking within and asking for guidance and awareness from there. We need to stop looking to external approval and conditioning to really live healthy lives.

I was learning about myself all the time, and Life gave me many experiences that I was able finally see the truth about being very codependent, investing a lot of time and energy to please others, and taking care of their misfortunes and responsibilities here in the United States. It was really an "Aha!" moment every time. Moving to the Guardian Angel church gave me the biggest lesson I learned about codependency. It was planned on the higher self realm that I can see it vividly to learn at last how to put boundaries, be truthful to myself, and be committed to my life. My inner being was waiting to say something, and it happened after living there for around one year. I was learning how to say no to things that don't serve me anymore. If I didn't do that, Life made it happen by itself. My ego was looking for the reasons or wanted to find some flaws in myself, but it was only the ego's old patterns learned from my childhood. If something was wrong around me, I took to myself. When I was standing up for myself and claiming my own rights, I was punished in different ways, and very often I heard words saying that it was my fault. So I was meeting new people who were friendly, but honestly, they took care of themselves. I always found out about it later, this or other way. I started learning discernment. These people many times mirrored my home patterns where I grew up. Seeing reflections of my parents, I was healing my self-esteem from childhood because I started noticing that there was nothing wrong with me, and I was very independent, loving, and standing up for my rights as a child and being here as adult person. I had my values as a teenager and as an adult person. As a child, I had no choice, only believing to the feedback of my parents that children don't have right to their own voice. I had no possibility to close doors behind me and not coming back to them. I was dependent on them. As an adult, I stood up for myself without fear anymore knowing that life wants me to be brave and speak up. Thanks to that, I was regaining my own power back and trust to myself step by step. Knowing this, it is a wonderful feeling. Life always wants us to gain our strength back. Also I praised myself and our Creator for knowing that we all have a choice and how important it is to our soul to act differently than other people instead of going down to their behavioral level stand for truth and respect.

On the first day, when I moved into the studio, I was introduced to a beautiful small town called Idyllwild in Riverside County. The town is situated six thousand feet above sea level. Driving up, we could feel the difference in the air pressure in our ears for a while. I invited Omkari to go with me. I was always sharing about myself and my good things with the people around me. I wanted them to experience good by getting wrapped up in their stories of how they were poor or messed up in their lives instead of taking care of my own energy and enjoying by myself that time. It cost me a lot of vitality. I bought three bracelets that lifted energy up to bring harmony to my being. It wasn't a fair exchange with her, and that's why I felt so low at that time. We had possibility to watch the sunset and sunrise from the same place. It was called a double view. The views were outstanding. The town is surrounded by woods. There are many places to hike. There are many art galleries there, and you can find a lot of wooden deer painted and decorated by people working there. There is a friendly and happy environment. A lot of tourists visit Idyllwild to relax and enjoy their time because of a lot of good restaurants and places to listen to music and have fun. When we went back to Los Angeles, I started unpacking and celebrating my new place. I was living in a small studio, where I had my own space to live and more intimacy for a while. The next day was my birthday, and people who I used to live with came to celebrate birthday with me. Also, Omkari, Joanna, and her friend Iwona were with us. I was thinking that time that I was celebrating my birthday and freedom, but it was not for a long time.

I had ups and downs during that year regarding my spiritual work and participation in the Landmark program, but it helped me digest the new learning process and assimilate more and more. I had a breakthrough with my mother through communication also. I invited her to the introduction to the Landmark Forum once or twice. As I mentioned before, since I was a child, I wanted her to do more. I knew that she deserved more in her life, but she didn't want more. She settled down for less. At that time, I spoke with Carlos about it. He was my coach then and now a friend. He said, "Magdalena, you make your mother wrong. Who does she resemble?" I answered, "Myself?" He said, "Yes, your mother is perfect and complete the way she is. Whatever experiences she had in her childhood, she determined a point of view about herself based on her parents and other people's negative feedback. That's why she is not able to see what you want for her. You love her, and clarify with her your inauthenticity about yourself. You are in a program in which you develop yourself. You are the star of your family. You know that, and you play small." So I called my mother. She was happy. We cleared the whole issue, and because of that, our communication again was filled with affection. A lot of my friends from Poland were probably surprised when I called them to clear my inauthentic way of being from the past and reconnected with them to share about myself.

One day, I made a promise to myself that this summer, I would swim in the Pacific Ocean. Since I was living in Los Angeles, I postponed my swimming in the ocean, waiting for some kind of healing. It had been three years. So I asked my friend Joanna, who lived in Torrance, if we could go to the beach. She said yes. We went to Hollywood Riviera beach, which was between Torrance and Palos Verdes. Thanks to that, Lauetta joined us. She had lived in Palos Verdes. At last, I was in the ocean. I could swim all day long. My body was so rejuvenated, and I realized how much I missed swimming. After that, I promised myself I would swim in the ocean again this summer. The opportunity came in two weeks' time. There were six of us. There was a lot of laughter and fun. We were enjoying the time and being together. Who would have thought that I would be that person who connected us all? I was there for only three years, and I was connecting people with one another. Later I realized that I have a gift for it.

Once, I spoke with my friend. We used to work together. She said that my prayers, which I posted on my Facebook profile, were beautiful. She started sharing about her spiritual journey and a new awareness. Also, she told me about her experience with coronavirus, which conflicted with what the TVs showed. She worked in the one of hospitals in Europe. She said that all the information about coronavirus being so dangerous was exaggerated by the mainstream media. At the beginning, she was panicked like all people who watched TV. But suddenly she got aware in the hospital she worked that the doctors were acting differently; they didn't wear overalls like what was shown on TV. The wards were nearly empty, and only a few patients and doctors treated it like a regular flu—without panic. When she started noticing it, she dug deeper and was in communication with the medical personnel regarding what was going on. She found out that this whole pandemic issue was really exaggerated. She remembered her son's words (he was working for a TV network in Poland). He told her many times before pandemic that the media added a lot of untrue information only to keep people watching and keep them busy. When he was telling her the truth, she didn't believe him until she saw with her own eyes the truth through her experience working in the hospital. TV showed different data regarding dying people and the number of illnesses compared to what she saw when she was taking care of patients. Thanks to that, she started believing her son and admitted that media can fabricate information to spread fear and that they do it on purpose. It was her awakening moment. She stopped believing in TV and started searching for true information. When we look for truth, we'll always find it. Sometimes it is so simple and obvious that people don't want to believe in it. When my friend became aware, she stopped wearing masks, which blocks disposal carbon dioxide, and received oxygen for our lungs to function well. She felt safe. Also, she spoke up loudly about it being on holidays in Poland, and it turned out that she met people who wore masks because they were afraid to get a financial penalty, not because of the virus. TV manipulates people through the news and other programs to keep them under the consciousness of fear and uncertainty—the same thing that the Catholic Church did many centuries ago to have power over souls and gain huge power and fortunes over unconscious people. These beliefs are still vivid in our subconscious minds. Some of us are awakening, but other people still live in an illusion of fear and condemnation. The church separated us from God, and TV uses the knowledge about our subconscious minds to program us how they want through news, marketing, and other programs shown on TV.

I had the opportunity to see in the United Stated how well-known and respected journalists of mainstream media repeated hundreds of times information about coronavirus and vaccinations to anchor the words into the watchers' consciousness, which is a gate to the subconscious mind. I was aware and had doubts about my convinced faith. And for other people who didn't know how all programming works, what they could create? We all are beholders. The more we think one thought the more neurons are created in our brains. This thought will pop up more often than we are aware of, and our subconscious will be ready to create experiences in our bodies and lives. Our natural state is health and not looking for new diseases. The subconscious mind accepts everything when the conscious mind lets the information in. That's why it is so important to filter what we hear—so our subconscious mind can create good and healthy experiences instead of misfortune in our lives. When the information are based on fear and repeated hundreds of times over and over, it can only bring the worst-case scenario.[1]

---

[1] February 5,2022 the day with energy Etznab 2 of Scared Mayan Calendar which is responsible for the Truth to be revealed. That day has started the proceedings of Grand Jury the Court of Public Opinion streamed on YouTube all over the world. It is compound from the international lawyers and the specialist who called the international justice regarding to the current situation in the world. They had a very strong evidences to do this and finish unexcited pandemic and unnecessary death of many people. They asked those who were victims of this situation in any kind to contact them on contact@grand-jury.net.

A few weeks later, after the conversation with my friend, a young man from India contacted me. He was in hospital diagnosed with coronavirus. He said that he probably was infected during the Indian Independence Day celebration. I asked him how he was treated in hospital. He said that every day, a blood test was taken, and he received *kadha*—an Indian drink that builds up the immune system. After five days, he was ready go home. The virus disappeared from his body. I received from God everything that I needed to write on this topic one after another. My good friend from Poland a few days later contacted me to send a link to a new book written by independent scientists and specialists in the medicine field: *False Pandemic: Criticism of Scientists and Doctors*. In the preface of the book, written by Dr. Mariusz Blochowiak, there was a Mark Twain's quote: *"Easier is to deceive people, than convince them that they had been deceived."*

Below are some excerpts from the preface of the book:

> *Our data suggest that Covid-19 has a mortality rate that is within the limits of seasonal influenza.*

> John Ioannidis, professor of epidemiology at Stanford University and one of the most cited physician scientists in the world said, "The virus influences our lives in an exaggerated way. This is completely out of proportion to the actual threat that comes from the coronavirus. The astronomical economic damage that is arising now is not in proportion to the threat of this virus. I am convinced that the coronavirus mortality will not be seen in the annual mortality in the record of an out-of-average increase in deaths."

> Everyone who died from the so-called coronavirus has had comorbidities.

The coronavirus is only exceptionally fatal, and in most cases is a largely harmless viral infection."

*There is no coronavirus pandemic...*in any country. While some regions of the world face greater problems than others, this is not due to the greater death rate of the coronavirus as such, but to additional factors "substrate" affected by the virus, e.g. a large number of nosocomial infections, poor health care, panic, the age structure of the society, the health status of the population, etc.

So TV and newspapers did a lot of good for the pharmacological industries in the past and current times all over the world to make people forget that they can be healthy all the time without medications. Thanks to media and governmental lobbying, seven billion people and the world economy are ruled by the decisions of a handful of people that have their own thoughts and goals. Some of them have sincere hearts we cannot generalize. We all are God's children, but they are not you. They are not in your mind. You have power over your destiny and your body's health. Stop giving the responsibility of your life to those who are not you. Take your life into your own hands to be happy and healthy.

Do you see any convergence of the events and the relevance of your life to them? Ask yourself this: How can billions of people be dependent on a minority who are included in these billions? They don't differ from us. How can billions of people allow their own lives to be ruled by fear and uncertainty by a few? Our global consciousness is rising up, and this is good. But not all people are aware of that. Those whose beliefs are based only on TV and radio cannot experience a true life and cannot see what is really happening in their own lives. They only duplicate old programming patterns and stay in the victim's consciousness, not taking responsibility for their own destiny. That's why they are dependent on opinions of others regarding what should be done or not. When it comes to global information, there are two currents of thought: those who are supported by rulers and those who are independent, including media. The independent media mostly invite to interviews scientists, doctors, and specialists who are very good in the field and look objectively at the current situation. It depends on their own credibility. Many times it turns out that the information can differ between independent media and the one people used to watch or listen to. These people who are dependent only on one source of information mostly accepted and do not listen to their intuitive guidance, and they often do not have the opportunity to make the right choices for themselves. When I participated in English classes in Evans Adult School, an experienced journalist was invited. She said, "It is important that a good journalist doesn't look for sensation, only for the facts, and that he or she looks at different sources to give more objective information that is not based only on one informational source." In the English textbook from Santa Monica College, we had the article "Statistic to Watch Out For." There were two subtitles for the article. The first was "Correlation is Not Causation," which was pointed out in the example where the sales of ice cream and bathing suits rising and falling together may correlate but don't prove that one causes the other. We know that the purchase of ice cream doesn't cause the purchase of bathing suits and vice versa. There is a third factor in this case that causes these two products to be bought more or less often: the warm weather, which is responsible for the correlation. The second subtitle was "Survey Data Is Easy to Manipulate and Misrepresent." The example given was of a toothpaste company that may proclaim that 80 percent of dentists recommend this brand. In the article, questions to ask such as these were given: Who conducted the survey? Was it the toothpaste company? The author of the article summarized that the chances were, they asked questions that would give them the results they wanted. Do we see the correlation between this article and what is happening in the world? Ask yourself how many times you were deceived by well-meaning people and, after listening to them, had to deal with consequences by yourself. I believe now it is high time to start being more trustful of your inner guidance instead of looking for solutions from others. Ask yourself, "What is my truth?" and be loyal to it. Thanks to that, you will always be guided safely to the right solutions, places, and people, and external circumstances will not affect you. Be yourself, and God will make the path for you to have peace, health, and harmony in your life. When we are anchored in our faith that we are protected and see in our bodies the perfection of God, any mentally made illness will not touch us, and the existing one will disappear. Our bodies are perfect. They are made of Light. That's why healing can occur in every moment. We only need to have faith in it. I know that we all take personally our bodies' illnesses and that we blame our bodies even caused disharmony in them by thinking negatively. We think that we are different. I had that kind of thought, but my willingness to accept that my thoughts caused chronic diseases was helping me to recover in the right time. Most people are not looking into places that they are supposed to. They look for answers outside themselves, not knowing that everything is curable from within. We were taught this way and got used to blaming it on circumstances in our lives and justifying ourselves with aging or misfortune holding the view that we have nothing in common with our diseases. First, we need to recognize. Our bodies only respond to our thought patterns and unintegrated emotions, which block flow of energy in our bodies, and what we put into our mouths as food and drink. Do we exercise and praise our bodies the way they are at the moment? Do we choose deliberately thoughts and activities that give us joy instead of stress? Do we support our bodies by stopping the misuse of alcohol and other addictive stimulants such as drugs, cigarettes, or junk food from well-known chains or stores? We need to learn how to discern for ourselves what is good for our bodies and not base it on what we were taught by our parents or relatives. The reason is that each body is unique and has its own guidance regarding what food or supplement is healthy for it. Tradition is good, but being attached to the way of food and how it's supposed to be served cannot deliver well-being for a long period of time to anybody. We need to look for our own solutions, which are the best for us and our bodies, the temples of the Spirit. The pill is supposed to be the last and not the first line of defense. At the moment, everything is upside down in our modern lives. Many times souls who identify themselves with their bodies, including its aging and diseases, have something to talk or complain about with others who are on the same level of consciousness. It is really a pity when immortal souls are so attached to their body's imperfection that if this imperfection would disappear, they would have nothing to talk about. They would feel lost. What's next? Sometimes people with this kind of consciousness, after healing, can bring subconsciously to their bodies another illness to have social contact with others and have another subject to talk about. A lot of them feel lonely, and if the illness would disappear, they would have no reason to complain. They would have to admit that there is nothing wrong with them and they can start living new life beyond their body's conditions. There is enough space to ask what is my purpose in life and how can I start anew? What kinds of dreams I had but have forgotten? How can I be more happy? What am I supposed to do to feel alive again and stop being afraid of life and circumstances that I face right now? Every question is answered. Listen to the answers. Your life will be changed, transformed, and become more meaningful. Some people, mostly younger ones, were awakened when they got cancer or other "incurable" illness. Then they started thinking, *What can I do for others before I leave this planet? How can I do some good in this world?* These kind of people open nonprofit companies. They create great and huge projects. The illness gave them the opportunity to stop being afraid and playing small. They had nothing to lose. In many cases, they healed their bodies because they had purpose to live. More divine light started flowing in their bodies and was able to cured them. Their minds were focused on the service and growing. Thanks to that, more thoughts were coming up about health and love. These people started taking care more about their bodies, and because of that, their bodies were healed naturally. Every emotional hurt that we had experienced during our lifetime stays in our bodies and without solving this, it very often changes into illness. Know that we are only the ones who can heal ourselves.

Many years ago I stopped believing in aging. I affirmed youth, and it became true for me. I don't use any antiaging cosmetics because I don't believe in this term. There is no age. Our bodies change naturally, and many of us have better bodies than they had when they were young. I believe in eternal youth, and my body manifests this. When I came to the USA, I was looking for facial creams which would moisturized and nourished my skin. I compared them. Some of them were cheaper than $20 and others cost $40–$50. I had opportunity to try under eye cream for $300. It was the newest invention. I paid for it $100 as promotion for a staff member. It was a generosity of the manager of the store where I was shopping. None of them gave my skin what it needed. Some of them made my skin burn. The more expensive ones. So now I use facial creams that every person can use at every "age." It is important for me that the ingredients are clean, without artificial and chemical improvements. I don't pay a lot for them. I stopped using makeup. I started to love my complexion, and I don't need any beautifiers at the moment. I love feeling natural. There is more freedom without worrying how do I look like to be accepted or not. I know that my body looks great, the way it is supposed to look like, and it is blessing to have this kind of freedom. I really love it and encourage everyone who reads this book to start looking at their bodies this way, as perfection. Then you can become friend with your body. If we know that every tension, pain, or illness is brought through our thinking and doing against yourself, then we can ask the body, "What do you want me to say? Where I was misled?" The answer will be always given. We are supposed to bless our bodies for giving us the signal to stop continuing practicing negative thinking and doing things that don't serve us. Our bodies are perfect because the Spirit creates them. We chose them for this lifetime, and as a result, we promised to take care of them and not compare them with others'. Everybody is perfect, complete, and can be healed by a thought. Even science is now so advanced that it can prove it.

When it comes to sun protector creams, I prefer to use marula oil or avocado oil as a base and add three to four drops of rosemary essential therapeutic oil. I use the mixture when I go to the beach. Rosemary therapeutic essential oil is great natural sun protector especially for UVA, which people are afraid the most. We don't have to use chemical cosmetics and put on our or our children's faces to protect their skin. This way we don't expose our skin to unnecessary side effects, which sun protector creams from department stores can cause. The nature gave us all to be safe.

Many years ago, I had problems with the lower part of my back. It hurt often. Then I learned and understood that the spine can hurt because of negative thought patterns, mostly worrying. The lower part of the spine causes pain when we focus on lack of money and worry about it. I started trusting Life and stopped worrying about how the bills would be paid because I am always supplied, and my back stop hurting me.

When I gave back to God all the burdens connected with the belief that I needed to carry my life and that of others on my shoulders, I felt all heaviness was released from them, and thanks to that, my shoulder blades became more flexible. I also started exercising and stretching, thanks to Self-Realization Fellowship techniques and Kriya Yoga.

When I stopped identifying myself with aging, I trusted more my body, and I started expanding it without worrying that it can be hurt. My body is made of Light. Light can be transformed and renewed always.

I used the affirmation, *"Divine light is flowing through me and radiating from me. It fills me within and without."*

Now I use more affirmations from Paramahansa Yogananda's *Scientific Healing Affirmations* pocket book, which helped me to realize that healing is certain in every "incurable" disease. There is no such thing like "incurable." Only our mind's perceptions are required to be changed. That's why Gurudeva's healing affirmations helped me understand who we are and what we are made of. Thanks to that, my mind had started to adjust to the truth. That's why my and everyone's body healing is certain. We can prevent mental disease by cultivating peace and faith in God. It can help us free our mind from all disturbing thoughts and fill it with love and joy. When we realize the superiority of mental healing over physical healing, our bodies will be cured.

Will, imagination, and faith are states of consciousness that actually and directly act from within. When we are willing to release habits that don't serve our bodies to make them healthy, we can start the journey to self-love. God knows His ways to free us from everything that we are willing to let go of. It is always the easiest and the more loving way, more than our minds could imagine. Paramahansa Yogananda explains in this small pocketbook why people fail to cure themselves through mental healing. He says,

> Autosuggestion and various affirmations are useful in stimulating the life energy, but people very often employ purely mental methods without consciously working with the life energy and are not able to establish physiological connection, they are not invariably efficacious. A cure is certain if psychophysical techniques are combine with the power of will, faith and reason to direct the life energy and to reach the superconscious mind. In the blissful state of Reality one comprehends the inseparable unity of mater and Spirit and solves all problems of inharmony.

Self-Realization Fellowship techniques given by guru Paramahansa Yogananda offer the operating mode for harnessing the will to direct the movement of actual vibrating life energy to any body part. By this method, we can feel in a definite way the inner flow of cosmic vibratory force.

> O Heavenly Father, O Cosmic Mother,
> O Master Mine, O Friend Divine,
> I came alone, I go alone;
> With Thee alone, with Thee alone.
> With Thee alone, with Thee alone.
>
> Oh, Thou didst make a home for me
> Of living cells, a home for me.

This home of mine is home of Thine;
Thy life did make this home;
Thy strength did make this home.
Thy home is perfect, Thy home is perfect.

I am Thy child, Thou art my Father;
We both do dwell, we both do dwell
In temple same,
In this temple of cells,
Oh, in this temple of cells.
Thou art always here,
Oh, on my throbbing altar near.

I went away, I went away;
With darkness to play, with error to play;
A truant child, I went away.
Home I came in shadows dark,
Home I came with matter's muddy mark.
Thou art near; I cannot see.
Thy home is perfect; I cannot see.
I am blind; Thy light is there.
'Tis my fault that I cannot see.
Beneath the darkness line
Thy light doth shine;
Thy light doth shine.

Together, light and darkness
Cannot stay, cannot stay.
Together, wisdom, ignorance,
Cannot stay, cannot stay.

Conjure away, oh, lure away,
The darkness away,
My darkness away.

> My body cells are made of light,
> My fleshly cells are made of Thee.
> They are perfect, for Thou art perfect;
> They are healthy, for Thou art Health;
> They are Spirit, for Thou art Spirit;
> They are immortal, for Thou art Life.
> (Paramahansa Yogananda)

I love use the last verse from this long affirmation as a mantra to remember that my body cells are made of divine light and God is Health and Life. You can find all the information and guidance on www.yogananda.org.

I remember how, after receiving my first lessons from Self-Realization Fellowship, I started putting my ego away and tried to understand what was said there and also practice the teachings given in the lessons to be able to meditate with Guruji Yogananda and ask him to be with me and guide me to healing and self-realization. Honestly, it wasn't easy at the beginning because my mind wanted to understand everything and translate this knowledge using the old way my mind worked, which still implemented my Catholic background and was behind about God, which didn't serve me at all. So there were ups and downs. Also, having guru, I had in my mind that I am not capable of deciding for myself. So I had a lot of resistance often, and even I knew that I was led to Gurudeva from very beginning. He was given to me directly by God. But the longer I was with the SRF teachings and the more I meditated and practiced Kriya Yoga, the more my mind started adjusting to higher vibrations and the more understanding came. And sometimes I really felt overwhelmed with joy and gratitude that I have my master, who helps me to practice Kriya Yoga correctly. I knew when I was doing it by myself and when Gurudeva was with me. These two practices were completely different. Thanks to my stubbornness and practicing techniques, I started noticing my thought patterns, which were hidden in my subconscious mind and was repeating subconsciously in the past for many years: "Life is bad. I don't want to live." I was observing how they flow through my solar plexus up to the ether. After noticing that, I started feeling compassion for myself, wondering what really was the bad thing I did that I was punishing myself with this kind of thinking. I didn't deserve at all to reject everything that was given to me, which is life itself. I realized that these thoughts started coming up to my consciousness when I was struggling in Spain and later in Poland as a young girl who fell in love with a person who wasn't for her. I didn't want to admit this to myself, and I was afraid of letting go. I had in mind what my family would think or say about me being so young and unable to keep my marriage. That it would be my fault. We always have people around who confirm our beliefs. The difference is only if we are aware and agree with them or let go and have the courage to live on our own terms. At that time, I believed others when they said that my life had to look that way, so I kept my toxic marriage and thought that life was cruel. But it turned out that it wasn't life. It was my ex-husband, who became my whole life to me that I had to ask him about everything and wasn't able to make my own decisions because I was worrying about how he would react. I didn't trust myself at all that I was doing it right, even if I did. I had him in my head all the time, what he would do or say, because of that. I was under so much stress by figuring out how to do the best I can so that there would be peace at home. I really had enough many times, and I didn't know that I had a choice to let go then. My condemnation thoughts and living all the time under stress led me to experience epilepsy longer than necessary. It became a chronic illness, and to heal this, I needed to become aware of that first. The longer we live and stay unaware after taking our journey to self-love and healing, the longer than usual it can take. It takes willingness from us to be healed consciously and have our own power over it instead of giving it to modern medicine. Many times it is required to use medication for a while but only to keep us going to the true healing and let us release things that don't serve us. It will not come overnight, but it will come with an awareness of ourselves and a willingness to believe and have faith that healing is certain. No one can heal us. We are the true healer of our bodies and lives. There is no third person who heals you. A true healer helps you release old blocks in your body and activate your own healing abilities. Your Consciousness heals it. You are the healer of your own body, nobody else. That's why it takes a lot of spiritual work on yourself and awareness of what was the true cause of the illness. I wasn't aware of my thought patterns, which caused my chronic disease and blocked my circulatory and sexuality meridian through which life energy (*prana*) supposed to flow smoothly. The meridian has its beginning in the heart. It runs down through the diaphragm, connecting the upper, middle, and back part of the triple warmer, which is responsible for the water channels throughout the body. It supports their cleansing and the proper secretion of body fluids. The triple warmer therefore combines respiratory, circulatory, excretory, digestive, and sexual functions as a whole. The branching of the circulatory and sexuality meridian runs around the ribs, around the armpits, along the inner side of the arm to the elbow joint, across the forearm, through the inner side of the palm, and to the tips of the fingers. On the surface of the hand, a short branch connects at the nail bed of the ring finger with the triple warmer. When the light flows without any blocks through this meridian, we feel inner peace, relaxation, trust in ourselves, and satisfaction. When the flow is blocked, people can experience in their bodies among others the following: encephalopathy, migraine, epilepsy, nausea and vomiting, asthma, hiccups, circulatory disorders, paralysis, states of exhaustion, circulatory collapse, or states of shock. As mental states it can be the following: melancholia, guilt, somnolence, envy, restlessness, and a feeling of tension.

I remember my disagreement when one of my first neurological doctors said to me that at the age of forty-four or fifty, my circulation would be worse because I had cold feet when she examined me. If I believed her, it probably would've happened this way, but I had always had it in me to reject in my mind what is opposite to my beliefs. At that time, I said nothing to her, but I knew that she wasn't right. Having knowledge, I understand now that the reason was that my circulation meridian was blocked and not because age states that. I feel better than when I was twenty-five or thirty-three years old. Now I am forty-eight. My circulation is in very good condition. Also, I have taught myself through energization exercises from Self-Realization Fellowship lessons how to bring life energy through my own will into defected parts of my body or when I feel cold or tired. I feel how energy flows through my body parts and meridian, which was blocked. I had my "Aha!" moment in the day of energy, Cimi 6. We receive this energy to planet Earth every twenty days to release things that block or limiting us. Then the soul as a human being can act freely or even heal the body when realization comes. I started crying with humility and joy from finding a solution for all people who suffer from this or other chronic diseases and can also be used for prevention. When I realized it, I felt pain in the place where my head was hit and felt life energy flowing in the branches into my brain, where the disconnection was before. And it was one day after when I was in a conversation with a doctor who I met after a service in Lake Shrine; she praised the technology of science and medications. She had patients with the same chronic diseases I had, and she told me the same thing I heard from others with whom I disagreed. So for me, it was only confirmation that my path wasn't the same path of a newly met person. I was looking for the Truth and healing to rely on my body without medications. The person's goal was quite different, and it was okay. We all receive what we ask for.

We need to remember that besides seven main chakras, our body contains twelve light channels called meridians, which Chinese medicine describes in a very detailed manner. Chakras absorb cosmic light, directing it to the body. The one in the medulla oblongata is called the mouth of God. Then through a subtle network of energy channels (meridians), the energy of light (life energy) is transmitted to all cells and organs of the body. Yin and yang energy flow as two different polar currents throughout the body and create a circulating system of liquid light. Six currents of female energy (yin) flow from the feet to the chest area, to the hands, and till the ends of the fingers from both sides. And six currents of male energy (yang) flow from the fingers up to head and from the head to the feet. The flow can be blocked by accidents, eating disorders, thoughts of worry, and stress. While understanding meridians and the cause of disharmony in my body, I received Trudi Thali's book *Opening the Light Body*. I recommend this book to each person who wants to consciously heal themselves. She gives practical guidance and information, which every person on the path to their own healing will understand.

The knowledge brings us the freedom of being less dependent on pharmacology and taking control over our health and lives. It requires only a willingness to change, and life will take its own course. Children who were born with epilepsy or other diseases can be healed by having aware parents, which, instead of going for pharmacological help only, start taking a child to meditation and practice with them energization exercises or other exercises to connect with their own source of healing as a stimulant of life energy. Using positive affirmations and feeling a connection with the Source of all cures. As a healthy supplement, I found out that CBD oil helps children with epilepsy a lot. We can use moringa or another tree fruit. For example, mangosteen, the juice supports the neural system and has other properties to regain balance in our bodies. We can also use herbs that have curing abilities. Children are very fast learners and accept what adults say. As a result, they can heal themselves very quickly. Mind and faith in the instructions brings the healing. Babies, which are still more in touch with the Spirit than the material realm, can be healed by a healer who knows that the Spirit is the cause of health.

Having knowledge and understanding about meridians, when I look back to see how my grandmother rejected her body and had circulatory collapse as a result, losing consciousness many times, I now can say that our thought patterns were similar; and it has nothing in common with genes and medical states. Our thinking is responsible for the health of our bodies. I was under my grandmother's protection or upbringing till I was four years of age. It is a time when the whole programming about life occurs. Everything that I have learned or accepted as true was from her and what was happening in the household. Later on, it was only a continuation of my mother's understanding, which she learned at her parents' home. That's why it is so important to break this cycle—so our children can have their own undisturbed pattern of thoughts to enjoy their own healthy lives. Nowadays I feel my grandmother's presence more often, and she is helping me release her beliefs as a person so that I can start living my life without her beliefs from my childhood. As I mentioned in previous chapters, clearing old patterns in our consciousness helps new generations be free of past beliefs and become closer to their own Source of Existence. Be sure that your ancestors and all of heaven are waiting for you to help you clear your own family lineage from thoughts and patterns that don't allow you enjoy your own life the way you want. I registered myself under Rose Cole Shamanic Academy to discover my dormant gifts and become of service to others as a medium healer through Guided Energy Medicine, which is compatible with Reiki that exists more longer than other healing practices on the planet Earth. I love to be a part of soul communities who are awakened and grow to move even higher with their consciousness and serve. It is wonderful to see how we all blossom and connect ourselves to our guides, who want to help us on the earthy realm. We all have divine support. We only need to ask them more often for help. They will respond with joy. One of my first guides was my grandmother. I recognized it when I started noticing signs connected to her. I attended a workshop from Shamanic Academy on her birthday. I noticed there was a picture behind the person who led the workshop. It looked like it was taken in the late '50s. The woman in the picture looked similar to my grandmother having her hand up. It looked to me like she was protecting herself from being hit. I knew that it was an issue in our family and that everyone accepted it as the way it was supposed to be. A woman had no right to speak. The next day, I found that out of five women, four were beaten by their partners in the United States. Some of them attempted to commit suicide because they didn't know that they have the right to reach for help. My first class was on the day of my grandmother's birthday Tzolkin energy (IK3), which represents psychic and telepathic abilities as well as communication skills and inspiration. With this day energy, I felt my grandmother's presence which, through the period a month, inspired me to look into my childhood in Jozefow differently that I remembered. Her energy helped me to solve all my misunderstandings from my childhood regarding my place of birth and the miscommunication with her, and I understood that I was really safe and loved there. My later experiences as a child blurred the truth.

During the whole year living in the church, I was able to travel three more times to Idyllwild. The second time I went by myself. Remembering my first visit with Omkari and how I felt down. I preferred to be by myself and enjoy the time. But for the two other times, I spent time with friends who all really felt good when we were with each other—Hind, with her son, and Alison, who initiated me to Reiki, to the second level there. The first attunement I had in Santa Monica. Being attuned to the second level Reiki let me channel energy into the clients to activate the natural healing processes of their bodies to restore physical and emotional well-being. Most of them were my friends and their and my family members. Reiki and other energetic healing modalities are what we can use beyond the geographic location of the practitioner and the client. We met with Hind during the Introduction Leaders Program, and we became friends at the end of the program. She connected me with Alison. The last time, I was with Nazanin, who was my buddy in the Introduction Leaders Program and become a good friend. We were hiking, swimming in the lake, and laughing a lot. I felt like I was a teenager then. We had a lot of fun. Also, I participated again in the Landmark Forum to understand more of what I didn't before and clear stuff with my friends this time, stuff I wasn't aware of. When registering for the Forum, I put my intention about my Self-Realization Institute opening, and I shared about it for the very first time. I can see that this institute will manifest by itself soon.

I proved many times to my closest family and some friends through my experiences that life is not what they think is. Life is full of miracles, but there are billions of people—living souls—who believe that they are mortal. We all live in the reality that our minds let us believe: what is possible and what is impossible for each of us. The more "bad" experiences happen in our lives the more disbelief there is that living is to thrive and enjoy in one's full potential and health. I love Mark Twain's quote mentioned before: *"Easier is to deceive people, than convince them that they had been deceived."* We forgot who we are by a veil of forgetting when we incarnated here, and we deceived ourselves that our true life is what we see or believe as an adult person. I have experienced many times when "reality" clashed with the truth. I have heard from people who admired me for my courage, but they didn't do anything to make their lives really fulfilled and happy. They believe in aging, misfortune, or luck. The fact is, they cover their unwillingness to change with the age, saying, "I am too old." You are young. This is an umbrella of their own fear—a fear of discovering the Truth, their true reality of who they are. They prefer stay in the consciousness of a victim instead of admitting that they have lived with a lie. Some of them may have tried once or twice to improve their lives, and they gave up, telling themselves that this or that is impossible. Life passes them by, and nothing new appears in their awareness. They are so attached to their old beliefs given by sociaty where they grew up that they cannot let go of them. This is our collective awareness right now. Do we really want to live in this kind of world where uncertainty, fear, diseases, and unforgiveness are the issue on a daily basis? Why can't we start trusting Life again and really look at it with hope and joy, knowing that everything is for a reason: to find God within us, nothing else.

An Ethiopian prime minister received the Nobel Peace Prize in 2019 for his work in ending the twenty-year postwar territorial stalemate between Ethiopia and Eritrea. I found out from the person who knows him and shared the happy news with us that the prime minister took one of the programs offered by Landmark group. He created then a possibility to keep peace in the borders. The result was the Nobel Peace Prize. Sharing this with one of my friends, I understood that the world is healing and transforming into a better place. What other people call an utopia, for me, it stopped being this way. Peace, love, and harmony is possible for everyone in a short time if only we stop waiting for others to change, we start changing ourselves by healing our old issues from the past, recognizing what is important for us and making choices on its behalf, and be open to love again. We all can start our new life again and again under the umbrella of the world community where money is the currency of love, where possibilities are for everyone, and where joy and respect for ourselves and others are gifts from within manifested through each of us. We can acquire all the wisdom, love, and power to create new world. The only reason that can stop us is fear and the misunderstanding of why each of us was born again on this beautiful planet.

Once, when I felt attachment to the time when I was hoping the Heal Your Life workshops would help me acquire income and pay my bills, I wanted to give up the Landmark program in which I was participating. At that time, Nazanin wanted to give up too. She had a lot of work responsibilities. We both came back to the program, and I am grateful for this. Thanks to that, we all had the opportunity to become closer with all the participants and each other. I know if I hadn't gone back to the program, I wouldn't be connected with Hind, Alison, and other people who play important roles in my growth and have good-quality friendships. I received a tip from a Los Angeles Landmark Center manager and a Leader Forum on how we can tune in to our creative nature to find solutions on a daily basis. He asked me to write down twenty actions that I could do to solve my financial challenge before the clients would come. He also mentioned that mostly, our ideas would stop coming to our minds after having eight or ten written down, but it is important to continue writing because then we can find the best and unexpected solution to our challenge.

As I mentioned, I received healing on many levels by allowing myself to dream and be led by my inner guidance to meet people who know the truth, and they weren't religious.

One day a combination of colors started attracting my attention. The first was red, which resonates only with money consciousness and is the lowest energy of material consciousness. The root chakra is red, which is the closest color to Mother Earth. But also, the color red represents Archangel Uriel. When my focus was changed from red, I started noticing other colors such as white, dark blue, and purple. It turned out at the end of the day that I was guided by the angelic energy of Archangel Uriel to focus on my assignment. I received support by subscribing to Angel Oasis emails, and I started feeling lighter and more joy in my heart when I was listening to the angelic music, which came with the Premium Guardian Angel Report I purchased for myself. It was all connected with Archangel Uriel. Later, I received angelic guidance when the book of Ella Selena fell off my windowsill. I opened to the page about how to connect with our guardian angel, and there was meditation for it. I know that my guardian angel does the best to communicate with me and help me by sending different people or books or bringing me to a master of the Self-Realization Fellowship. My chronic issue was healing through practicing the techniques, using affirmations, and taking another step, which was Kriya Yoga.

Previously, when I started working with Louise's affirmation from her book *Heal Your Body*, I didn't resonate with it at all. I was repeating it, but they were empty words: "I choose to see life as eternal and joyous. I am eternal, joyous, and at peace." The reason was that I didn't know who I really was. The words such as "eternal" had no meaning for me because I identified myself with the body, which looked so solid, and I didn't know how I could heal my issue through this simple joyous affirmation. But when I received the knowledge of who we are through Paramahansa Yogananda's lessons and practicing them, it gave me more understanding of the disharmony in my body, which occurred after hitting near the medulla oblongata my thought patterns, after which later caused me to shut myself down to stop myself from dealing with life and its challenges. I was secluded and alone even though I dealt with many people. Now I know that I am a Spirit, a soul incarnated on the planet Earth and connected with all other souls as people, nature, and the cosmos, which is made from Light.

Now I can accept her suggestions from the book about the probable cause of epilepsy being the sense of persecution, a rejection of life, a feeling of great struggle, and self-violence. I became aware of these thoughts after practicing Kriya Yoga. Louise received that wisdom after she joined the United Church of Religious Science, founded by Ernest Holmes in 1927, and searched for truth. Thanks to that, she healed herself from cancer that appeared in her genitals. She found the core issue of her disease, such as resentment and unforgiveness toward her tormentors, among others, the person who raped her when she was five years old, and later, her stepfather. She shared her story in the book *You Can Heal Your Life*. Nowadays, Religious Science is known as Centers of Spiritual Living. It has become a global community comprised of more than four hundred spiritual communities, teaching chapters, study groups, and other ministries in thirty countries.

Sacred Mayan calendar indicates what kind of thoughts are responsible for pain in our bodies. The body is called as a human *holon*. As an example, let's focus on our hands and feet. Every negative thought has reflection in our hurt finger or toe. Every archetype is correlated with our fingers and toes as I mentioned before.

Right hand:
Thumb finger—AHAU—willingness to retaliate, expectation
Index finger—IMIX—distrust, envy, mother complex
Middle finger—IK—conflict, alienation
Ring finger—AKBAL—complaining, pressure, blame
Small finger—KAN—lack of faith, disbelief

Right leg:
Big toe—CHICCHAN—envy, lust, slander
Second toe—CIMI—fear of…, vindictiveness
Third toe—MANIK—workaholism, avarice
Fourth toe—LAMAT—meticulousness, grudges
Small toe—MULUC—hypocrisy, false humility

Left hand:
Thumb finger—OC—selfishness, victim attitude
Index finger—CHUEN—fear, intrigue, maneuvering
Middle finger—EB—manipulation, false godliness
Ring finger—BEN—loneliness, overload
Small finger—IX—dishonesty, pose, materialism

Left leg:
Big toe—MEN—addiction, blindness
Second toe—CIB—instability, bias
Third toe—CABAN—exaggeration, hasty conclusions
Fourth toe—ETZNAB—deception, masks
Small toe—CAUAC—routine, resistance, powerlessness

There are accidents when people are hurt, but mostly, these accidents and incidents they attracted to themselves unknowingly by the law of attraction. Some of these is a journey of their soul to fulfill their destinies on the plane realm. What is the difference between these two examples: the first ones, people who act in aggressive way, their anger and negative thoughts bring to them an experience to watch out. Mostly, they come out from the accident safe and sound or with a few scratches or broken leg or hand. Life was giving them a sign to be aware of their thoughts and words. The others pass away or become a disabled in some way. At this point, their life can be transformed in a new one, if they allow it. There are many people, who through disability, became transformation for others. They become of service to others who were disabled from birth. They found strength. They realized that they could use their body differently and evolve in it to enjoy their lives and support others in it. They couldn't control anything anymore the way they used to. Thanks to that, they surrendered and the soul could take their life over for good of others. For the soul, how the body would look like or in what condition it is in is not important. It is possible for it to complete its task for this lifetime regardless of it. Some disabled people became cured again in order to testify the Spirit's power over matter. Mostly, they became spiritual teachers and healers. They find their soul's destiny this way. We are never victims of our circumstances or illnesses unless we believe in them.

We can ask about children who were born with disfigured bodies or diseases. The body was chosen by the soul who wanted to have experiences of an imperfect body on order to realize that the body is not the issue anymore when we know who we are. Healing can occur quickly or not, but the soul's destiny will be fulfilled. Also in the spiritual world, it is said that we come to this world with some kind of disease or imperfection of our bodies to emphasize that in the previous incarnations our deeds were wrong. When we see disfigurement in the body of the person, it doesn't mean that this person is "bad" at the present life, only there is an outside mark of previous incarnations and what this soul wanted to accomplish in this incarnation can only be found by seeing God's perfection. Disfigured body is not important, because the power of God will always find the way to express Itself in this world. Our bodies are pure illusion of God's creation. The disable children or people are examples of God's perfection expressed through their art or any kind of creative work.

The body is the temple of God in which He is embodied as a unique soul on this planet.

We all are lotuses, which wouldn't be so beautiful and not able to blossom without the mud. This wisdom comes from Asian culture, where among others Parmahansa Yogananda came from, India, one hundred years ago, September 19, 1920. We can see on the stained glass in Lake Shrine and other temples the lotuses one next to another. As an interesting fact, the Self-Realization Fellowship monks wanted to have lotuses on the lake at the Shrine, but water was too salty. They wanted to emphasize that Guruji's teachings who wanted to release all of us from the mud of delusional life and let us blossom freely in consciousness of Spirit.

He said, *"It is better to die, if death has to come, with the conviction of perfect health than with the thought that a mental or physical aliment is incurable. Though death may be the necessary end of the according to present human knowledge, still its 'destined hour' may be changed by the power of the soul."*

The soul is "I," and the mind is only a tool to be connected to the soul's wish. Here we have the answer to the curable miracles of the bodies and how people who were in coma or diagnosed as a dead person come back to life. Jesus said, *"Man shall not live by bread alone, but by every word that proceedeth out of the mouth of God."* It means that our body receives cosmic energy every day, and it is received through the medulla oblongata (mouth of God), filling our whole body from within. And we're supposed to learn how to rely on it more than food or sun, which are external sources. The same is with healing. We're supposed to rely on this healing modality rather than medications. The dynamo of our bodies is cosmic energy; external sources like food, medications, or supplements are like small batteries in comparison to the force of life with which we are connected to. All external methods of stimulation only cooperate with the life energy but are valueless without it. This cosmic energy (the

Word) in Hindu or Western religions are called respectively *Aum* or *Amen*. This word encompasses the whole creation where we live in and Christ Consciousness as the one son of God. How we can start relying more on life energy is explained in Self-Realization Fellowship lessons written by Paramahansa Yogananda.

Reading spiritual books like Jonnette Crowley's *The Eagle and the Condor*, Matt Khan's *Whatever Arises Love That* and *A Love Revolution That Begins with You*, Drunvalo Malhizedek's *Serpent of Light*, Paul Selig's *I Am the Word*, Don Miguel Ruiz's *The Mastery of Love* and *Four Agreements*, and many other authors, I didn't know from where they got their knowledge and why they were so certain at what they claimed. I wanted to know as well. Reading some of their books, I was curious how they received guidance, pictures of themselves from the past incarnations, and how they had these experiences. I had in my mind that the spiritual world was out there, like God was introduced in my case by Catholic Church. At that time, I thought that they were chosen or unique. I didn't recognize myself that I was the same as they were. I really thought that they were from a different planet. My upbringing as a sinner and bad person imprinted by the Catholic religion and my parents by giving me negative feedback in the name of love; I darkened my true nature and the true nature of every person who was taught that Jesus is only the Son of God. I don't blame my parents or church anymore. We all are victims of victims and misperception of who we are.

As a result, there were lack, judgment, and comparison with others in my awareness all the time. These authors knew something that I wanted to know. What did they share was amazing and promising, but in my consciousness, it was impossible for me. They spoke about God as a Spirit with a loving energy. When they shared about their awakening experiences for me, it sounded like they spoke a different language unknown to me before. I wanted know what they knew, but in my mind, I was only an ordinary person who had the courage to take the first step to trust life and only dreamed about what these people knew and experienced during their spiritual journey. As a result of their experiences, they had become spiritual teachers and guides. In the end, it turned out that this ordinary dream wasn't only a dream. I really started awakening. I got pictures, and through them, I knew what I was supposed to do. My soul started to adjust my body. I surrounded myself with the guidance of my higher self and listened to my intuition more often. I started feel more. Because of that, the spiritual world has become more and more real for me. I can only confirm that none of us is different from each other, only our awareness and understanding of the real world is different. As Jesus said, *"There are many mansions in my Father's Kingdom."* He meant that there are many levels of our consciousness. Many rose over their ego and found themselves as a child of God who we really are Pure Spirit, Christ.

Coming to California for me was a huge learning experience regarding spirituality and levels of consciousness. There is mecca of spirituality here. People have access to every tool and technique that exists to level up their consciousness. I was a newcomer who started learning about the origin of our existence, and I had more clarity and tools about how the mind works compared to others. Being spiritual doesn't mean that you are aligned with what you teach. It is very important to stay on the path, continue the journey, and practice what you have learned or taught. Otherwise, they will only be empty words, and nothing will change in our lives unless we find a true understanding of why we are here and what the purpose is behind learning or teaching. Many people come to the spiritual world to adjust their lives and become a better human being, which is very important, but they're still operating on the human level of consciousness regarding their bodies and health issues. Also, there are those who see only the Spirit, and they don't deal with things very well on the earthy realm. There are also those who can find a balance between the two realms and make their own choices regarding what health means, what beauty means, and what success really is for them. We all receive according to our understanding of how our life is supposed to look like. Unless something new appears in our consciousness, we cannot have it, understand it, or want it. It needs to arise truly from our heart as a desire that we want to have more clarity, asking for God's discernment if it is for us or not. We have people from the lower consciousness of society where violence exists to the higher one where there is communication and compromise. But there can be a lack of love and understanding for one another and only a calculation of what is for oneself. There are people with a level of consciousness where love and communication exist, but they don't have good health and so on. When we turn to the Spirit, it will show us where our misunderstanding of life or what really life is for. In the sacred Mayan calendar, every birth metric starts with an interpretation of the wave in which we incarnated. There are four subjects to evolve during our current lifetime, and collectively, they are called *solar family*. The sooner we understand our own journey the sooner life will become easier for us, and we will be guided individually and make our own choices as well as understand that what others do or not do is their karmic subject to evolve in this lifetime. We cannot save anyone from their own soul's journey. That's why it is very important to stop taking responsibility for others. We can guide them when they ask, but we cannot persuade them to do things we think would be the best for them. Maybe we are right, but they need to understand for themselves in a way that is very often different from ours. Each of us is responsible for our individual life and our soul's calling, where health and well-being are.

I asked Spirit what kind of affirmation I supposed to use to be focused, joyous, and healthy. I received the answer:

> *I can bring peace to your mind when you ask Me. I really want you to focus on Me and I Am the doer of all. I will guide you and support you. Your focus is on Me and your heart, and joy will be great. Health is My birthright, keep thoughts about health. Your mind needs peace. This is the most important. When you achieve this, be careful with yourself by doing things what make you happy and joyous. Health is certain. Be patient. I promise you your brain is whole and complete. Your mind needs healing which is certain. Your mind is divided between circumstances and Reality, which is Me. When you achieve balance, everything will heal.*

How can I achieve balance? The answer:

> *Achieving balance is the way of being. It is a way of joy and believing in Me. This balance is certain in Me, no other way. I want you to be now peaceful. It keeps you steady. You can move everything when you are peaceful. You are really brave and I encourage you to see everything as anew. I am creating you with love and compassion. I can bring more possibility to your life when I Am peaceful in you.*

Later I received this affirmation: "*My body is filled with love and God's perfection. I am the health of my body. I choose thoughts about health. My mind receives thoughts about my body's divine perfection.*"

My mother is one of the people who always says that she doesn't believe in spirituality. She believes in science and "reality." But there is one thing she trusts me with are her dreams. She always had dreams. When we started being more and more connected, I listened to what my mother said regarding her dreams that concerned me in current circumstances. She'd provide guidance for me when I neglected a thought, or she'd have a dream about something I was planning to do. She has a lot of spiritual gifts, and she rejects them by choosing not changing her thought patterns about life and herself. She is a very wonderful person, and she forgets that. When my book was ready to be submitted to a publisher, I opened my account on the GoFundMe platform to receive support and be able to pay my first installment to the publisher so that the process of editing would start. When I was looking for a publisher and an opportunity to pay for my book, I found out that a lot of writers have their own sponsors so the books can see the dailylight of day. The first person who transferred money was my brother Piotr, but the next day, unexpectedly I received money from our father. I was amazed with it. He always surprised me. I needed to adjust my thinking that he really cares and wants me to move forward with my life courageously. At the beginning, I didn't have it in mind to mention how I paid for a publisher for this book. But a few days later, I received a thought to do that, and I was postponing. I didn't think that it would be so important. But I was speaking with my mother, and she mentioned that she had a dream. For the very first time, she dreamed about the parents of my father. They showed themselves in her dream two to three days later after transferring the money. They knew that I would understand their appearance as a message for me. That's why I realized that it was important to mention it. Another karmic issue between our families was cleared, which was about neglecting the child who didn't belong to its father's family. Our ego doesn't see the bigger picture and why we are asked to do or not to do some things, but our soul knows. That's why I repeat that it is important to understand that our journey on the planet Earth has a reason—to bring harmony in our families and evolution in the universal consciousness.

People can hear on TV or read in the newspapers about children being molested by priests or other well-known personages, unaware that it also was happening in their homes when they were children. During the one year I lived in the studio attached to the church, I had a lot of energetic clearing from my childhood when I was working with Louise Hay's book and practicing Kriya Yoga. Two or three months before my Reiki initiation, I started feeling uncomfortable in my feminine parts, specifically in my womb and genitals. This feeling was on an energetic level, very subtle but noticeable. I didn't know what the reason was. I found out when I was traveling with my two friends to Joshua Tree Park. There is a very strong vibration energy there. People compare it to Sedona's, where there are a lot of vortex portals. Americans like going there for healing, meditation, and relaxing.

When we were driving to Joshua Tree Park, I started talking with one of my friends about work with the inner child, that we needed to start trusting our feelings because this small child in us has something to tell us. This child knew what was happening in our childhood, but we didn't listen or were so young that we didn't know how to call out things that were done to us by others that weren't right. For most of my childhood, I heard from my parents that what I said was impossible, that people could act or say this or that to me.

Even though my mother wanted to believe what I said, sometimes she made the conclusion that it probably was just my fault or that the person didn't mean that. All the time, others were being justifying.

When we have that kind of feedback from our parents, we stop trusting ourselves and start thinking that we are wrong and justifying adults bad behavior toward us. As a child, we start believing that people have the right to act or speak to us disrespectfully, and we go along with it for most of our lives as an adult person. We accept this as natural way of communication with us, forgetting that we lost our worth and inner guidance as a child when strangers or parents behaved insolently toward us. So now we let people behave rudely around us, and we go along with it because we think that it can only be this way, not knowing that our inner guidance would disagree with it. But we don't listen to our inner child, our soul, who knows what the cause of our behavior is and blocks what we have right now. Therefore, my friend mentioned also about molesting, and energy in my womb moved in a discomforting way. I shared this with her. She said to me, "Magdalena, ask about the issue. Start writing, and you will know." I received an index card from her. Thus, I asked and received the answer. Yes, I was molested as a child. I asked who it was. The answer was, "The person who you admired the most as a child." I didn't want to hear it. I was rejecting my knowing. I put out the intention to release energy from my being a molested person or child, and I was in denial mode, thinking that it was impossible. When we got to our destination point and entered the house, I started introducing myself to new people. The last person to whom I introduced myself had the same name of the person who molested me as a child and looked very similar. I stopped pretending that it never happened and accepted that my childhood idol was the one who robbed me of my innocence. I felt a lot of compassion for myself. The universe showed me what I asked for and also showed me how I can forgive at the same time. There were about twenty or more people in the house, and we got out to walk in the labyrinth under the moonlight. We were sitting in the center, and there was a twelve-year-old girl with us. She resembled me when I was her age. She arranged a game to hug one another. She started from the left side, and each of us who received a hug from the person who was on the left was supposed to hug the person on their right. I didn't know who was on my right. It was dark, but when I turned to give that person a hug, it was the same person God used as a tool to show me my executor. So I hugged the person and forgave the executor. Since then, I stopped having this uncomfortable feeling in my genitals and womb.

Throughout June, I had a lot of new opportunities to see more of Los Angeles. I was working at night three times a week in Beverly Hills, and after that, I spent a lot of time with Malwina, her husband, and her son. I met them when they rented a parking lot for their RV. They travelled around the USA to see new places and find a new home since they had decided to sell their apartment in the Los Angeles area. They decided to move to the East Cost at last. But before that, Malwina introduced me to new places and stores. It was a lot of fun. She was able to understand and heal her pain from the past during this time. I miss her very much. She is so smart and such a wise person. She is a very openhearted woman. There was and still is an unconditional friendship between us.

My friend Alison repeated the word "mindfulness" very often, and I never asked her exactly what it was. But I learned about it during my English classes in Santa Monica Collage. It turned out that mindfulness is very well known and used also by teachers and students in schools (in Santa Monica Collage for sure), and the University of California (UCLA) is a facilitator of mindfulness classes. I was curious when a spiritual tool was introduced to schools. I asked the person whose mindfulness is her passion, and she was invited to our Zoom class. She said that mindfulness started being popular in North California ten years before and was widespread thanks to well-known celebrities among others. Oprah Winfrey invited them to her talks, and they shared about the benefits of mindfulness, which is used in dance also. Goldie Hawn and Wendy Holden wrote a book called *10 Mindful Minutes: Giving Our Children—and Ourselves—the Social and Emotional Skills to Reduce Stress and Anxiety for Healthier, Happier Lives*. What is mindfulness? The definition we received was this: Mindfulness is paying attention to the present moment, experiencing with openness, curiosity, and willingness to be with what is.

The person mentioned that children intuitively know how to ground themselves, an example, they love to play with water; put their hands on wheat and rice; or walk barefoot on the grass or at home. Thanks to that, they feel connected and present. As the girl in Joshua Tree Park unknowingly showed me how to forgive, we can take our children as an example to show us how we can reconnect with ourselves and planet Earth to play and stop pretending to be as serious as we are. Life takes care of us. It's time to come back to health and joy. I noticed that in California, some doctors prescribe to their patients meditation to reduce stress and anxiety also like how, in the past, Louise Hay's book *Heal Your Body* was given under the counter by doctors when they weren't able to help their patients. In most cases, the patients cured themselves thanks to that. When our minds start to worry and we feel anxious, we can use Louise Hay's advice: *"Don't scare yourself. Stop terrorizing yourself with your thoughts. It's a dreadful way to live. Find a mental image or thought that gives you pleasure and immediately switch your scary thought to a pleasure thought."* Or we can use Patricia Crane's affirmation: *"My mind is a powerful healing tool. I am divinely guided. I love myself in this moment. I am willing to be quiet and hear my own guidance"* or *"My intuition guides me more each day. I feel loving presence of Spirit in my daily life."*

In my healing process, I chose a sunflower as a sign for me that my body is completely healthy. I had the opportunity to see this flower all the time when I was living in the small studio. It gave me confidence that my body was healing. The affirmation I used when the process started in the Guardian Angel Church was this: *"My healing is in the process, and I live in completely healthy body the rest of my life.*

The Divine Healing Energy I am so blessed that I am a part of You. You fill out every atom of my being and every cell of my body. You flow through me in every moment of my existence. I am so grateful that I can see, I can hear, I can experience through my body's all senses. I can walk, I can drive, I can be in every place where I want to be, because my body works. Now I claim healing in my every cell and organ which have not functioned well. I believe that healing can occur even in one day. In what my mind believed as impossible, in this moment I accept as possible and true. The healing of my whole body is happening NOW. *I live joyously in my restored body. I love every organ, I love every tissue, I love every joint and nerve. I bless health in the bodies of others. All is created from the Divine Light. Every day is expression of me in the healthy body. I can jump, I can run, I can dive, I can exercise. My body is rejuvenated easily. I feel like my cells are becoming anew. I accept my health in my whole body* NOW. *I am at peace and so be it. Amen!*

—*Divine Healing Prayer by Magdalena Julita Byra*

CHAPTER 13

Life Always Speaks to You

The reality of my life cannot die, for I am indestructible consciousness.

—Paramahansa Yogananda

During the last month of me staying in the Guardian Angel church, something happened that was tragically funny; it was like everything was falling apart in my life. I lost my income again, and it was on the day with Akbal energy, which means intuition and abundance. The person who let me go accused me of stealing the empty plastic bag, which we could receive in each grocery store for free. When I was hearing it, I really was amused because I knew that it wasn't the person; it was Life taking me into another direction even though I wasn't ready to let go yet. It was the second time I lost income in a year and in the same area, Beverly Hills, without it being anybody's fault. The first time was one year before, when in springtime the coronavirus was announced as a pandemic even though we had coronavirus seasons earlier like flu each year, according to epidemiologists. And this time was the second time where Life left me without income and gave me instead a new direction to focus on. I registered myself to Shamanic Academy on that day. But I needed to find a way to get by and be able to meet my needs to overcome my current situation and follow the new direction which was connected to my heart. Before losing my job for nothing, I had signs twice a week or two earlier.

First, I noticed something on the tarot deck, which I had for the very first time in my hands. I saw a card, and it told me, "It is a karmic family issue." I was playing with them to learn more about them. Then one or two days later, I noticed a description somewhere saying, "Be careful with your money." I knew that something was going to happen, but I was not expecting that it would be so fast, unpredictable, and in a somehow comic way. One week later after losing the job, I received a notice saying that if I didn't pay rent, according to the short-term agreement, I would need to leave the place in two days. I signed the short-term agreement, only for the church that they could have any document. I didn't need it. I had been living there for over seven months without a lease, and I was able to keep my word regarding paying rent and duties. What I put on myself unknowingly became my burden—an obligation instead of favor. It was Guardian Angel church's committee ordinance.

I was really surprised how I was treated by people for whose businesses I was in charge of for the upkeep of the church during the last eleven months. When I lost the job, I recieved support from Santa Monica Collage to pay my rent. I asked the priest who I treated as a friend for the key to the mailbox. I was waiting for the check. I didn't receive a key, and the check was returned to Santa Monica College. Everything lasted longer than it supposed to. How did it start? Everything went south because of money and a lack of trust and appreciation for people who took care of this place. That's why I was guided at the end of my stay there to give the priest the Self-Realization Fellowship the Horn of Plenty bank box filled with collected money by me throughout forty-two days. The affirmation on the box can help one's rise consciousness to find abundant God in them and everywhere. As child of God, who really knows God, can receive much more than we allow ourselves to ask. When we act on its own with consciousness of lack, it will never be enough and we hurt others on the way. I asked about moving my rent to the end of month because all my bills were at the beginning. I wanted to stop being late with rent payment a week or two when the additional cost came to me for the immigration lawyer service. I thought that I was treated equally and that my time given to this church was appreciated by all. It turned out that everything was covered by the person who was in charge; she brought me there to have someone who could trust to take care of the church's businesses, which the person tried to manage from far away. I realized it when I was in front of the ten people from church committee, who wanted to know why I dared to ask about a favor to move my payments to the end of month. At the end, the payment wasn't changed but was unwritten agreement that all tenants there can pay till fifth day of the month. Some of the committee members gave their own examples not being treated fairly here by landlords because of that, they weren't able to understand why they could act differently. I said, "This is not about others, only about you, how you want to treat another person." Knowing that we all are souls on the evolutionary plain. That's why it is important to act differently from these who didn't act like we expected to, even they could. Thanks to our experiences; we can evolve in compassion—understanding how it feels like, when we have no help or roof over our head in some cases.

After this meeting, it was quiet for two weeks. Later, I had a conversation with the church priest where he belittled my work and left me with impression that I was not worthy of asking what I wanted. I was shocked. I left the conversation to calm down in my room and I received a thought: "He protects himself." After this incident, the same day committee of the church decided behind my back that I would not take care about the site during filming industry shooting, even we signed a new lease with church week before. They found solution by giving my responsibility to a new person who was living there, and he was very inventive and charismatic young man. I knew that my time there was going to be finished soon. I thought that it would be at the end of the year, but Life had another plan. Four days later, I received a call with a request to open the gate for the cleaning lady the following day. I had this in my calendar, but I forgot it. I was on an important call with Shamanic Academy, and I didn't open the gate. I realized it when I heard people on the stairs from the church community who asked me to open the hall. They opened the gate by themselves. Meanwhile, I received a text message that I didn't open the gate purposefully, and it was unfair toward the person. Reading the text message, I was surprised that the person who knew me over the year accused me about doing things deliberately against her. That day was my birthday, and I realized that I trusted the wrong people. Two days later, I found out that my lease would not be prolonged. I was given two weeks to find a new place to live. So my stay in the Guardian Angel Church was terminated in the way like many people were treated by their landlords. The committee knew that I didn't have income, and they left me without a place to live. I really felt compassion for the person who took on herself the responsibility of throwing people away on the street. It wasn't first time. How did I recognized at last that I trusted wrong people? This birthday, I started the day with an energy mirror (ETZNAB 12); it's my twelfth year in connection with my intuition. The whole year topic was "Exposing Falsehoods." I was shown very vividly that people who I trusted weren't on the same stage of the awareness I was. I started using more often the prayer from Gurudeva to God to teach me about discernment. I found a temporary place to live thanks to my new friend in two to three days, but I wanted to stay there till I would take a driving test at Hollywood DMV. The church committee agreed to that. I received few more days to finish up my things there. At the day of my driving test, I wasn't able to have the exam because Edward, my first landlord, who taught me most of the time how to drive here, forgot documents. It was a very funny situation. Edward also was the person who lent me money so that I would be able to pay the first rent payment of the new place. I am really grateful for him. He helped a lot of people here. Edward came to the United States about thirty years ago to teach mostly Polish immigrants' children Polish folk dances. He is a professional folk dancer. This is his passion, and he collects information from Polish villages and the people at the Subcarpathian region about folk dances to write a book. He is over seventy years old and has a lot of plans. He never is bored. I grew up in Subcarpthian Voivodeship while he was born there. By the way, I was registering myself to pass the driving test three more times, and I didn't have the possibility to drive for the second time also. I was laughing to myself, watching how Life was making corrections to grant my wishes in the best way. I drove twice driving test in Hollywood DMV. I didn't pass. After that, I decided to schedule my final driving test in Culver City. I passed it with peace and joy. It was a pleasure to drive with the examinator from there. My Californian driving license was a Christmas gift. Life has a good of sense of humor.

After that situation with the members of the church where I used to rent a studio, I realized that it was the first time since I came to the United States that people treated me like a child, doing everything behind my back and making decisions about my life and myself without giving me the right to stand up for myself. They made assumptions of what I do or don't do without asking me. Honestly, it was the second time with the flower community where we were playing in giving and receiving the year before, but this time, it was in an even more comic way. When I stood up for myself, everything fell apart, including the friendships. I had a similar situation with a beautiful Omkari when I spoke up for myself and told her how I was really feeling about her behavior toward me in front of my friends. Also, when I chose to market my workshops instead of spending more time with her, she felt uncomfortable and disappeared from my life. Wishing me well, she said that I was the one who caused the end of our friendship, which was very codependent from the beginning. I wished her to do what she loves. We cannot be friends with all, only with those who really care about us. I had very important lessons about friendships and who was really for me. I noticed as an adult person, I let others rule my life and unknowingly allowed them to decide for me without asking what is good for me and what kind of values I have which I gained through awareness books and many development trainings to shine my light and lead others to their freedom. I needed to relearn that I was first, to honor my boundaries, and to be truthful to myself, and then when I have time, I can meet the needs of others. There is no other way.

Malwina has her philosophy of keeping as much as she can independent from others. When you have money, you can pay for everything. Thanks to that, you become less codependent on other people for your needs. And I can testify to her advantage that I haven't met such a caring and generous person for a long time since I started living in Los Angeles. Now I have a lot of new friends who love you because you are yourself, and when they can, they help without asking for anything in return. It is a real friendship and I appreciate them.

After losing my job and having many things taken away including duties and the place where I used to live, I was wondering for a moment what was happening. Why was this last month so chaotic? And suddenly I came to a realization that it was my thirteen month of Tzolkin year, which I started the topic to my freedom, independency (BEN11). I understood that life took away everything and everyone who wasn't aligned with my real purpose. So looking at the whole situation, I realized that those who I knew and treated as a friend, their awareness and reactions to me or situations helped Life release me from them without any bad feelings. No one was guilty. Instead I received people who had the same or a higher level of consciousness than I did as well as the opportunity to be surrounded with those who really wanted to learn from me the true meaning of life.

Also, I realized that I had the same experiences to a person who stayed prior to me in the church and to a person who I replaced in the job in Beverly Hills. I was hired after a woman was fired and accused of taking a night tablet, and she worked for months there. Regarding the studio that I was renting, before me was staying for a month or so, a man who was addicted to the drugs. He was but harmless but loud. And one day the member of the church committee threw him away, even he paid a rent. The person who asked her to get rid of the man was the one who rented him the room at first place. It understandably that the church supposed to have a good opinion, so the same member of committee who got rid of me also threw him away on behalf of all church committee before me. Previously, when I heard about these two situations, I thought that I have nothing in common with them. But life showed me differently. I was arrogant, thinking that I was dissimilar than the man who was the drug addict and the woman who was letting go of from the job. There was a third factor in those situations. First of all, the person who fired people accused for things they didn't do because of not having control over her life even though she had all the love and support from others.

Second, the person who was taking care of the church's businesses was afraid of losing control of it. Fear itself is the enemy to us, but the fear of losing something worsens people's behavior in the situations in which they don't know how to act. People react instead of calm down and to try looking into the whole situation peacefully and from different perspectives. Then change can occur for the better one and the best solusion for all involved. It calls communication. People, so many times, imagine things which are not true instead of communicating with the one who bothers us the most. Thanks to that, we can realize no one wants to threaten us. This is the ego playing imagine things about people which are not true to protect ourselves. People live their whole lives in this illusion without realizing that ego is not the place that we wanted to act and can trust.

I know that Life always speaks to me. I could neglect these two phone call conversations with people from whom I found out about firing and eviction at the beginning, but now I know that I am not different from others. Even though my ego wanted to feel better because of my inner work and understanding, the Spirit tells me all the time to look into others and myself with my heart instead of my egoic mind, which differentiates all of us for the better or the worse ones. I knew that I was in the right place to learn. I was supposed to be in this church. When I moved there, I noticed a huge fabric with an angel carrying two children across the bridge and the words *"In all thy ways acknowledge Him, and He shall direct thy path."* The same but smaller picture was hanging on the wall in my grandparents' home. Seeing all the contrast, life gave me possibility to find a way to become more compassionate for others and myself. We don't know what these people are dealing with, and we judge them by appearance.

So life took away from me the things and people that didn't serve me anymore. I needed to accept it even if it wasn't easy I treated those people like true friends. I was helped and favored by people because I was meeting their desperate needs. I prayed to God about dicerement, and my prayer was fulfilled by recieving a very clear insight which helped me to recognize instantly in the future which people are like minded and which favored me because they were desperated to meet only their own needs. Then I was able to say "stop" faster and leave without turning back and regeret. This is how life exposes lessons to us and we don't have to reapet them over and over. Creator wants us to see the pattern what we have and shows us how we ended up in the certain life circumstances in the past. Unanawere that we created it by fales beliefes about ourselves. Noticing this, we start letting go of people who are not for us without blaming anyone. Thanks to that we start evolving and moving to higher levels of our consciousness. We start to realize that Life is firendly, loving, and helps us to release what is not true for us anymore. This is a beautiful process of becoming a friend with Life called God. We see what is good for us and what is not.

All of this is a learning process. I love people and wanted to trust them that they have the same level of integrity in their behaviors, but some of them showed an unseen shadowed side when things didn't go their way. That kind of behavior discredits the connection and trust like a lot of us lost with our parents because their behavior was against our will, only forcing us to do things their way. They didn't give us a choice or respect. Life helps us to grow and move beyond the limitations of others and go to the better experiences and people who we can trust and rely on beyond changing life circumstances. Life taking away things from my field emphasized the things I was dreaming about. I started noticing a new direction and received more support in it. Even on the last day of my thirteenth month, I received a call from a publisher and found out that I had a new project director for my book. The first one left since new opportunities came up for her. Last year I was focused on having my website. Thanks to Fatimata, I was connected to Vania, who created her website, and she developed for me a beautiful one: www.lifespeakstoyou.com. I placed the affirmation there, which came from me during my second Qigong healing session. I was on four or five sessions and invited friends to it. Thanks to those healing modalities, I was regaining my power as a soul to operate from my higher self's level of awareness instead of the survival part of my brain, which we have at the back, and most people operate from there. I had a new awakening then, and the affirmation was this: *"My name is Magdalena. I am the mas-*

ter of my life, and I am free to create my life anew, filled with joy, love, and fulfillment." All the guilt I was carrying for years being here was released then. I felt like a newborn person. Also, when creating the website, I started feeling Mary Magdalena's energy again. Her symbol was the lily, and I felt like I was opening myself and blossoming like this beautiful flower. I want every woman to start using the statement for herself and feel this way, knowing that she is beautiful and has the right to blossom. That's why I decided to put the whole affirmation and the direction of where our power is on the landing page of my website:

> My name is_____.
> I Am the master of my life, and
> I Am free to create my life anew,
> filled with joy, love, and fulfillment.
> My power is in my heart.

Once, Fatimata texted me to share her dream with me. She said that we were both on the stage and that I was speaking powerfully and using Reiki to heal others. At that time, I started being interested in learning how to speak publicly and joining women's circles. Fatimata didn't know about it. After her message, I opened Instagram. And I didn't know why, but right away, out popped an angelic card—"The Speaker," and the description said that a part of my work is speaking. It was only a confirmation of my path after Fatimata's message. I recognized when I started being interested in public speaking that it was the effect of my intention, which I put out loudly in the circle with all the healers who I was with in Joshua Tree Park. We all were sitting in the labyrinth and shared about our origin and what we were going to do after our healing, which also occurred there.

My purpose of speaking started opening up my understanding of where my focus was supposed to be, who I wanted to serve, and why. My assignment is empowering women who lost themselves in others, forgetting about their true purpose in the world. Those who suffer from society's beliefs and misunderstanding that they don't have the right to shine want to love with all of themselves and be loved and respected by others instead of getting disapproval, making them out as wrong for everything they have done or not done. As a result, they feel confused and shut down their inner guidance. They suppress all their feelings, and their bodies stop functioning well. There are women who have dreams but took onto their shoulders the whole family and have no rest for themselves. There are always demands from the nearest ones and little support in return. When women are not awakened, life seems very hard and cold to them. It is very hard to stand for themselves when they don't have support from the nearest ones who only put them down and say things about aging, about the time to learn and grow they had when were "young," and how now it is too late. Those kinds of statements or beliefs kill an immortal soul that wants to learn and experience new things to expand.

Life gave me an opportunity to be accepted as the trusted author on www.SelfGrowth.com. I submitted my first two articles there. Also, on this platform, I can post information about my workshops. I am a part of the Heal Your Life trainers and coaches website, where my clients can find me: https://www.healyourlifeworkshops.com. We received a Heal Your Life learning portal online where clients, after receiving the code for themselves, can use it for six months. Every week, there are five topics such as DISERVABILITY, LOVE, PROSPERITY, LOVING YOUR BODY, and HONORING BOUNDARIES. They are unlocked in sequence after finishing one week, then another and another. The clients who know Louise Hay's philosophy can practice by themselves, and others can receive support weekly by the Heal Your Life teacher through Zoom like me. I subscribed to the SanityDesk platform, which gave me all the software support, and there were people who helped me with my funneling and copywriting. I have access to social media education and support from marketing specialists to put my small business on social media and Google to grow in the near future. I also signed myself to be a certified marketer on their behalf to help other entrepreneurs put out their messages and attract right clients, who resonate with them to change their lives for the better one in different proffessions and industries all over the world. I connected with the Beverly Hills library to submit my Heal Your Life workshops as a project to lead them there. Also, it opened the possibilities to lead the workshop in the library on Santa Monica Blvd. near the place where I used to stay in Hollywood. I found a small hall to lead workshops in. I received support from coaches from Centro Community Partners to create my business plan when I was applying for a SEED grant which I received through the Immigrants Rising organization. They want to transform the lives of undocumented immigrants through education and supporting them in launching their own businesses to make a difference in their lives and in others'. My company's name is LifeSpeaksToYou, LLC like the title of the book, to help all of us remember that Life communicates with us all the time and that we only need to become aware. You cannot cheat Life; it always gives you feedback through others and your current circumstances. The only one who you cheat is yourself. Start being honest with yourself, and you will find out how much and how long you have been deceiving yourself that someone from outside will save you so that you can be happy. Ekznab, the archetype in Mayan calendar, refers to looking within you through other people and outside life circumstances. From within, you will see outside yourself. Your experiences are only reflections of your inner world: thoughts, emotions, and beliefs. Life speaks to you by mirroring your beliefs from those you were brought up and how they treated you as a child. Life speaks to you through nature, which is thriving, beautiful, abundant, and loving. Life speaks to you when, in your experience, there is a lack of affection, and it shows you that you need to work on it, giving more affection to yourself instead of putting up with it or demanding from others who have that lack also. Life speaks to you when, in your life, there is a lack of joy. It is information on how far you've escaped from yourself. Life speaks to you when, in your experience, there is a lack of understanding or respect. Ask yourself how disrespectful you are to yourself and others only mirror you how low you treat yourself or your time. Life speaks to you through the discomfort of your being to show you the truth about yourself. Life speaks to you through you experiencing a lack of health: it says that you were warned and you disregarded your body completely without giving it a good thought, nourishment, and rest to recharge from within. It is your vehicle through this life time. Can you imagine when you start seeing these signs and knowing that there is no other person outside who can stop you from hurting yourself, only you? Fall in love with yourself and life, then Life will shows you how much love you.

We grew up on the fairy tale stories about Prince Charming, who solves all the problems for us. There is someone out there who can help us. But there is only one person who can change your life circumstances and transform them. This person is YOU. The change starts from each of us unlearning old programmed thoughts and beliefs that don't serve us to learn the new ones, which would create new habits, and they will benefit you and others. Everyone has their own journey, and we cannot live or learn for them. They script themselves on this planet to their own learning and overcoming misunderstanding of what life is and how they can change themselves from within so external circumstances will change for them. Our children, at twenty years old, start going on their journey. We are not responsible for them to control their lives. We are responsible to teach them to trust their inner guidance to love them and encourage to their best potential without worrying if it happens or not. Then they will be safe and happy that we want for our children. Sacred Mayan calendar says that it depends on which month of our birthday our childern were born; they came to teach us something. In my case, Martin was born in my second birthday month. He came to help me learn self-control, self-awareness, and self-determination. That time I didn't know I had in my mind my husband and his idea how children supposed to be brought up. Even I felt differently by my heart but my mind didn't listen to. So the learning process from our children lasts until they reach twenty years of age and then they have their own lives. As I mentioned above, we missed the purpose of having children. They came to make us better people on evolutionary playground on this planet Earth and help see possibility of reaching the starts and not learn from us, wounded children who had implemented beliefs by our society. That's why if we are not aware of that we are messing up. Now there is time to change the whole coding old paradigm and give ourselves and our children unconditional love. It will heal all the world.

Being here in my awareness appeared the university where I would like to graduate from a bachelor's degree, and after that, I would decide to do a master's degree or not. I asked my mother to mail me my transcript evaluation so I would be able to translate to English because it may help me obtain my bachelor's degree in two years instead of four. *Everything is always working out for me.* But now I am focusing to awake my dormant gifts as a healer and awakening soul under wisdom of Shamanic Academy call. I applied in June 2021 for a marriage nullity in Our Lady of the Bright Mount Church, Polish Roman Catholic church in Los Angeles. The day I received that information from the Polish parish priest that my marriage nullity was granted had released me from the burdens multiplied by cosmic portal. I felt like all karma was raised. I felt lighter and happier. I was like a new person. I received a new life. I was so much grateful for this day. I didn't realize that by saying yes when I meant no, I put a huge burden on my life for over twenty-seven years. I was free on March 8, 2022. After that information we were waiting for ten days, whether there would be an appeal from the other party or not, I prayed with my friend Jo to be free. The parish priest called me on April 1, 2022, saying that any appeal was not submitted, and my marriage nullity was recognized on March 25, 2022. The day with energy of forgiveness, CIMI 11. The phone call I received with the information on the day with BEN5 energy meant to step toward freedom. My desire is to write a book series for children to help them start feeling a connection with all nature. My prayers are for those who want to move forward with their life to find healing in themselves. I have learned a lot, and in many aspects of life, there is still much to learn. We all have many things to learn and experience. Thanks to that, our awareness is growing, and our skills and creative side can be reborn in us. This book is for you to wake up and be trustful. If you don't have anything, you have nothing to lose, so follow your heart. You will be supported always. If you have something and feel attached, let it go and don't carry your burden as you're growing. If you have children and you are afraid of letting go of a relationship that is not working, let it go for yourself and your children and trust. Your partner will benefit also. We all need to be healed from wounds from our childhood. That's why your relationship doesn't work. The perfect partner for you is waiting on your path to a healthy and happy life. You first need to let go of what doesn't serve you to receive what is aligned with your highest good because that benefits all. Life is for you and is waiting for when are you willing to let go of control and start floating on its waves of love. Start investing in yourself, in your growth. It will benefit you always. You will meet new people and new opportunities that will come as blessings in disguise. By reading this book, you were with me on this journey. I believe that you noticed, with trust and a willingness to evolve, that everything opens up and that money will come from different places. Be kind with yourself and love yourself the way you are right now. I invite you to become aware of your own journey ahead of you. I am thankful that you took this book and read it to the end.

I believe that this book can change many lives including yours. Be yourself and stop doubting in yourself. You can do this. You are a unique expression of God. Let Him guide you to your greatness. You are a soul with gifts and talents that the world hasn't seen yet. Each of us was born as a genius with unlimited potential. Only beliefs from our childhood that we carry as an adult person determines how our lives look now. From being on this journey, I learned that great names started their awakening after they reached their forties, fifties, or even seventies, and they were able to impact the world in an amazing way. Take, for example, Louise Hay, Dr. Wayne Dyer, Nelson Mandela, and many others. Their path for the first part of life was as an ordinary person, or they had huge burdens to overcome, which would allow them to be able to show us that the only thing that matters is LOVE. Each of us has different paths. Some souls start their spiritual journey at a younger age, but most of us wake up after our thirties, forties, or fifties when we've received so much pain that we need to start thinking and acting differently. It is never too late to live a fearless and healthy life. You have a story to tell. Don't wait for your greatness. *Start now.*

The Values That I Have Obtained on My Journey

1. *Maintaining a daily connection with God* through thoughts, techniques in SRF lessons, Kriya Yoga, meditation and study SRF lessons as often as possible to be aligned with my guru and his teachings to keep walknig on the path of self-realization.
2. *Speak truth always.* There is nothing to lose. People start valuing you when you speak truth.
3. Be honest and transparent.
4. *Trust Life* no matter in what kind of circumstances I am facing right now. I will be guided to the better ones. Keeping faith in God's love. He always responds to my prayers. I can ask, believe in it, and enjoy the process, and I will manifest what I asked for by taking actions and expecting the best outcome of my work and endeavors. Do it with awareness of who I want to become (ask for what I want instead of what I don't want and surrender totally to God and His guidance. Practice, practice, practice).
5. *Love life and appreciate everything and everyone.* Wake up and go to bed with gratitude.
6. *Trust myself, my feelings.* They are my true guidance.
7. *Listen to my heart* and make choices on its guidance.
8. *Listen to my intuition always.*
9. *Be certain that the choices I make are right for me.* Others would benefit also.
10. *Be courageous always.*
11. *Be loving and supportive for myself.* Feel love. It benefits all in our planet.
12. *Be on time.*
13. *Be peaceful and patient.*
14. *Choose food* through my body's guidance and intuition.
15. *Speak and think positive words.* They are in harmony with the core values, and they nourish me. The words are vibration, and they attract good or negative experiences in my life. It depends where my focus is.

16. *Focus on gratitude*, the most powerful tool.
17. *Appreciate myself* for everything that I have done.
18. *I love order and good quality* in every situation.
19. *Practicing persistence and commitment* in my work to bring fulfillment to my life.
20. *Give Love* to everything that I do and everyone. To love has become my natural state of being.
21. *Be creative and joyful.* Find good in everything. Mostly in the times which things are not going my way. It is time to surrender and the best way will be shown.
22. *Self-reflection.*
23. *Set up new habits* such as visualization. Use more often positive affirmations and mirror work as a daily routine.
24. *Be connected* with others and share myself. They love my presence.
25. *Be discerning* when I interact with others to learn that not everyone is my best friend. Thanks to that, I will learn with whom I can have a deeper connection as friends and co-workers. I will know how to keep good friendships and nourish them.

You have own values to obtain to live happy, fulfilled life, and be aligned with your true purpose on our planet Earth. Our Creator wants us to shine and bring His values to our lives and our envioronment by allowing Him to change our misconception of Himself and ourselves to elevate us as His One Beloved Son.

Today is a beautiful day. The day which I have never lived. Every day I grow and love my Self beyond words. I love the way I talk. I love the way I look. I love everything that I do. I Am so happy that always I make right decisions. I know that I Am guided through my heart and intuition. There is no blame, there is no shame, there is no guild. I Am pure Spirit, a precious child of God, who is expressing Itself in the unique way on this planet, Mother Earth. Today my thoughts are focused only on Love, Joy, Happiness, because I Am a part of it and I Am created of it. My life becomes more and more easier. I rejoice to meet new opportunities to grow, forgive and love. I Am grateful that I receive help to overcome every obstacle in my life. I become more stronger and stronger to fulfill my destiny, the reason I came here. Today I claim with trust and believe that I will find inner joy in every situation. I Am a Light of the world and nothing will obscure this light in me. I let go of every problem to God. There is no obstacle to the Great Mind of God. Now, I accept it and believe, knowing that every question and need are answered in the right time. Thank you, thank you, thank you, Father, Mother, Friend, Beloved God.

—Prayer by Magdalena Julita Byra

Afterword

This book was written for you to find God within you. My journey started with the intention of healing and ended with these questions: Who am I? And who is God? As I mentioned above, every question is answered, and the answers were given to me. I share with all of you this message to invite you to a new world that has started being created anew—a world of harmony, love, joy, and peace and with the freedom of being yourself to become aware of you being the creator of your destiny as an indestructible soul on the planet Earth. The beautiful spark of Divine Light never left on its own; we are always loved, protected, and supported even when we are in the deepest despair. I was there, and it turned out that I was never left alone. I love my whole family, but my mother and son had the biggest impact in my life. I had a great mirror of myself in my son, how I communicated with my mother. And I see myself in my mother, how I can give up being right when I communicate with my son. Being aware of helping to heal seven generations back and forward of my family lineage to elevate higher in Spirit and also on the planet Earth in the next incarnation gives me the possibility to always look within me.

I took this journey to share with you how life can be shaped to your own design by making your own choices and fulfilling your role in this world. It is never too late to start. Thanks to these two people, the book was written to make others stop judging you for where you are right now and for those who believe that life has more to offer than what you have experienced but you lost hope and don't know how move with your life. A lot of people don't understand even if they love you, and not everyone is ready to dare to believe that the circumstances of life can be changed and that it starts from them releasing their subconscious pattern of beliefs. There are many levels of consciousness, and each of us has to evolve in our own by ourselves. We can ask these questions: Is what I believe really true, or am I repeating the pattern of beliefs of my family and the people I surrounded myself with? What is the best path for me? Do I really want to live my whole life as a victim of my current circumstances? What can I do for myself right now to start living aligned to my life's purpose here? Why am I afraid of letting go of things that don't serve me and make me unhappy and unhealthy? How long do I want to wait, pretending that my life is dependent on others' feedback and acceptance of what I do or don't do? How long will I let others dictate how my life is supposed to look like? How long am I willing to keep beliefs about myself based on my family's understanding that I don't deserve a fulfilled life and I am only a woman or a man? What would it be like if my life really has meaning and I was able to express myself in my way and not the way how others expected me to? Ask yourself what it would be like to live on your own terms without bothering with what others would say about you and without carrying guilt around yourself. Guilt and shame are the lowest level energy which drag us down. Ask yourself when you started feeling so lost that now you keep control of everything and everyone to survive in this world. Ask yourself, and the answers will come to your head. Or you can use a piece of paper and write them down. You will start finding your true yourself layer by layer, peel by peel. We don't know how long we will live. God wants us to live for over one hundred years in healthy bodies, according to the Mayan galactic metric, which is Tzolkin. So it would be unreasonable not to try anew and awaken these dreams that we were born with. We forgot about them due to responsibilities we took on for ourselves and when we got lost in duties for others.

We cannot live blindly anymore and pretend that we have nothing in common with the quality of our lives as a soul on planet Earth. We are responsible for our lives here and now. You are here to evolve in your consciousness so that you can take it with you after you have been released from your body one day to benefit in the spirit world, nothing else. Honestly, it starts with a dream in your heart that you buried after you had started playing the role that society gave you without asking yourself if it was yours. The dream is still within you to unfold.

We can be good mothers, wives, fathers, and husbands and be fulfilled. This is our main purpose. When we don't know how to begin the journey, we can start with what we used to love or like to do and then practice gratitude for it. After that, another desire will arise—another thing we would love to do, and then another. There is no ending. Every year, we evolve whether we want to or not. There is always a small shift in our consciousness. We behave differently from how we did in previous years. There is no aging; it is just our consciousness rising. We can quicken this process by being willing to grow from within, and then we can have a different way of being. Why? Because the Universe takes away what doesn't serve us and gives something better, which requires a higher level of consciousness. Can you imagine living in this awareness? Stop counting the years that passed. Just ask yourself, "Who can I become now? or "What do I like now?" We are here to evolve and be a role model for our children. We cannot teach them something if we don't do it and only preach. They learn from us what to do or what not to do. Their lives will be the same as our lives when they grow up, and they will have the same relationship patterns we have. Do you really want that kind life for your child, a life like the one you have right now? When you take care of your daughter or son, stop teaching them to count how many things they have and pleasing them with new toys, clothes, or make-up. Just spend more time with them. Show them you love them so that they can feel your love not only in words. Be understanding of them and encourage them to look differently into life instead agreeing with them that it was someone else's thought that they experienced unfairness. They are vibrational beings like you are. With the way they feel about themselves, they take in experiences in their lives to confirm their beliefs. Teach them the truth and explain to them that by loving themselves, they will be able to rely on themselves and will have better experiences. They will know how to stand up for themselves because they will have their self-worth and self-love as a human being. That prevents them from hurting themselves through bad habits, disrespect, and settling down for less, like only earning money to get by from month to month or buying better cars when they have more money. When you show children love and respect, you can congratulate yourself. They only need these two things to learn how to live a happy and good life and create healthy communities and societies. When you want your child to be courageous, first, you must become this way. When you want to see your child successful or express themselves artistically, first, you must stand up for your success or artistic way of expression. When you want to see your child be a good orator, it is required for you to stand up first and speak. Then you'll understand that it wasn't about your children; it was only about you and your inner child, who was neglected for so long and wasn't be able to truly express themself in this life. Look within yourself first and love yourself unconditionally with all your imperfections to be fulfilled in this world.

Now I can see and understand how everything was connected to my family roots and home in Jozefow. The whole transformation of my life started from there in 2016—the monarch butterfly that sat on my lap in the garden and a dream about white wolves that same night, which represents household protectors. In my dream, I was protecting my mother and son from a horde of wolves and could run through without hurting my closest ones. I understood the dream at last. I realized that I was the protector of the lineage of the past generations and future generations of my family. Now I am connected to all members of my family and have regained my family from my father's side, and I really love them all. It was a huge healing process, and I have started coming back home to my origin as a person. From the sign as fabric of the guardian angel in the church, which was the same as the picture in my grandparents' home, to the Shamanic Academy adventure, which I started with the workshop called Awaken in my grandmother's birthday, I can see how much I have received love and support from the living members of my family and ancestors to clean our lineage from things that were not glorious, which our family will be proud of in the future by a new awareness of being human as a woman and a man.

My mother has gifts, and one of them is dreams. But she is not aware of how many people she could help with it. Thanks to her gift, our family members who have passed on can communicate with us. I remember what my mother shared after my uncle's sudden transition. He showed himself in her dream and was surrounded with the Light, and he assured her that he was really happy now. It was a message for her older sister to stop crying and worrying after his passing.

In my journey to publish my book, I have learned a lot regarding funds. A lot of writers have sponsors or platforms so their work could be published. Many artists support themselves through GoFundMe or other crowdfunding platforms. Others who are known for their work have their own sponsors. I started learning how to publish book on Amazon.com. When I couldn't find the right publisher who wouldn't cost thousands of dollars and make me pay in installments, I wasn't afford for it. I put out the intention that the book would be published in the right way and the best way for everyone. I stopped being attached and released the intention to God and His angels. At last I found the publisher Newman Springs Publishing in New Jersey thanks to Ella, who knew better how to maneuver social media at the time. She treated them as a friend, and thanks to that, the right ad popped up in front of her eyes. She contributed a lot in my life during my stay in their church. For these good things, I really appreciate her and her husband. During connecting myself, more and more with my project of Self-Realization Institute or even writing the book I started learning things which I haven't been taught before. My mind started being open for a new information. What I found out was that many huge projects had to involve the whole community and sponsors to start existing. People start from nothing. They only have an idea of themselves that is greater than they are at the present moment. In the old-world paradigm, we were taught that to start something new, we need to earn, save, or take credits and rely only on ourselves. But this is not true. There are many people, companies, and unknown philanthropists that want to support you in your uniqueness and what you have to offer. We can stop being afraid to ask. We cannot do everything by ourselves if we are committed to our lives and start daring to dream big. This was another lesson I had learned by participating in the Landmark programs. We are not alone. When we learn how to release fear and go for what we want, magic happens, and doors will open one after another as I mentioned before.

Last year, when I was in a Santa Monica College Zoom class, one of the participants said some beautiful words: "*Through art, you can express yourself in a unique way.*" It was Patricia who said these words. She came to the United States from Ecuador about three to four years before. Her both brothers are artists, and she used to write a lot. Now she is in the process of writing her own book to contribute to her father's life, and what matters is only love. When Patricia shared that she loved visiting museums and places with art, I recognized that, as an adult person, I never felt attraction to museums or understood art. I only went to tick the box saying that I was in a known place such as the British Museum in London or the American Museum of Natural History in New York City or learn more about the United States' history by going to the Statue of Liberty in New York. I was in Getty Villa in Malibu to admire and do some sightseeing mostly not because of the value of the exposition. I believe that there are a lot of tourists who go to see places only because they are very well known, but they don't see value in it themselves. I was one of them. But after Patricia's words, something changed in my perception of art. I understood that the whole life is art, and as a creative beings, we can express ourselves in unique ways on a blank canvas without guilt and judgment from others. As there are so many pictures in the world and so many of them being different, we can treat our life experiences as one of them. We can create one thing on a canvas and paint something new—another picture of an experience in our lives, and it all will lead us to the beauty of the Spirit, which is in each of us. My father's stepdaughter, Anna, graduated from art school. She lives in Warsaw. Her life was a huge mess because of programmed societal beliefs of what life is supposed to look like, but she found her own path to healing and now expresses her Light through her art. She says that she was born with the mission of transmitting love and Light through her pictures. She explained to me the whole process of creating her paintings, and after that, she uses a prayer to bless and send healing, loving energy from her heart to the newly painted picture. It brings healing and harmony into the rooms where they hang. Thanks to that, people benefit being in their space with inner peace and harmony around. She is a true Light worker. Her pictures was bought by many people abroad who were appreciative of her creative work. Her website is www.annapawlakobrazy.pl. I wish all of you healing so that we can have more Light workers on planet Earth that old programming which harms us all will disapear much quicker. There are many of us, but we need you to find your own calling and express your gifts on this beautiful planet where we all live. We are here to praise God and spread His love through us and our work to everyone. I call on all of you once again.

Wake up! You are immortal child of God!
Wake up! You are Divine Light for which this world is waiting for!
Wake up! Don't let us wait for you so long! I bless you All, Amen.

Acknowledgments

I would like to thank all the beautiful souls on my journey who reached out to help me even though they didn't know me. From many, I had received shelter, a manifestation of income, and trust. Thanks to them, I was able to continue my path, and they helped that the book is written and published, that the message of Truth who we are reached you. I appreciate all the beautiful souls who believed in me when I was doubting myself, thinking that I wasn't really needed here to give wisdom and support to those who were on a path of rediscovering themselves. Thank you to all my friends and the people who I wasn't able to mention in my book. Our encounters changed a paradigm of my life. I also want to appologize those who felt neglected or used by my low behavior. Please forgive me. I would like to thank to my first book project director, Tracy Brown, for standing up for me, believing that my book could be edited in a professional way. I received new editors thanks to her request. I am thankful for their work and patience on me. Thank you to Adam McGeegan a new project director of my book and thank you to all the staff who stood for this book in Newman Springs Publishing at the first place so my message would be spread to the world. It is only a confirmation that we meet the right people in the right time—people who are aligned with our purpose and help in its fulfillment. I would like to thank all the teachers, masters, and healers who enabled me to understand who I am and healed my life and my body step by step. Thank you.

I have unlimited gratitude toward all my family members who supported me in the writing process financially and showed their love for me. And thank you to those members of my family who weren't able to be a part of my new life adventure as an author. There is time for all of us to wake up. I keep love for you in my heart.

Thank you to my father, Wieslaw Ferens, for his love for me. Our contact helped me to keep connection with my brothers and my soul sister through this journey: Michal, Piotr, Anna, and her mother, Teresa. I want to thank my son, Martin Zieba, who has become for himself a captain and leader in his life endeavor. I was unaware that you were living for my dreams for most of your adult life instead of living yours and follow your passion as was architecture and drawing. Being connected to your dreams, you would be supported through your father's family and life itself to express yourself in a creative way. Thank you, and I love you. If wasn't for you, my life wouldn't be different from before. A huge thank you to my mother, Elzbieta Kruszewska, for overcoming resistance, which allowed her to trust me, support me through good words (and not only in the new adventure), and show only love to me. Thank you for being with Martin when I wasn't with him. I love you. Thank you to my both brothers, Bartosz and Pawel, for our sibling relationship became much closer. Here I would like to also mention my stepfather, Leszek Kruszewski, who passed away in 2017. His life had meaning. Huge thanks for bringing me up and showing his love to me the best way he could. Thank you for our good times when you taught me how to swim on my back, run and we had good play times sometimes. Thank you for taking care about my mom. If it wasn't for him, I wouldn't see any connection between my childhood and my adult life. I would live in illusion without doubt. Thank you to my ex-husband who didn't know that love is who we are. If wasn't for his behavior, I would not stand up for myself and my son over ten years ago and I didn't know that I have a calling to fulfill in this life time. Thank you. I would like to thank my grandparents, Jozefa and Jan Byra; they brought me up at the beginning of my life. Even if they are in the Spirit, I see and feel more connection between these two worlds, especially my grandmother is with me all the time lately. Lastly and mostly, I am sending gratitude to my godfather, Henryk Byra, the one who kept our family the best he could so each of us stood for one another. He did his best to bring harmony to our individual family lives. He never judged, only believed that everything can be solved by dialogue and respect for one another. He was the one who took care of me with my grandmother after I was born, and my mother was taken to hospital at that time. He was the one who indulged me with some money so that I could have it for myself. In the home I grew up in, there were different ideas about what I deserved. He was the one who was interested in our family genealogical tree to remember each of the members and be connected to their tree roots. He is the one who I asked for help every time, and he said yes. He is the one who keeps his son, Tomek Byra, in his heart to remind each of us that life is too short for wasting and keeping grudges toward one another because one day, it could be too late to say "I love you" or "I am sorry" to the person we admired the most. Namaste, all.

I want to give a huge thank you to you, my readers. To those who are looking for change in this world, I believe that you read this book and that the message can be spread to others who are on different stages of awareness to give them the promise that healing can occur in their lives, bodies, and on this planet by implementing the new tools into their lives given in this book on a daily basis. The most important message is that life is for us, and we are safe. God, angels, our guides, and masters are with each of us to guide and protect us in the reincarnation adventure on the planet Earth. Thank you! Amen.

List of Books

- *The Secret*, *The Power*, and *The Magic* by Rhonda Byrne
- *The Master Key System* by Charles Haanel
- *Wishes Fulfilled* by Dr. Wayne Dyer
- *Four Agreements* and *The Mastery of Love* by Don Miguel Ruiz
- *You Can Heal Your Life and Heal Your Body* by Louise Hay
- *Conversations with God* and *The Little Soul and the Sun: A Children's Parable* by Neale Donald Walsch
- *Wallace D. Wattles Trilogy: The Science of Getting Rich, The Science of Being Well,* and *The Science of Being Great* by Wallace D. Wattles
- *Think and Grow Rich* by Napoleon Hill
- *Living on Your Own Terms* by Osho
- *The Alchemist* by Paulo Cohelo
- *Who Do You Think You Are?* by Rick Nichols
- *Dying to Be Me* by Anita Moorjani
- *Your Soul's Plan: Discovering the Meaning of the Life You Planned Before You Were Born* by Robert Schwartz
- *This Thing Called You* by Ernest Holmes
- *Prosperity* by Charles Fillmore
- *I Am the Word: A Guide to the Consciousness of Man's Self* by Paul Selig
- *Akashic Records: One True Love* by Gabrielle Orr
- *A Course in Miracles* by Helen Schucman
- *Life Visioning: A Four-Stage Evolutionary Journey to Live as Divine Love* by Michael Bernard Beckwith
- *Opening Light Body: Spiritual Healing of Subtle Body through Meridian Activation* by Trudi Thali

- *Sh*t the Moon Said: A Story of Sex, Drugs, and Ayahuasca* by Gerry Powell
- *The Magdalene Line Series: The Expected One, The Book of Love*, and *The Poet Prince* by Kathleen McGowan
- *The Power of Thank You: A Story of Gratitude, Love, and Self-Realization* by Rodolfo A. Esteves
- *The Tapping Solution* by Nick Ortner
- *The Untethered Soul: The Journey Beyond Yourself* by Michael A. Singer
- *Meet Your Angels by Ella Selena* (There is only the Polish version, according to my knowledge now.)
- *Ordering from the Cosmic Kitchen: The Essential Guide to Powerful, Nourishing Affirmations* by Patricia Crane:
- *Autobiography of a Yogi, Specific Healing Affirmation, Metaphysical Meditations*, and *The Yoga of Jesus* by Paramahansa Yogananda
- Self-Realization Fellowship / Yogoda Satsanga Society lessons
- *The Law of Attraction* by Esther and Jerry Hicks
- *Pearls of Wisdom* by Patricia Crane and Rick Nichols
- *Crystals for Beginners: The Guide to Get Started with the Healing Power of Crystals* by Karen Frazier
- *The Empath's Survival Guide: Life Strategies for Sensitive People* by Judith Orloff
- *Calling in "The One": 7 Weeks to Attract the Love of Your Life* by Katherine Woodward Thomas
- *Creative Visualization: Use the Power of Your Imagination to Create What You Want in Your Life* by Shakti Gawain
- *Fall in Love with Life* by Ewa Foley
- *The Photographs, Tomek Byra 2000–2002* by Tomasz Ferenc and Henryk Waniek
- *The Eagle and the Condor* by Jonnette Crowley
- *Whatever Arises, Love That: A Love Revolution That Begins with You* by Matt Khan
- *Serpent of Light* by Drunvalo Melchizedek

- *10 Mindful Minutes: Giving Our Children—and Ourselves—the Social and Emotional Skills to Reduce Stress and Anxiety for Healthier, Happier Lives by Goldie Hawn and Wendy Holden*
- *Being Supernatural by Dr. Joe Despenza*
- *The Gene Kays Embracing your Higher Purpose by Richard Rudd*
- *The Mayan Oracle, Return Path to the Stars by Ariel Spilsbury and Michael Bryner*
- *Three Magic Words by Uell Stanley Andersen*
- *The Presence Process by Michael Brown*

About the Author

Magdalena Julita Byra is a Heal Your Life workshop leader, Reiki and Guided Energy Medicine practitioner, and author. Living in Poland, she discovered in 2010 the truth about how life really works. She started implementing it into her life with the great results. After years of developing herself using the tools she teaches now, life put her on the true path of her soul calling and brought her to the United States to awaken her dormant talents and gifts. Here, she found her life purpose, to empower and support every woman in her own journey to self-love, rediscovering, healing, expanding, and finding a life purpose. She spreads her message of love and life understanding to bring love and peace to the world through realization that we are all one on evolutionary realm as a soul in a human body.

www.ingramcontent.com/pod-product-compliance
Lightning Source LLC
Chambersburg PA
CBHW031613160426
43196CB00006B/114